complete book of Thai cooking

complete book of Thai cooking

Over 200 delicious recipes

Linda Stephen

For complete cataloguing information, see page 277.

Disclaimer
The recipes in this book have been carefully tested by our kitchen and our tasters. To the best of our knowledge, they are safe and nutritious for ordinary use and users. For those people with food or other allergies, or who have special food requirements or health issues, please read the suggested contents of each recipe carefully and determine whether or not they may create a problem for you. All recipes are used at the risk of the consumer.

We cannot be responsible for any hazards, loss or damage that may occur as a result of any recipe use.

For those with special needs, allergies, requirements or health problems, in the event of any doubt, please contact your medical advisor prior to the use of any recipe.

Editorial: Shelley Tanaka
Design & Production: Daniella Zanchetta/PageWave Graphics Inc.
Food Photography: Colin Erricson
Food Styling: Kathryn Robertson
Prop Styling: Charlene Erricson

Cover image: River Kwai Chicken and Mango Stir-fry (page 158)

We acknowledge the financial support of the Government of Canada through the Book Publishing Industry Development Program (BPIDP) for our publishing activities.

Published by Robert Rose Inc.
120 Eglinton Avenue East, Suite 800
Toronto, Ontario, Canada M4P 1E2
Tel: (416) 322-6552 Fax: (416) 322-6936

Printed in Canada
1 2 3 4 5 6 7 8 9 TCP 16 15 14 13 12 11 10 09 08

To the people of Thailand, who have always shown me great kindness and hospitality.

Contents

Acknowledgments

Thanks to so many for their help with this project.

- Sompon Nabnian of the Chiang Mai Thai Cookery School and the Jasmine Rice Resort, Chiang Mai.
- Pipith Kaewta, our knowledgeable, always cheerful guide, who has become a dear friend.
- Michael Gaehler and Marcel Huser of the Chedi Hotel, Chiang Mai.
- Kayla Shubert at the Tourism Authority of Thailand, Toronto.
- Kanta Leelaphat and Kanjana Wanthanatanti at the Educational Travel Center, Bangkok.
- Navamas Lakanantkoon (Rutch), for sharing her love of cooking.
- Nay Durant, for answering endless questions about Thailand.
- Rick Blackwood of Mike's Fish Market, St. Lawrence Market, Toronto.
- Dedicated and efficient recipe testers and sounding boards Francine Ménard and Rhonda Caplan.
- Gordon and Penny Matthews, Adelaide, Australia, for first suggesting that I "stop off" in Thailand.
- Bonnie Stern, for her constant support over the years.
- Bob Dees, Marian Jarkovich, Arden Boehm and the team at Robert Rose Inc.; Andrew Smith, Joseph Gisini, Kevin Cockburn and, especially, Daniella Zanchetta at PageWave Graphics; Colin Erricson, Kathryn Robertson and Charlene Erricson.
- Bill Vronsky, once again, for computer assistance.
- Brenda Stanford, for support on the home front.
- My family, for bearing with my sighs while I worked on this book.
- My editor, Shelley Tanaka, for her skill, patience and good humor, and for assuring me that it was okay to take a day off now and then.

Introduction

TWENTY FIVE YEARS AGO, I was about to return home after spending a year working in a hotel kitchen in Australia. I wanted to make a stop along the way, and Gord Matthews, a fellow chef, strongly recommended that I visit Thailand. I did, and ever since I have felt an affection for all things Thai — the people, the colors, the flowers, the calm temples and bustling streets, the vibrant markets, the textiles, the beaches, the palms (though maybe not the humidity so much!). And I have become smitten with zestful, light, fresh Thai food.

I took a few cooking classes in Thailand, ate copiously, and when I returned to Canada I couldn't wait to start reproducing the dishes I had eaten there. In the mid-eighties, this meant special trips to Toronto's Chinatown to find certain ingredients (including cilantro), and trying to decipher the few Thai cookbooks that I had managed to find (mostly literal translations that were challenging to understand).

Today it is no longer necessary to travel to Thailand to experience Thai flavors (though it is always a bonus). We have Thai cookbooks and Thai restaurants, and Asian ingredients are now readily available in North American supermarkets and in Asian stores in smaller communities. Several companies produce their own line of Thai ingredients, and Western restaurants often feature dishes that include Thai flavors. Thai is not so mysterious now.

Since that initial trip, I have returned to Thailand several times, with groups and with friends. I never tire of going there. Although some areas remain much the same, Thailand is constantly changing to accommodate and entice new and repeat visitors. More luxury hotels and resorts are being built, more cooking classes are being offered, and more varied tourist opportunities (home stays, working with elephants) are available.

Not everyone shares my enthusiasm for Thai cuisine. Some are allergic to peanuts, some people don't like hot food or cilantro. But Thai food is extremely adaptable. The heat of a dish can always be reduced by omitting chilies or curry paste. Cilantro can be reduced or replaced with parsley. Peanuts can be left out of garnishes and sauces. The final chapter of this book — Beyond Thai — includes recipes that add Thai flavors to popular Western dishes. And many Thai dishes can easily be adapted for vegetarians by using soy sauce instead of fish sauce and tofu instead of meat.

The goal of this book is to make it easy to cook Thai food at home. Ingredients are for the most part easily accessible, and techniques have been streamlined so that you can create delicious Thai dishes in your own kitchen — from family dinners to special-occasion meals.

What I do notice whenever I serve Thai food or dine in Thai restaurants is that people seem happy. Thais love to cook and to socialize with family and friends over food. The heat and spices tend to perk up appetites, and spirits.

Now Thai food is something everyone can enjoy more often.

About Thai Food

PACKED WITH FLAVOR, color and texture, Thai food appeals to all the senses. Thailand does not have a colonial past, and the cuisine has retained its distinctive identity. At the same time, Thai cooking does reflect the influence of other countries, specifically India, China and Portugal.

The secret is to create a balance of flavors so that nothing is overwhelming. Sweet, sour, salty, hot and sometimes bitter add layers of flavor and aroma. Sweet comes predominantly from palm sugar, fruit and sometimes honey. Sour is added with lime and tamarind. Salty is provided by fish sauce (nam pla), shrimp paste and, to a lesser extent, by oyster sauce, yellow bean sauce and condiments such as preserved salted vegetables. Hot is added with chilies in various forms, and pepper. And bitter is gently provided through the addition of herbs and dark green vegetables.

The goal is to achieve harmony in a dish, to appeal to both the palate and the eye, and to make the dish memorable.

The distinctive Thai tastes come from traditional ingredients such as cilantro, Thai basil, lemongrass, lime leaves, galangal, ginger, coconut milk, fish sauce, tamarind, palm sugar, garlic, shallots and dried spices (mostly used in curry pastes). Chilies add the heat, but not all dishes are predominantly hot. Before the introduction of chilies by Portuguese traders, peppercorns added heat, and they are still used today.

The marvelous array of fresh vegetables and fruits available in Thailand add texture, color and taste. The country's rivers and coastal waters are rich in fish and seafood. And although meat and poultry are also used, they are added to dishes in small amounts — cut into bite-size pieces and incorporated with other ingredients to make a curry or stir-fry.

Rice is the mainstay of Thai cuisine. There are several festivals that celebrate rice, from the beginning of the rice-planting season, to the plowing and finally the harvest. Eaten every day, it forms the center of the meal, accompanied by other foods such as a simple sauce or curry dish. Noodles take second place to rice, but they are eaten twenty-four hours a day — for breakfast, lunch and snacks. Noodle dishes are sold from mobile noodle carts, at floating markets, in restaurants and at markets and food stalls. A variety of seasoning condiments is always offered so diners can tweak the flavors to their individual tastes.

THAILAND IS SHAPED LIKE an elephant's head and is about the size of France. It is a diverse country divided into several regions. The North (which neighbors Laos and Myanmar) is cool, green and mountainous; the Northeast is a vast plateau (that can be drought-prone) flanked by the Mekong River; the Central Plain has its fertile river basin with rice-growing areas and orchards; and the tropical South is a peninsula with steamy dense jungles and famous beaches. Although these are distinct regions, cooking techniques and ingredients overlap. Bangkok is the cosmopolitan melting pot of all regions — a bustling metropolis that boasts one of the newest and largest airports in the world, yet where flowers and foods are still sold from wooden long-tail boats on the Chao Phraya River.

Thai cuisine has long been known for elaborate dishes garnished with intricately carved fruits and vegetables. This elaborate Royal Palace cuisine originated in the king's palace, a city within a city where young women were trained in the refinements of food preparation and presentation as well as other household skills. This cuisine is still evident today in fine restaurants as well as in hotels and resorts that have the large staffs required to prepare these labor-intensive dishes. Generally, palace cuisine is less spicy and slightly sweeter than other Thai cooking.

Food is a significant part of everyday life in Thailand, too. People are always snacking. Traditional Thai meals at home are generally informal, simple and practical. They may consist of a single dish, such as bowl of noodles or rice, or several dishes, but all are carefully prepared and look as good as they taste, even if simply garnished with fresh herbs.

And one cannot talk about Thai cooking without mentioning street food. Street vendors are a common sight in cities, villages, markets, waterways and even on country roadsides. These "shops" take many forms, including trolleys, bicycles, carts, boats and bamboo and basket carriers. Some may become more permanent stalls in night markets and at streetside, with small tables and chairs set out for customers.

People from all walks of life line up at these places. Simple snacking foods, rather than a "put together" dish, are often cooked over a brazier and artfully displayed on banana leaves or in assorted baskets. These foods (often skewered and accompanied by a dipping sauce) include meatballs, satays, roasted meats, sausages, dried squid, smoked fish, grasshoppers, cockroaches, grilled corn, spring rolls, steamed buns, dumplings, pancakes, deep-fried and grilled bananas, sticky rice in banana leaves, fruit, fruit juices, desserts and more. There is energy, fragrance, noise and excitement day and night — the complete opposite of culinary boredom.

Eating Thai Style

THAIS LOVE TO SNACK, but they still eat three main meals a day. Breakfast and lunch are simple. A rice-based soup containing bits of chicken, fish or pork and accompanied by seasoning ingredients might be breakfast. Lunch might be a rice or noodle dish. The evening meal is the main meal of the day. It is not separated into courses. All the dishes are brought to the table at the same time — including soup — and are eaten warm or at room temperature. Along with rice, there might be soup, a salad, a steamed dish, a stir-fry, a curry, some sauces and possibly a deep fried dish. Everything is shared. Dessert may simply be fresh fruit or a small custard type dish. Tea, water and fruit juices accompany the meal.

Spoons and forks are the eating implements, with the food being pushed onto the spoon with the fork. Knives are not used. Chopsticks are reserved for noodle dishes. In the North and Northeast, sticky rice is served. Since it adheres to itself, it is eaten by rolling a small amount of rice into a ball by hand. Then it is flattened slightly and dipped into a sauce or used to pick up small pieces of food.

Life has become busier in large cities such as Bangkok and Chiang Mai. More noticeable now are prepared sauces, pastes and dressings that were traditionally prepared in the home. These are of very good quality and offer a shortcut for the cook. It is also not uncommon for a meal to be supplemented with take-out items purchased from a market stall or supermarket. And some people may never cook at home, content with the vast array of inexpensive, good-quality street food.

Cooking Thai Food

EVERYWHERE YOU GO in Thailand, whether it is a small village, a large supermarket in Bangkok, a street market or a tourist attraction, there are always busy hands sorting, preparing and cooking. Much of the cooking is done in open-air kitchens.

In Thailand it is rare to see a cook with a cookbook. Instead they are likely cooking dishes that have been in the family for generations, making adjustments as they go to accommodate the number of guests and the availability of fresh ingredients.

In that spirit, you can use the recipes in this book just as a starting point. As your comfort level improves, feel free to let dishes take on a character of their own.

The following tips will make the process easier:

- Most Thai dishes require chopping, mincing and slicing ahead of time, but the trade-off is that they only require quick last-minute cooking. Have all ingredients assembled and at stove side, in the order that you will use them, before you start to cook. Have serving dishes and garnishes ready in advance.
- Most recipes call for heating the wok before adding the oil. Heating the wok ahead means the cooking process starts right away. Medium-high heat is usually recommended; high heat is too hot for nonstick skillets (it may damage the surface) or for heavy skillets that hold the heat very well. However, if the wok is too hot when you start to cook, ingredients (such as garlic) may brown too quickly. Make adjustments according to your own stove and pans.
- Plan a menu that includes some dishes that can be prepared in advance (salads), some that can be kept hot or reheated after cooking (curries), and one or two last-minute dishes (stir-fries or deep-fried dishes); rice can steam while the last-minute dishes are being prepared. (You'll also find menu ideas suggested throughout this book.)
- Do not double recipes that are cooked in a wok; a sufficiently high heat cannot be maintained, resulting in stewed or overcooked dishes. Instead, for larger quantities, use a second wok and have a friend cook alongside, then combine both dishes for serving.

Equipment

- **Wok:** Select a large wok (at least 14 inches/35 cm) with a flat bottom and a second short handle so cooked food can be easily transferred to serving dishes. If you don't have a wok, use a large, deep skillet.
- **Mortar and Pestle:** Heavy granite mortars and pestles are used throughout Thailand to grind herbs, seasoning ingredients and spices into pastes. Blenders or food processors with small capacities (some large food processors also have an insert for smaller amounts) can be used, but the pastes may not be as smooth (you may need to add a small amount of liquid). Scrape down the sides of containers and bowls as necessary. The tall ceramic mortar with a wooden pestle is used for making salads, especially green papaya (page 70).
- **Spice or Coffee Grinder:** Use these for grinding whole dried spices such as peppercorns, cumin seeds and chilies, as well as small amounts of peanuts and roasted rice (to make rice powder). It is best to keep a grinder just for spices.
- **Electric Rice Cooker:** An excellent piece of equipment if you cook rice often. Select one with a large capacity, as it can also be used for smaller quantities. These cookers free up your time and attention for the rest of the meal, and they keep rice hot. (Be sure to buy one with a "keep" feature.) Otherwise, steam rice in a saucepan with a tight-fitting lid (page 114).
- **Rice Steamer:** This cone-shaped basket with a tall pot is used for steaming sticky/glutinous rice (page 117). Soaked rice is placed in the basket set over boiling water. As an alternative, place the soaked rice in a wire mesh sieve (lined with cheesecloth if necessary) set over (not in) boiling water in a Dutch oven or large saucepan.
- **Utensils:** Wooden and metal utensils are used for stir-frying and for lifting and turning food. Slotted spoons and wire mesh strainers are used for lifting ingredients from hot oil or skimming scum from the surface of stocks. Tongs of varying lengths help turn and lift foods when grilling. Small tasting spoons set beside the stove are for the cook to "season to taste." Bamboo skewers of varying lengths are handy for satays, sampling and for testing doneness.

Ingredients

Ingredients used in Thai cooking have become more available in recent years. However, when developing the recipes for this book, care was taken to use accessible ingredients whenever possible. Shopping was done at supermarkets, health food stores and Asian grocers. Some ingredients involved a trip to Chinatown or an Asian supermarket in larger centers, but many of these ingredients can be kept in dry storage or frozen, and seasoning sauces keep well when refrigerated after opening.

Banana Leaves

Large, long green leaves used to wrap raw and cooked foods, as liners when steaming foods, and for presentation. Always used fresh in Thailand, they are available frozen in Asian supermarkets. Defrost and rinse well before using. They can also be refrozen.

Basil

Sweet Thai basil (bai horapah) is the most common basil used in Thai cooking. It has purplish stems and flowers, shiny green leaves and a slight anise but almost citrusy flavor. It is used in curries, soups and stir-fries, usually added at the end of the cooking time. Seeds are available and it is quite easy to grow in home gardens. If you can't find it, use Italian basil.

"Holy basil" is less common in Western markets. It has small, serrated leaves with a dull finish. Use it quickly as it has a short refrigerator life. It adds a slightly hot, peppery flavor to dishes and is added to curries and stir-fries.

Black Fungus (Wood Fungus)

A dried fungus that needs to be reconstituted in warm water before using. It is available whole or in strips and used in spring rolls, soups and stir-fries. It adds texture and volume and absorbs other flavors in the dish. Mostly found in Asian stores.

Chilies

Fresh and dried chilies add the heat to Thai food (although not all Thai food is hot). Thai markets abound with fresh red, green and even orange chilies in various sizes.

The most common are bird's eye. They are less than an inch long. Medium and longer chilies are also available, but in general, the smaller the chili, the hotter it is. If you can't find them, use serranos or jalapeños.

The seeds (which are the hottest part) can be removed if you wish. After working with chilies, wash your hands and under your nails well with hot soapy water. Wash cutting boards and knives, too. Do not touch your eyes or face. Plastic gloves can also be worn.

See also Hot chili sauce, Roasted chili powder, Sweet chili sauce.

Cilantro

Also called coriander or Chinese parsley, all parts of the plant (leaves, stems, roots and seeds) are used in Thai cooking. Roots and stems (which have a stronger flavor) are used in curry pastes, but if the bunch does not have roots, use a combination of stems and leaves. (Well-washed cilantro roots also have a longer refrigerator life than the stems and leaves, and some cooks wrap the roots well, freeze them for up to six weeks and chop frozen.)

Fresh cilantro leaves are a common garnish for many dishes.

See also Coriander seeds.

Coconut Milk

In Thailand, freshly grated coconut is soaked in water and squeezed or pressed to extract the first pressing of coconut milk. The grated coconut is then pressed again, producing a thinner and lighter milk.

Many brands of coconut milk (sold in cans and Tetra Paks as well as frozen) are widely available. Some are already blended, but most canned coconut milk separates on standing, with the thick milk rising to the surface (some recipes will specifically call for this thicker milk). To blend the thick and thin, stir well to combine or transfer to a measuring cup or bowl and whisk lightly.

Refrigerate extra coconut milk for up to three days or freeze. Sometimes frozen coconut milk separates. Stir before using.

Coriander seeds

The dried seeds of the cilantro/coriander plant are often used as an ingredient in curry pastes. Ground coriander is also used in curry powders and as a flavoring ingredient. For the fullest flavor, toast the seeds in a dry skillet over medium heat for 3 to 4 minutes, or until fragrant. Cool and grind to a powder in a spice grinder or with a mortar and pestle.

Curry Paste

Curry pastes (pages 196, 205, 211 and 214) are a combination of wet ingredients (such as chilies, garlic, shallots and herbs) and dry spices. Each paste has its unique blend of ingredients. It is traditionally made in small amounts with a mortar and pestle. Increasingly available now are high-quality commercially prepared pastes, available in packages, tubs, jars and even frozen. For the best flavor, it is often cooked in thick coconut milk or oil at the beginning of a recipe. If you are using commercial products, which tend to be saltier than homemade, cut back on the initial quantity of fish sauce or soy sauce, and adjust to taste at the end of the cooking time.

Curry Powder

Curry powder (page 266) is used in some dishes, marinades and sauces. Thais usually buy it ready made. It is available in Asian shops, but most are not hot.

Fish Sauce

Fish sauce is the salt of Asia and one of the most important ingredients in Thai cooking. It is used both in cooking and as a table condiment. Made of fermented salted anchovies, the amber-colored liquid varies depending on the manufacturer. Use it sparingly until you know how salty your product is.

Vegetarians can replace fish sauce with soy sauce or salt.

Galangal

Similar in appearance to ginger (it is also known as Siamese ginger), galangal is used in curry pastes and soups. It has a lemon-ginger flavor and is available fresh, frozen or as dried slices. Galangal powder is a poor substitute. Use fresh ginger instead.

Galangal is fibrous, so it can be removed before serving. Both fresh and frozen are often available in supermarkets. Look for a smooth skin.

Garlic

Thai garlic is smaller and has a thinner skin than the garlic we are familiar with. It is just smashed but not peeled. Crisp fried garlic — storebought or homemade (page 146) — is a common garnish. Pickled garlic is also used in recipes or eaten as a snack.

The recipes in this book have been tested using regular garlic.

Hoisin Sauce

A thick, reddish brown sauce made from soybeans and used primarily in Thai-Chinese dishes, such as stir-fries and marinades. Refrigerate after opening.

Hot Chili Sauce

Hot chili sauce, known as Sriracha (after the seaside town where it originated), is a puree made from chilies, sugar, vinegar, garlic and salt. It is used in cooking but is also served as a condiment to add extra heat at the table. It is the Thai ketchup or hot sauce. Once opened, refrigerate it.

Lemongrass

Another mainstay of Thai cooking, stalks of fresh lemongrass are available in Asian stores and regular supermarkets. Look for stalks that are flexible and not too dry. Cut off the base and peel off some of the tough outer leaves to reach the tender white part. This can be cut in lengths (which are removed prior to serving or just pushed aside when eating) or very finely chopped (prechopped lemongrass can sometimes be found in the frozen section). Wrap lemongrass well and store in the refrigerator for a few days or freeze for a couple of months (use it straight from the freezer). Lemongrass can also be grown in the garden, but it will not withstand frost.

Lime Leaves

An essential flavoring in Thai cooking. Sometimes called kaffir or wild lime leaves, the shiny double (figure-eight) leaves impart a citrus flavor. They are generally added whole or torn into large pieces. If you are using them fresh in a salad, the vein should be removed and the leaf finely shredded, as it tends to be chewy.

Fresh leaves can be challenging to find; frozen are more readily available. Wrap extra fresh leaves well in small amounts and freeze for future use. Strips of lime zest can sometimes be used, but dried lime leaves are a poor substitute.

Mushrooms, Dried Chinese

Dried black shiitake mushrooms add texture and a rich, smoky flavor to dishes. Reconstitute them in warm water for 25 to 30 minutes, or until softened. Remove and discard the stems and use the mushrooms whole or sliced. The dried mushrooms will keep indefinitely if wrapped well in plastic bags. Some cooks keep them in the freezer. Fresh shiitake mushrooms can be substituted, but the flavor is not as rich.

Oyster Sauce

Originating in China, oyster sauce is a common ingredient in Thai dishes. The thick, dark, rich sauce is often used with soy sauce or fish sauce. It contains oyster extract along with other ingredients, but does not have a fishy flavor. Available in Asian stores and many supermarkets; some Asian stores also stock a "vegetarian" oyster sauce.

Palm Sugar

The sap from sugar palms is boiled down, then poured into forms or tubs. In Thailand, palm sugar is available in various stages of firmness, from very soft to firm. It is also available in jars. If the palm sugar in jars is too hard, microwave on Low to soften. If the cakes are hard, either shave with a knife, grate or pound with a pestle or rolling pin. If unavailable, substitute brown sugar or maple syrup.

Peanuts

In Thailand, peanuts are often purchased raw and deep-fried, but most of the recipes in this book use salted or unsalted roasted peanuts. Store peanuts in the freezer. For those with peanut allergies, use soy nut butter, available at health food stores.

Roasted Chili Powder

Made from ground dried chilies, this chili powder is hot and not the same as Mexican chili powder. Purchase it in Asian supermarkets or make your own (page 48). It is a popular condiment; diners season their dish to taste at the table.

Sesame Oil

Sesame oil is extracted from roasted sesame seeds. This amber oil is added as a last-minute seasoning, as well as being used in marinades and salad dressings. In Thai recipes it is mostly used in Chinese-influenced dishes. It is not used for frying, since it burns easily.

Shallots

Reddish shallots are used extensively in Thai cooking, and crispy fried shallots are a common garnish. You can buy them in Asian grocery stores or make your own (page 147). The recipes in this book were tested using medium-size shallots.

Shrimp, Dried

In Thailand, small dried whole shrimp are sold loose in markets. The best ones are bright pink. Used as a seasoning to add saltiness, they are often softened in water before being added to a dish. Available in Asian supermarkets, sometimes in the refrigerated section. Refrigerate after opening.

Shrimp Paste

A strong pungent flavoring added in small amounts to dips, soups, sauces and curry pastes. Mostly sold in jars, it comes as a grayish paste, but some brands containing soy bean oil are more pink and not quite as strong. Refrigerate after opening. Use anchovy paste as a substitute.

Soy Sauce

Soy sauce comes in varying degrees of color and strength. Select one that is not too salty. Dark soy sauce is thicker, less salty and slightly sweeter than light soy sauce. It adds color to a dish, so is not usually used in light-colored dishes.

Sweet soy sauce is thick, sweet and syrupy and is used in stir-fries, noodle dishes and marinades. It is similar to the Indonesian ketcap manis. If you can't find it, use two parts regular soy sauce and one part molasses.

Sweet Chili Sauce

Storebought or homemade (page 45) sweet chili sauce is another popular condiment or dipping sauce, especially served with chicken, fish and spring rolls. It is a translucent sauce made from chopped chilies, water, vinegar, sugar and salt.

Tamarind

One of the "sour" ingredients used in Thai cooking. Found in markets as fresh or dried pods, it is commonly sold as a dried pulp that contains seeds and fibers. The pulp can be wrapped well and stored in the cupboard like dates or raisins.

When softened in warm water and pressed through a sieve (page 167), tart tamarind paste (also called tamarind juice, puree, concentrate, liquid or water) is extracted. The prepared version can be found in Indian and Asian stores. As a substitute, use lime juice or white vinegar.

Preserved tamarind, coated in sugar, and ripened tamarind pods are used in desserts.

Tapioca Starch

Made from dried cassava root, tapioca starch (sometimes called tapioca flour) is used in batters, coating mixtures and desserts. It has a slightly glutinous consistency. Found in Asian stores, some supermarkets, bulk food stores and health food stores. Use cornstarch if you can't find it.

Turmeric

Fresh turmeric (both bright orange and white) is a rhizome related to the ginger family. Found fresh in Thai markets, it is less available in Western stores, but can sometimes be found in the frozen section. It has a peppery aroma. If you use fresh or frozen, peel, slice thinly and chop finely. It is popular in dishes of Indian origin. In this book, ground turmeric powder is used.

Take care when working with turmeric, as it can discolor clothing, work surfaces and some utensils.

Food Safety

- Wash your hands for 20 seconds before starting to cook and after coughing, sneezing, using the restroom and touching pets.
- Keep work surfaces, cutting boards and counter surfaces clean. Sanitize them with a mild chlorine bleach solution (especially when working with meats, poultry and seafood). Mix 1 tsp (5 mL) bleach with 3 cups (750 mL) water and store in a well-labeled spray bottle.
- Use two cutting boards: one for raw meat, poultry and fish; one for cooked foods, fresh vegetables and fruits.
- Keep cold foods cold, below 40°F (4°C).
- Keep hot foods hot, above 140°F (60°C).
- Keep raw meat, poultry and seafood separate from one another, other foods and cooked foods. Use clean utensils and dishes when switching from raw to cooked foods.
- Defrost meat, poultry and fish completely under refrigeration and keep in the refrigerator until cooking.
- Refrigerate leftovers as quickly as possible. Cooling to room temperature on the counter invites bacteria growth. Use leftovers quickly.

About These Recipes

The recipes in this book were created using accessible ingredients, with Western cooks and home kitchens in mind. Most ingredients can be found in well-stocked supermarkets, Asian grocery stores and some health food stores.

- Fresh chilies vary in size, so unless they are being used as a garnish, the measured volume has been given. The recipes were tested using very small chilies, but seeding these can be tedious, so the seeds are included in the suggested measure. However, the seeds are hotter than the flesh; to reduce the heat you can remove them before chopping, or reduce the amount.
- The recipes were tested using a variety of homemade and commercial curry pastes. Some commercial pastes are quite salty, so if you are using them, reduce the amount of fish sauce in the recipe and then adjust seasonings to taste at the end of the cooking time. (Different brands of fish sauce also vary in saltiness.)
- Unless fresh or frozen ingredients are specified, either can be used (frozen ingredients should be defrosted before using, unless otherwise specified). Fresh herbs are always used. Do not substitute dried.
- Deep-frying is less common in Western homes than in Thailand. In this book, most recipes use techniques such as steaming, stir-frying and braising, but deep-frying is used for some appetizers and for whole fried fish. For deep-frying tips, see page 37.
- Most recipes will yield four to six servings (with the occasional serving more or less) assuming that you are also serving rice (unless it is included in the dish). In Thailand rice is almost always the main feature of the meal, with several meat and vegetables dishes accompanying it in small quantities.
- In general, Thai homes do not have freezers, and Thai cooks do not usually cook too far ahead of meal time. However, some recipes can be made ahead and left to stand for a short while, or they can be reheated (e.g., some curries, soups, desserts and sauces). Where practical, suggestions have been given for preparing some items ahead, or for freezing for later use.
- Many of the recipes in this book can easily be adjusted for vegetarians, by replacing fish sauce with soy sauce or salt, oyster sauce with vegetarian (mushroom) oyster sauce, and chicken stock with vegetable stock or water. Use curry pastes that do not contain fish sauce or anchovy paste.

Appetizers, Snacks and Sauces

Shrimp Crackers

Makes about 7 dozen

Instead of bread, the first food that might appear at Thai restaurant tables is a basket of shrimp crackers accompanied by peanut sauce (though not every eatery serves them free of charge).

Make Ahead
Cooled crackers can be stored at room temperature in a tightly covered container for up to 3 days.

3 cups	vegetable oil	750 mL
8 oz	shrimp (prawn) crackers, plain or colored	250 g

1. In a wok or deep saucepan, heat oil to 365°F (185°C).
2. To test oil, gently place a cracker in wok. It should sink and then rise quickly to the surface, puff and expand. Once oil is ready, cook several crackers at once. Remove from oil with a wire mesh strainer and drain on paper towels.

Corn Pancakes

Makes 4 to 6 servings (16 to 18 pancakes)

These pancakes are sold by street vendors, either pan-fried or deep-fried. Serve them with cucumber relish (page 46) or sweet chili sauce (page 45).

2	eggs	2
2 tbsp	fish sauce	25 mL
2 tbsp	chopped fresh cilantro leaves and stems	25 mL
2	cloves garlic, minced	2
1/4 tsp	black pepper	1 mL
3 tbsp	cornstarch or rice flour	45 mL
2 cups	corn kernels	500 mL
4 oz	chopped (or baby) cooked shrimp (optional)	125 g
2 tbsp	vegetable oil (approx.)	25 mL

1. In a bowl, beat together eggs and fish sauce.
2. Add cilantro, garlic, pepper and cornstarch and mix thoroughly. Stir in corn and shrimp, if using.
3. In a large nonstick skillet, heat oil over medium-high heat. Cook pancakes in batches by dropping large tablespoons of batter into hot skillet. Be sure to include some egg mixture in each spoonful. Flatten slightly. Cook for 2 minutes per side, or until golden brown.

Fish Cakes with Green Beans

Makes 20 small fish cakes

Fish cakes are served as street food snacks as well as in restaurants and homes. There are many versions — spicy or mild, deep-fried or pan-fried, with curry or without. Although often served as an appetizer, they can also be served as a main course. Serve with cucumber relish (page 46).

12 oz	white fish fillets, (e.g., cod or halibut), cut in 1-inch (2.5 cm) pieces	375 g
1 tbsp	fish sauce	15 mL
2 tsp	red curry paste	10 mL
1	egg	1
1 tbsp	cornstarch	15 mL
1 tsp	granulated sugar	5 mL
3/4 cup	finely sliced green beans	175 mL
1/4 cup	chopped fresh cilantro leaves	50 mL
3	lime leaves, center vein removed, finely shredded	3
2 tbsp	vegetable oil (approx.)	25 mL

1. Pat fish dry. Chop fish coarsely in a food processor.
2. Add fish sauce, curry paste, egg, cornstarch and sugar. Pulse to combine, but do not puree.
3. Transfer mixture to a bowl and add beans, cilantro and lime leaves. Mix thoroughly. Shape mixture into 20 patties (about 1 tbsp/15 mL each), wetting your fingers as necessary.
4. In a large nonstick skillet, heat oil over medium-high heat. Add fish cakes, in batches, and cook for about 2 minutes per side, or until golden brown. Drain on paper towels. Serve warm or at room temperature.

Coconut Dumplings

Makes 24 dumplings

A cross between a pancake and a dumpling, these are served everywhere in Thailand, sometimes with a savory (green onions, shredded dried shrimp) or sweet topping (toasted coconut, cooked pumpkin or corn). At Pak Klong Talat market in Bangkok, we bought some that were made in a special cast-iron skillet with two dozen indentations. Batter was poured from a tea pot, the pan was covered with a lid, and the dumplings were steamed until almost set, before being topped with a thick cream and steamed for another couple of minutes. The cook deftly popped them out, topped them with diced pumpkin and handed them to us in a little container so we could snack and walk. The indented pans are difficult to find, so use mini muffin pans instead. The dumplings will still be tasty, though the bottoms won't be quite as crispy.

Base

1/2 cup	rice flour	125 mL
1/4 tsp	salt	1 mL
1/2 cup	coconut milk	125 mL
3 tbsp	water	45 mL

Topping

1/2 cup	thick coconut milk (page 18)	125 mL
2 tbsp	granulated sugar	25 mL
Pinch	salt	Pinch
2 tbsp	vegetable oil or melted butter	25 mL

Garnish (optional)

Chopped peanuts
Chopped green onions
Shredded coconut, toasted (page 245)

1. To prepare base, in a bowl, combine flour, salt, coconut milk and water.
2. To prepare topping, in a separate bowl, whisk together coconut milk, sugar and salt.
3. Brush 24 mini muffin cups generously with oil. Spoon about 2 tsp (10 mL) base mixture into cups.
4. Bake in a preheated 400°F (200°C) oven for 8 minutes. Spoon about 1 tsp (5 mL) topping mixture over base. Return to oven and bake for 3 minutes. Let stand for a few minutes before carefully removing from pans.
5. Sprinkle with peanuts, green onions or coconut or leave plain. Serve warm.

Chicken Satays

1 1/2 lbs	boneless, skinless chicken breasts	750 g
3	cloves garlic, peeled	3
2	shallots, peeled	2
3 tbsp	coarsely chopped fresh cilantro roots or leaves	45 mL
1/2 cup	coconut milk	125 mL
2 tbsp	soy sauce	25 mL
2 tbsp	vegetable oil	25 mL
1 tbsp	granulated sugar	15 mL
1 tsp	curry powder	5 mL
1/2 tsp	ground turmeric	2 mL
1/2 tsp	ground coriander	2 mL

1. Cut chicken breasts into strips about 4 inches (10 cm) long and 1/2 inch (1 cm) wide. Place in a bowl.
2. In a food processor or using a mortar and pestle, blend garlic, shallots and cilantro to a paste. Add coconut milk, soy sauce, oil, sugar, curry powder, turmeric and coriander. Puree until smooth.
3. Pour marinade over chicken and stir to thoroughly coat chicken. Cover and refrigerate for up to 4 hours.
4. Thread chicken strips onto thirty 6-inch (15 cm) presoaked bamboo skewers. Brush with remaining marinade.
5. Grill, turning several times, until cooked through and slightly charred, about 7 minutes. (To cook under a broiler, line a baking sheet with foil and broil about 4 inches /10 cm from heat, turning several times.)

Makes about 30 appetizers

Satays made their way to Thailand from Indonesia and Malaysia. Although not strictly Thai, they are very popular. Peanut sauce (page 47) is the usual accompaniment, but cucumber relish (page 46) is also served. Soak bamboo skewers in water for an hour before threading and cooking the satays. Beef, pork or whole shrimp can be used instead of chicken.

Galloping Horses

Makes 6 to 8 servings

There are many versions of this sweet, spicy, sour, nutty and salty appetizer. Pork is often used on its own, but you can also substitute chicken or a combination of pork, shrimp and chicken. Add extra sugar if you prefer a sweeter topping. Pineapple or mandarin oranges can be used instead of oranges.

4	oranges	4
2 tbsp	vegetable oil	25 mL
4	shallots, finely chopped	4
3	cloves garlic, finely chopped	3
2 tbsp	finely chopped fresh cilantro leaves	25 mL
8 oz	lean ground pork	250 g
2 tbsp	palm or brown sugar	25 mL
2 tbsp	fish sauce	25 mL
1/4 cup	chopped roasted peanuts	50 mL

Garnish

2	fresh red chilies, thinly sliced	2
	Fresh cilantro leaves	

1. Trim ends from oranges. Remove peel and pith. Cut each orange crosswise into 4 or 5 slices. Arrange slices on a serving platter or individual serving plates.
2. Heat a skillet over medium-high heat and add oil. Add shallots, garlic and cilantro. Stir-fry for 1 minute. Add pork. Stir-fry for 4 to 5 minutes, or until pinkness disappears.
3. Stir in sugar, fish sauce and peanuts. Cook for 3 to 4 minutes, or until meat is almost caramelized with sugar.
4. Mound a spoonful of pork mixture on each orange slice. Garnish with a chili slice and a cilantro leaf.

Fresh Spring Rolls

Makes 12 rolls

Although more Vietnamese than Thai, fresh spring rolls often appear on Thai restaurant menus. They are like a salad wrapped in rice paper. They are very popular in North America because they are not deep-fried, making them healthful and light. Working with the wrappers may require some experimenting — soften them until they are pliable but not so wet that they tear. Always have extra on hand. (Having the ingredients prepared and then letting guests assemble their own can become a party on its own.) Cooked chicken, tofu or mango can replace the shrimp. Serve with peanut sauce (page 47) or sweet chili sauce (page 45).

Make Ahead

Rolls can be assembled, covered with a damp tea towel and plastic wrap and refrigerated up to 4 hours ahead. If rolls become a bit dry, drizzle or spritz lightly with cold water to soften before serving.

2 oz	dried rice vermicelli noodles	60 g
12	8-inch (20 cm) round rice wrappers	12
6	small Boston or leaf lettuce leaves, ribs removed, halved	6
1/4 cup	peanut sauce, sweet chili sauce or hoisin sauce	50 mL
1 cup	grated carrot	250 mL
1/4	English cucumber, cut in strips	1/4
1/3 cup	shredded fresh mint leaves	75 mL
1/3 cup	shredded fresh cilantro leaves	75 mL
12	large cooked and peeled shrimp, halved lengthwise	12

1. In a bowl, cover noodles with very hot water and let stand for 10 to 12 minutes, or until softened but still firm. Rinse with cold water and drain.
2. To assemble rolls, place wrappers one or two at a time in a shallow dish of very warm water. Soak until softened, about 30 seconds, then gently transfer to a dampened tea towel.
3. Place half a lettuce leaf on lower third of wrapper. Spoon about 1 tsp (5 mL) peanut sauce over lettuce. Arrange some noodles, carrot, cucumber, mint and cilantro on top.
4. Fold up bottom of wrapper to encase filling (be firm yet gentle) and fold in sides. Place two pieces of shrimp cut side down across upper third of each wrapper (this is so shrimp will show through wrapper). Roll up wrapper and then place seam side down on a serving platter. Continue making rolls with remaining ingredients.

Spring Rolls with Pork and Shrimp

2 oz	bean thread (cellophane) noodles (page 111)	60 g
1/3 cup	dried black fungus strips	75 mL
2 tbsp	vegetable oil	25 mL
1	onion, chopped	1
1 cup	grated carrot	250 mL
1 cup	finely chopped cabbage	250 mL
8 oz	lean ground pork	250 g
8 oz	peeled raw shrimp, chopped	250 g
2	green onions, chopped	2
2 tbsp	chopped fresh cilantro leaves	25 mL
2 tbsp	oyster sauce	25 mL
2 tsp	fish sauce	10 mL
1/4 tsp	black pepper	1 mL
2 tbsp	all-purpose flour	25 mL
3 tbsp	water	45 mL
20	9-inch (23 cm) square spring roll wrappers	20
6 cups	vegetable oil	1.5 L

1. In two separate small bowls, soak noodles and fungus strips in hot water for 15 minutes, or until softened. Drain well. Cut noodles into short lengths.
2. Heat a wok or skillet over medium-high heat and add oil. Add onion, carrot and cabbage and stir-fry for 2 minutes.
3. Add pork and shrimp and stir-fry, breaking up pork, for 2 to 3 minutes, or until pork is cooked, vegetables are soft and juices have evaporated.
4. Stir in noodles, fungus, green onions, cilantro, oyster sauce, fish sauce and pepper. Cook for 2 minutes, or until liquid evaporates. Turn mixture into a shallow dish to cool.
5. In a small bowl, combine flour and water. Separate wrappers but keep covered with a damp tea towel to prevent drying. Place a wrapper on counter with pointed end toward you. Spoon about 2 tbsp (25 mL) filling in center of wrapper. Fold one end over mixture, tucking in slightly to firm mixture. Fold in 2 sides and roll up to encase filling. Brush inside of tip with flour mixture to seal tip and place seam side down on a baking sheet. Keep covered to prevent drying. Repeat with remaining filling and wrappers.
6. In a wok, heat oil to 365°F (185°C). Cook rolls in batches, turning, for 3 to 4 minutes, or until crisp and golden. Drain on a wire rack. Serve whole or cut into 2 or 3 pieces.

Makes 20 spring rolls

Although Chinese in origin, deep-fried spring rolls are a popular item on Thai menus. Crispy and golden, they are difficult to resist. Many versions can be found in the frozen section of supermarkets, but homemade are better.

Spring roll wrappers come in various sizes and are often found in the frozen section. This recipe uses a package that contains 20 wrappers. If there is any filling left over, eat it or use it as an omelet filling.

Serve these with sweet chili sauce (page 45).

Fresh shiitake mushrooms can be substituted for the dried. Just trim off the tough stems and slice the mushrooms thinly.

Thai Potstickers

Makes about 30 potstickers

Potstickers (a popular dim sum item) have been part of Thai cuisine for a long time. Considered a snack food, they can also be served as an appetizer or as a main course with a salad. Some potstickers are steamed or deep-fried, but in this recipe they are simply pan-fried. Any combination of ground pork or turkey, finely chopped shrimp or drained cooked crab meat can be substituted for the chicken. The round dumpling (sometimes called perogy) wrappers can be purchased fresh or frozen.

Make Ahead

Potstickers can be assembled and placed on cornstarch-dusted parchment paper. Cover lightly with plastic wrap and refrigerate for up to 3 hours before cooking.

8 oz	ground chicken	250 g
1/4 cup	finely chopped water chestnuts or bamboo shoots	50 mL
2 tbsp	chopped green onion	25 mL
2 tbsp	chopped fresh cilantro leaves	25 mL
1 tbsp	chopped fresh gingerroot	15 mL
1	egg white	1
1 1/2 tbsp	cornstarch	22 mL
1 tbsp	fish sauce	15 mL
1 tbsp	oyster sauce	15 mL
30	round dumpling wrappers	30

Chili Dipping Sauce

1/4 cup	homemade (page 45) or storebought sweet chili sauce	50 mL
3 tbsp	rice vinegar or lime juice	45 mL
2 tbsp	soy sauce	25 mL
1 tsp	sesame oil	5 mL

2 tbsp	vegetable oil (approx.)	25 mL
1/4 cup	water	50 mL

1. In a large bowl, combine chicken, water chestnuts, green onion, cilantro, ginger, egg white, cornstarch, fish sauce and oyster sauce. Mix thoroughly.
2. Arrange wrappers on a flat surface. Place a generous teaspoon of filling in center of each wrapper. Brush edges with water. Fold in half and press to seal, making three or four decorative pleats. Stand potsticker pleated side up, making a flat bottom. Place (without touching) on a parchment-lined baking sheet.
3. To prepare dipping sauce, in a bowl, whisk together chili sauce, vinegar, soy sauce and sesame oil.
4. In a large nonstick skillet, heat vegetable oil over medium-high heat. Add potstickers (in two batches if necessary). Cook for 2 to 3 minutes, or until lightly browned on bottom.
5. Add water to pan and cover immediately to prevent splattering. Cook for 4 minutes, or until filling is firm and water has evaporated. Remove cover and continue to cook for 1 to 2 minutes, or until bottoms are crisp, without letting potstickers stick. Serve with dipping sauce.

Shrimp in a Blanket

Makes 20 appetizers

These crisp parcels of seasoned shrimp wrapped in wonton skins make an elegant and irresistible appetizer. They are easy to assemble, but for a more elegant presentation, leave the tails attached (provide a little dish so guests can dispose of them). Serve with a dipping sauce (page 36).

1/4 cup	chopped fresh cilantro leaves	50 mL
2	cloves garlic, minced	2
1 tbsp	chopped fresh gingerroot	15 mL
1/2 tsp	green or red curry paste	2 mL
1/2 tsp	sesame oil	2 mL
20	3-inch (7.5 cm) square wonton wrappers	20
1	egg white, beaten	1
20	large shrimp, peeled and deveined, with tails intact	20
4 cups	vegetable oil	1 L

1. In a bowl, combine cilantro, garlic, ginger, curry paste and sesame oil.
2. Arrange wrappers on a flat surface and brush with egg white. (Work quickly to prevent drying out or assemble in two batches.) Place 1/2 tsp (2 mL) cilantro mixture in center of each wrapper. Pat shrimp dry, straightening slightly, and arrange on top, leaving tail to overhang edge at one point of wrapper. Fold opposite point to almost cover shrimp and filling, then fold in sides to make a triangle, pressing to seal edges.
3. Heat oil in a deep saucepan or wok to 365°F (185°C). Cook shrimp in batches for about 2 minutes, or until golden and crisp. Drain on paper towels.

Deep-frying Tips

- Heat oil in a flat-bottomed wok, deep saucepan or electric deep-fryer to the suggested temperature (for the best results, use a thermometer). Most recipes suggest a temperature of 365°F (185°C).
- For the best results, test one or two items before really starting to cook.
- Add items a few at a time to maintain the oil temperature. If too many items are added at once, the oil temperature will drop and the food will absorb too much oil.
- Have paper towel-lined baking sheets ready to absorb excess oil, or place cooked items on a baking rack set over a tray.
- Do not leave hot oil unattended, and have a lid available for possible splattering and flare-ups. Turn handles away from the edge of the stove.

Grilled Skewered Shrimp

Makes 30 appetizers

At a resort at Cha Am, on the Gulf of Thailand, the fish choices on the menu were abundant. This is a version of a shrimp appetizer we were served. After marinating, these shrimp could also be cooked in two batches in a wok and served as a main course. They are also good served cold on their own or as part of a salad. Soak the bamboo skewers in water for an hour before threading and cooking the shrimp.

30	extra-large shrimp, peeled and deveined, with tails intact	30
1/4 cup	packed fresh cilantro leaves	50 mL
2	cloves garlic, peeled	2
1/2 tsp	chopped fresh red chilies	2 mL
1 tbsp	fish sauce	15 mL
1 tbsp	lime juice	15 mL
2 tsp	palm or brown sugar	10 mL
1/4 tsp	black pepper	1 mL

1. Pat shrimp dry and place in a shallow dish.
2. In a blender or small food processor, combine cilantro, garlic, chilies, fish sauce, lime juice, sugar and pepper. Puree to form a paste. Spoon paste over shrimp and toss to coat. Refrigerate, covered, for up to 4 hours.
3. Thread each shrimp onto a 4-inch (10 cm) presoaked bamboo skewer, inserting whole skewer from head to tail so shrimp is straight and will not twirl on skewer when cooking.
4. Grill shrimp for 1 to 2 minutes per side, or until pink and just cooked.

Shrimp Toasts

Makes 32 toasts

More often associated with Chinese dim sum, Thais have a version of this popular appetizer, too. Some cooks combine shrimp and pork. Bread is not a traditional Thai ingredient, but it is available in Thai supermarkets. Try to use thinly sliced sandwich bread.

2 tbsp	chopped fresh cilantro roots or stems	25 mL
2	cloves garlic, peeled	2
½ tsp	black pepper	2 mL
1 lb	shrimp, peeled and deveined, cut in pieces	500 g
2	green onions, coarsely chopped	2
1	egg	1
1 tbsp	fish sauce	15 mL
8	thin slices stale white sandwich bread, crusts removed	8
4 cups	vegetable oil	1 L
	Fresh cilantro sprigs	

1. In a food processor, process cilantro, garlic and pepper to a paste.
2. Add shrimp and process until coarsely chopped. Add green onions, egg and fish sauce and process until finely chopped.
3. Spread mixture evenly over top of bread slices. Cut each slice into 4 squares or triangles.
4. In a deep saucepan or wok, heat oil to 365°F (185°C). Add toasts about 6 to 8 at a time, shrimp side down. Cook for 1 to 2 minutes per side, or until golden. Drain on paper towels. Keep warm in a 200°F (95°C) oven.
5. Garnish with fresh cilantro sprigs.

Make Ahead

Shrimp topping can be made several hours ahead, covered and refrigerated until ready to assemble toasts. Although best served shortly after cooking, the cooked toasts can also be refrigerated and reheated in a preheated 400°F (200°C) oven for 6 to 8 minutes, or until hot.

Golden Baskets

Makes 24 baskets

Delicate little baskets filled with a fiery shrimp filling make a wonderful appetizer. To tame the heat, simply reduce the amount of hot chili sauce. Traditionally the container is made from a crisp pastry shell, but wonton wrappers, spring roll wrappers and even phyllo pastry can be used. Try to find thin wonton wrappers, as they will be more delicate. The shrimp can be replaced with ground chicken.

Make Ahead

Shells can be baked up to a day ahead and stored in an airtight container.

24	3-inch (7.5 cm) square wonton wrappers	24
2 tbsp	vegetable oil, divided	25 mL
1/4 cup	chopped red bell pepper	50 mL
2	cloves garlic, finely chopped	2
8 oz	shrimp, peeled, deveined and chopped	250 g
1/2 cup	corn kernels	125 mL
2	green onions, chopped	2
1 tbsp	chopped fresh cilantro stems or leaves	15 mL
1 tbsp	fish sauce or soy sauce	15 mL
1 tbsp	lime juice	15 mL
1/2 tsp	palm or brown sugar	2 mL
3/4 tsp	hot chili sauce	4 mL
Garnish		
24	fresh cilantro leaves	24
24	thin slices fresh red chilies (optional)	24

1. Fit wonton wrappers into 24 lightly greased mini muffin cups so points extend beyond edges, keeping baskets as open as possible to allow room for filling. Brush lightly with 1 tbsp (15 mL) oil. Bake in a preheated 375°F (190°C) oven for 8 to 10 minutes, or until golden brown. Cool.
2. Meanwhile, heat a wok or skillet over medium-high heat and add remaining oil. Add red pepper and garlic and stir-fry for 1 to 2 minutes, or until softened.
3. Add shrimp and stir-fry for 1 to 2 minutes, or until just cooked.
4. Add corn, green onions, cilantro, fish sauce, lime juice, sugar and chili sauce. Stir-fry for 2 minutes.
5. Spoon filling into prepared cups. Garnish with cilantro leaves and red chili strips, if using.

Crispy Wontons with Tamarind Sauce

Makes 36 wontons

Many tasty morsels in Thai cuisine are wrapped. Wrappers can be spring roll sheets, wonton sheets, bean curd, pandanus leaves, banana leaves and even lettuce. Since many delicate crispy pastry treats can be tied with chives or thin green onions, they are also called beggar's purses. Chives do contain some moisture, which may cause the oil to splatter, so you can omit them if desired.

Make Ahead

Filling can be made several hours ahead, covered and refrigerated until assembling. Sauce can be made a day ahead, covered and refrigerated.

Tamarind Sauce

1/3 cup	tamarind paste	75 mL
1/4 cup	water	50 mL
1/4 cup	palm or brown sugar	50 mL
1/2 tsp	finely chopped fresh red chilies	2 mL
1/2 tsp	fish sauce	2 mL

Wontons

12 oz	shrimp, peeled and deveined	375 g
2 oz	lean ground chicken or pork	60 g
1/3 cup	chopped water chestnuts	75 mL
2	green onions, finely chopped	2
1	clove garlic, minced	1
1 tbsp	oyster sauce	15 mL
1/4 tsp	black pepper	1 mL
36	3-inch (7.5 cm) square wonton wrappers	36
36	long chives (optional)	36
6 cups	vegetable oil	1.5 L

1. To prepare sauce, combine tamarind paste, water and sugar in a small saucepan. Bring to a gentle boil, stirring to dissolve sugar. Remove from heat and stir in chilies and fish sauce. Cool to room temperature.
2. To prepare filling, in a food processor, chop shrimp to a coarse paste. Transfer to a bowl.
3. Add chicken, water chestnuts, green onions, garlic, oyster sauce and pepper. Mix thoroughly.
4. Working in batches, place 1 tsp (5 mL) filling in center of each wonton wrapper. Brush remaining wonton lightly with water. Gather wonton into a bundle and pinch gently to form a waist. Tie with a chive piece, if using. Continue with remaining filling and wontons.
5. In a wok or deep saucepan, heat oil to 365°F (185°C). Cook wontons in batches for 3 to 4 minutes, draining on paper towels. Keep warm in a 200°F (95°C) oven while cooking remaining wontons.
6. Serve wontons with sauce.

Thai Omelets

Makes 4 servings

Eggs — from tiny quail eggs to chicken and duck eggs — are used in many Thai dishes. A simple omelet is a common dish, but these are a step up. Ground chicken or turkey could also be used. Serve with hot chili sauce.

Make Ahead

Filling can be prepared, covered and refrigerated up to a day ahead.

Filling

1 tbsp	vegetable oil	15 mL
1	onion, chopped	1
2	cloves garlic, finely chopped	2
8 oz	lean ground pork	250 g
2 tbsp	fish sauce	25 mL
1 tsp	palm or brown sugar	5 mL
1/2 cup	chopped tomatoes	125 mL
2	green onions, chopped	2
1 tbsp	chopped fresh cilantro leaves	15 mL
1/2 tsp	black pepper	2 mL

Omelet

5	eggs	5
1 tbsp	fish sauce	15 mL
1 tbsp	water	15 mL
2 tbsp	vegetable oil, divided	25 mL

1. In a wok or skillet, heat oil over medium-high heat. Add onion and garlic. Cook, stirring, for 2 minutes, or until soft.
2. Add pork and cook for 4 minutes, or until pinkness disappears.
3. Add fish sauce, sugar, tomatoes, green onions, cilantro and pepper. Cook for 4 to 5 minutes, or until juices evaporate. Spoon into a bowl and cool.
4. To prepare omelets, in a bowl, whisk together eggs, fish sauce and water.
5. In a wok or small skillet, heat one-quarter of oil over high heat. Add one-quarter of egg mixture to pan. Tilt and swirl pan to coat with egg mixture. Cook egg until set, easing uncooked part to edge of pan. When cooked and slightly golden on bottom, spoon one-quarter of filling into center of omelet. Fold over edges to encase. Flip onto a serving dish. Continue with remaining egg mixture and filling.

Son-in-Law Eggs

Makes 4 to 6 servings

A traditional dish served at weddings, this also makes a light supper served with steamed rice. Generally the eggs are deep-fried, but in this recipe they are pan-fried. You can also omit the frying and just cut the hard-cooked eggs in half.

Make Ahead

This dish can be served cold. Prepare the sauce, cool and pour over eggs just before serving.

2 tbsp	vegetable oil	25 mL
6	hard-cooked eggs, peeled	6
1/4 cup	tamarind paste	50 mL
2 tbsp	palm or brown sugar	25 mL
2 tbsp	fish sauce	25 mL
2 tbsp	water	25 mL
3 tbsp	crisp fried shallots (page 147)	45 mL
1 tsp	chopped fresh red chilies	5 mL
	Fresh cilantro leaves	

1. In a wok or nonstick skillet, heat oil over medium-high heat. Dry eggs well with paper towels. Add eggs to oil and cook, turning frequently, for 3 to 4 minutes, or until blistered. Transfer to a paper towel-lined dish and cool slightly. Cut eggs in half lengthwise and place on a serving dish.
2. Pour off all but 1 tbsp (15 mL) oil. Add tamarind paste, sugar, fish sauce and water. Bring to a gentle boil, stirring to combine ingredients.
3. Spoon sauce over eggs. Garnish with fried shallots, chilies and cilantro.

Just Appetizers

Deep-fried Cashews (page 225)
Shrimp Crackers (page 28) with Peanut Sauce (page 47)
Chicken Satays (page 31)
Shrimp Cakes (page 191)
Son-in-Law Eggs (page 44)
Fresh Spring Rolls (page 34)
Vegetable Curry Rolls (page 260)
Pork and Tomato Dip (page 45)

Pork and Tomato Dip

Makes 2 cups (500 mL)

This is a dipping sauce from northern Thailand, but it is not like a Western dip. Often served warm or at room temperature with crisp slices of cucumber, carrots, cabbage wedges and fried pork rinds, it can also be served with plain rice or noodles. With added water, it becomes the Thai equivalent of pasta sauce.

2 tbsp	vegetable oil	25 mL
3	shallots, chopped	3
4	cloves garlic, chopped	4
2 tbsp	chopped fresh cilantro stems or roots	25 mL
1 tbsp	red curry paste	15 mL
8 oz	lean ground pork	250 g
1 cup	chopped tomatoes	250 mL
1⁄2 cup	coconut milk or water	125 mL
2 tbsp	fish sauce	25 mL
1 tbsp	palm or brown sugar	15 mL

1. Heat a wok or large skillet over medium-high heat and add oil. Add shallots, garlic and cilantro and cook for 1 minute. Add curry paste and cook for 30 seconds.
2. Add pork and cook for 2 minutes. Add tomatoes, coconut milk, fish sauce and sugar. Bring to a boil, reduce heat to medium and cook, stirring occasionally, for 8 to 10 minutes, or until thickened.

Sweet Chili Sauce

Makes 1⁄2 cup (125 mL)

This all-purpose condiment (which is also available bottled) is often served with fish cakes, spring rolls and barbecued poultry and meats.

Make Ahead

Sauce can be refrigerated for up to 2 weeks.

1 cup	rice vinegar	250 mL
3⁄4 cup	granulated sugar	175 mL
1⁄4 tsp	salt	1 mL
1 tbsp	finely chopped fresh red chilies	15 mL
2	cloves garlic, minced	2

1. In a saucepan, combine vinegar, sugar, salt, chilies and garlic. Bring to a boil. Reduce heat and simmer, stirring occasionally, for about 15 minutes, or until thick. Cool.

Spicy Cucumber Relish

Makes $1\frac{1}{2}$ cups (375 mL)

This most often accompanies fish cakes, but it is also delightful served with grilled fish or chicken. Cut the cucumber lengthwise into quarters before slicing for a more delicate appearance.

1/4 cup	rice vinegar	50 mL
2 tbsp	granulated sugar	25 mL
2 tbsp	water	25 mL
1 tsp	fish sauce	5 mL
1 1/2 cups	thinly sliced English cucumber	375 mL
1/4 cup	finely chopped carrot	50 mL
2	shallots, thinly sliced	2
1 tbsp	chopped fresh cilantro leaves	15 mL
1/2 tsp	chopped fresh red chilies	2 mL
2 tbsp	chopped peanuts	25 mL

1. In a small saucepan, combine vinegar, sugar, water and fish sauce. Bring to a boil and stir until sugar dissolves. Remove from heat and cool for 20 minutes.
2. In a bowl, combine cucumber, carrot, shallots, cilantro, chilies and peanuts. Add cooled sauce and stir to combine.

Hua Hin Peanut Sauce

Makes $1\frac{1}{2}$ cups (375 mL)

This is a version of a peanut sauce served by a Thai street vendor at the night market in Hua Hin. It has more texture than others because peanuts are used instead of peanut butter.

3/4 cup	roasted unsalted peanuts	175 mL
1 1/2 cups	coconut milk	375 mL
1 tbsp	red curry paste (page 196)	15 mL
2 tbsp	palm or brown sugar	25 mL
1 tbsp	fish sauce	15 mL
1 tbsp	tamarind paste or lime juice	15 mL

1. In a food processor or by hand, coarsely chop peanuts (if you are using a food processor, be careful not to chop too much or you will end up with peanut butter).
2. In a saucepan, combine coconut milk and curry paste. Add sugar, fish sauce, tamarind paste and chopped peanuts.
3. Bring to a boil, reduce heat to medium and cook, stirring often, for 6 to 8 minutes, or until sauce has thickened slightly.

Peanut Sauce

2 tbsp	vegetable oil	25 mL
2 tbsp	chopped fresh gingerroot	25 mL
3	cloves garlic, chopped	3
4	green onions, chopped	4
1/2 cup	peanut butter	125 mL
1/2 cup	coconut milk	125 mL
1/4 cup	coarsely chopped fresh cilantro leaves	50 mL
2 tbsp	lime or lemon juice	25 mL
1 tbsp	fish sauce	15 mL
1 tbsp	soy sauce	15 mL
1 tbsp	brown sugar	15 mL
1/2 tsp	hot pepper sauce	2 mL

1. In a small skillet, heat oil over medium heat. Add ginger, garlic and green onions. Cook for 2 minutes, stirring occasionally, until softened. Cool for 20 minutes.
2. In a food processor, combine cooled ginger mixture, peanut butter, coconut milk, cilantro, lime juice, fish sauce, soy sauce, sugar and hot pepper sauce. Puree until smooth. (Sauce will be thick. For a slightly thinner sauce, add a small amount of water.)

Makes 1 1/2 cups (375 mL)

Peanut sauce is served with satays, spring rolls, raw vegetables and shrimp crackers (page 28). There are many variations (both homemade and storebought), but this is a great all-purpose version that uses readily available ingredients.

Make Ahead

Sauce can be made ahead, covered and refrigerated for up to 4 days or frozen for up to 4 weeks. Stir well after defrosting.

Roasted Chili Paste

Makes 3/4 cup (175 mL)

Traditionally, this condiment (Nam Prik Pao) is made from whole garlic and shallots dark-roasted in the ashes of a fire. Several commercial varieties are available, but homemade has a fresher taste. The paste is often used in soups, rice, vegetables and stir-fried dishes.

Make Ahead

Paste can be prepared, covered and refrigerated for up to 2 weeks.

1/2 cup	dried red chilies	125 mL
1/2 cup	garlic cloves, unpeeled	125 mL
1/2 cup	shallots, unpeeled, halved lengthwise	125 mL
1/3 cup	vegetable oil	75 mL
1 tsp	fish sauce	5 mL
1 tbsp	palm or brown sugar (optional)	15 mL

1. In a dry wok or skillet over low heat, cook chilies for 5 to 6 minutes, stirring often, until skins darken and become brittle. Remove from pan.
2. In same pan, cook garlic and shallots for 6 to 8 minutes, stirring often, until they soften and dark spots appear. Remove from pan.
3. Remove stems (and seeds, if desired) from chilies and peel garlic and shallots. In a food processor or using a mortar and pestle, pound or process until a smooth paste forms.
4. In same skillet, heat oil over medium heat. Scrape in paste. Add fish sauce and sugar, if using. Cook for 4 to 5 minutes, stirring, until paste darkens. Remove from heat and cool to room temperature.

Roasted Chili Powder

Roast dried red chilies in a dry skillet over medium heat for 3 to 4 minutes, or until lightly colored. (Turn on the fan or open windows, as there is some smoke, or roast on an outdoor grill.) Transfer roasted peppers to a dish and cool. Grind in a spice grinder or coffee grinder, leaving small pieces of seeds and pepper. Store in a covered container in a dry place.

Soups

Chicken Stock

Makes 12 cups (3 L)

There are always large vats of stock simmering in Thai restaurant and hotel kitchens. Although some Thai soups use water as a base, chicken stock is more common, even for fish and seafood soups.

Make Ahead
Stock can be refrigerated for 2 days or frozen for up to 4 months.

4 lbs	chicken pieces	2 kg
16 cups	cold water	4 L
4	stalks celery, cut in large pieces	4
2	stalks lemongrass, cut in 2-inch (5 cm) pieces	2
4	onions, cut in large pieces	4
4	fresh cilantro stems, including roots	4
3	thin slices fresh gingerroot	3

1. In a large Dutch oven or stock pot, combine chicken, water, celery, lemongrass, onions, cilantro and ginger.
2. Bring to a boil, skimming surface if necessary. Do not stir. Reduce heat and simmer (with bubbles just breaking surface) for 3 hours.
3. Strain stock, cool and refrigerate. When cold, skim fat from surface.

Vegetable Stock

Makes 5 cups (1.25 L) or more

A simple stock ideal for vegetarian soups.

Make Ahead
Stock can be covered and refrigerated for 3 days or frozen for up to 4 months.

6 cups	cold water	1.5 L
2	onions, chopped	2
2	carrots, chopped	2
2	stalks celery, chopped	2
4 oz	fresh mushrooms, sliced	125 g
2	cloves garlic, peeled	2
2	stalks lemongrass, cut in 2-inch (5 cm) lengths	2

1. In a large saucepan, combine water, onions, carrots, celery, mushrooms, garlic and lemongrass.
2. Bring to a boil. Reduce heat and simmer for 1 hour. Strain stock.

Spicy Shrimp Soup

1 lb	shrimp, peeled and deveined, shells reserved	500 g
5 cups	chicken stock or water	1.25 L
3	stalks lemongrass, white part only, cut in 1-inch (2.5 cm) lengths, divided	3
8	lime leaves	8
6	thin slices galangal	6
2 tsp	thinly sliced fresh red chilies	10 mL
1 1/2 cups	sliced fresh mushrooms (about 4 oz/125 g)	375 mL
3 tbsp	lime juice	45 mL
2 tbsp	fish sauce	25 mL
1 tsp	granulated sugar (optional)	5 mL
2	green onions, finely chopped	2
3 tbsp	fresh cilantro leaves	45 mL

1. In a saucepan, combine shrimp shells, stock and 1 stalk lemongrass. Bring to a boil, reduce heat and simmer for 20 minutes. (This adds more shrimp flavor to the soup, but some cooks omit this step.) Strain into another saucepan.
2. To flavored broth, add remaining lemongrass, lime leaves, galangal and chilies. Bring to a boil, reduce heat to medium and cook for 10 minutes.
3. Add shrimp and mushrooms and cook for 2 minutes, or until shrimp is just cooked.
4. Stir in lime juice, fish sauce and sugar, if using. Remove from heat.
5. Serve garnished with green onions and cilantro. Guests can add extra lime juice, fish sauce and chili paste (page 48) to taste.

Makes 5 to 6 servings

Tom Yam Goong is the popular seafood soup filled with classic Thai flavors. In Thai markets and supermarkets, bundles of flavorings (such as lemongrass, lime leaves, galangal and other ingredients) are held together by elastics, ready to season a particular dish. Usually the pieces of lemongrass, lime leaves and galangal are left in the soup and the diner simply pushes them aside. If you prefer a more delicate appearance, strain the stock before adding the shrimp and mushrooms. In Thailand, fresh straw mushrooms are used, but since these are not usually available, use the smaller button mushrooms. Firm white fish, such as cod or halibut, or thinly sliced chicken can be used instead of shrimp.

My Hot and Sour Soup

Makes 6 to 8 servings

I have taught Thai and Thai-inspired classes for many years, adapting recipes according to the tastes of the group and the availability of ingredients. This soup is a delicious way to introduce people to a wide spectrum of Thai flavors. Everyone can adjust the heat with a side dish of sweet or hot chili sauce. The sweetness of the corn and pineapple is balanced by the lime juice, fish sauce and chilies.

For a vegetarian version, use vegetable stock, tofu instead of shrimp or chicken and soy sauce instead of fish sauce.

5 cups	chicken or vegetable stock	1.25 L
2 tbsp	sweet chili sauce	25 mL
6	lime leaves	6
3	stalks lemongrass, white part only, cut in 1-inch (2.5 cm) lengths	3
1/4 cup	thinly sliced galangal	50 mL
1 tsp	chopped fresh green or red chilies	5 mL
1 cup	thinly sliced fresh shiitake mushrooms	250 mL
1/2 cup	corn kernels	125 mL
8 oz	diced shrimp or chicken	250 g
2 tbsp	fish sauce	25 mL
1/2 cup	diced fresh pineapple	125 mL
1/4 cup	lime juice	50 mL
2 tbsp	chopped fresh cilantro leaves	25 mL
2	green onions, thinly sliced	2

1. In a saucepan, combine stock, chili sauce, lime leaves, lemongrass, galangal and chilies. Bring to a boil. Cover. Reduce heat and simmer for 20 minutes. At this point broth can be strained if you wish.
2. Add mushrooms, corn, shrimp and fish sauce. Simmer for 2 to 3 minutes, or until shrimp is just cooked.
3. Add pineapple, lime juice, cilantro and green onions and heat for 1 minute.

Chicken and Coconut Soup

2 cups	coconut milk	500 mL
1 ½ cups	chicken stock	375 mL
3	stalks lemongrass, white part only, cut in 1-inch (2.5 cm) lengths	3
8	thin slices galangal	8
10	lime leaves	10
3	shallots, thinly sliced	3
12 oz	chicken breasts or thighs, thinly sliced	375 g
1 ½ cups	thinly sliced fresh shiitake mushrooms (about 4 oz/125 g)	375 mL
3 tbsp	lime juice	45 mL
2 tbsp	fish sauce	25 mL
½ tsp	palm or granulated sugar (optional)	2 mL
2 tbsp	fresh cilantro leaves	25 mL
½ tsp	chopped fresh red chilies (optional)	2 mL

1. In a large saucepan, combine coconut milk, stock, lemongrass, galangal, lime leaves and shallots. Bring just to a boil. Reduce heat and simmer for 10 minutes.
2. Add chicken and mushrooms and simmer for 10 to 12 minutes, or until chicken is tender and just cooked.
3. Remove from heat and stir in lime juice, fish sauce and sugar, if using.
4. Serve soup garnished with cilantro. Stir in chopped chilies, if using, or let guests add their own.

Makes 4 to 6 servings

This soup, Tom Kha Gai, probably rivals Tom Yam Goong (Spicy Shrimp Soup) in popularity. It is rich and comforting, with galangal, lemongrass, lime leaves and coconut milk. It is not a spicy soup, so diners can spice up their own servings with fresh chilies or chili sauce. Some versions include tomatoes. This is another soup where the seasonings are left in the soup and the diner eats around them but, for entertaining, the seasonings can be removed before serving.

Pumpkin and Coconut Soup

Makes 5 to 6 servings

The combination of pumpkin, coconut and shrimp makes a luscious soup that is almost a meal in itself. It is not spicy. If fresh pumpkin is not in season, use butternut squash.

1 lb	pumpkin, peeled and cut in 1-inch (2.5 cm) pieces	500 g
2 tbsp	lime juice	25 mL
2	shallots, peeled	2
2	cloves garlic, peeled	2
1/2 tsp	chopped fresh red or green chilies	2 mL
1/2 tsp	shrimp or anchovy paste	2 mL
2 tsp	fish sauce	10 mL
1 tsp	granulated or brown sugar	5 mL
12 oz	small shrimp, peeled and deveined, divided	375 g
3 cups	coconut milk	750 mL
2 cups	chicken or fish stock, or water	500 mL
1/2 cup	fresh sweet Thai basil leaves	125 mL

1. In a bowl, combine pumpkin and lime juice. Let stand while preparing paste.
2. In a food processor or using a mortar and pestle, combine shallots, garlic, chilies, shrimp paste, fish sauce, sugar and half the shrimp. Puree or pound to a paste.
3. In a saucepan, combine coconut milk and stock. Stir in paste. Heat to just below boiling, stirring often.
4. Add pumpkin and simmer for 15 minutes, or until pumpkin is just tender. Do not overcook or pumpkin will fall apart.
5. Add remaining shrimp and cook for 3 to 4 minutes, or until just cooked.
6. Stir in basil just before serving.

Corn and Crabmeat Soup

Makes 5 to 6 servings

A quick soup that can be prepared in a few minutes. Some cooks add a 19-oz (540 mL) can of cream corn for a creamier soup. Finely chopped shrimp can replace the crabmeat.

1 tbsp	vegetable oil	15 mL
4	cloves garlic, chopped	4
5	shallots, chopped	5
4 cups	chicken stock	1 L
2 cups	corn kernels	500 mL
8 oz	crabmeat, flaked, cartilage removed	250 g
2 tbsp	fish sauce	25 mL
1	egg, beaten	1
2 tbsp	chopped fresh cilantro leaves	25 mL
Pinch	black pepper	Pinch

1. In a saucepan, heat oil over medium-high heat. Add garlic and shallots. Cook, stirring, for 3 minutes, or until golden.
2. Add stock and corn and bring to a boil. Add crabmeat and fish sauce. Cook for 1 minute, or until corn is just tender. Stir in beaten egg and cook for 1 minute.
3. Stir in cilantro and pepper.

Spinach and Tofu Soup

Makes 4 servings

A mild, delicate soup to serve with a meal that includes spicy or curried dishes. Some versions include a few dried shrimp (page 22) simmered in the stock.

4 cups	vegetable or chicken stock	1 L
8 oz	firm tofu, cut in 1/2-inch (1 cm) pieces	250 g
2 tbsp	soy sauce or fish sauce	25 mL
1/4 tsp	black pepper	1 mL
10 oz	baby spinach leaves	300 g
2	green onions, thinly sliced	2

1. In a saucepan, bring stock to a boil. Reduce heat to medium. Add tofu, soy sauce and pepper. Cook for 3 minutes.
2. Stir in spinach and cook for 1 to 2 minutes, or until just wilted.
3. Serve garnished with green onions.

Rice Soup

2 tbsp	vegetable oil	25 mL
4	cloves garlic, thinly sliced	4
4 cups	chicken stock	1 L
4 oz	ground chicken or pork (optional)	125 g
2 cups	cooked rice	500 mL
2 tbsp	fish sauce	25 mL
1/4 tsp	black pepper	1 mL
Condiments		
2	green onions, finely chopped	2
2 tbsp	chopped fresh cilantro leaves	25 mL
2 tsp	chopped fresh red chilies	10 mL
2 tbsp	chopped fresh gingerroot	25 mL
1 tbsp	pickled radish root (optional)	15 mL

1. In a small skillet, heat oil over medium-high heat. Add garlic and cook, stirring, for 1 minute, or until golden. Remove garlic from pan and drain on paper towels.
2. In a saucepan, heat stock over medium-high heat. Add chicken, if using, stirring to separate. Add rice. Bring to a low boil and cook for 4 to 5 minutes, or until chicken is cooked.
3. Add fish sauce and pepper. Taste and adjust seasonings if necessary.
4. Serve garnished with reserved garlic. Top with condiments, or let diners add their own.

Green Chilies with Vinegar

Serve this as a condiment with soups, rice or noodles.

In a small bowl, combine 1/2 cup (125 mL) rice vinegar, 1 tbsp (15 mL) fish sauce, 1 tsp (5 mL) granulated sugar and 2 tbsp (25 mL) thinly sliced fresh red or green chilies. Cover and refrigerate for up to a week.

Makes about 2/3 cup (150 mL).

Makes 4 to 6 servings

When I accompanied a group to Thailand for the first time, we arrived in Bangkok very late at night after thirty hours of traveling. The next morning, before embarking on a full day of sightseeing, we first needed a restorative Thai breakfast of rice soup (Khoa Tom). On the table were small dishes of condiments to adjust the sweetness, spiciness, heat and saltiness of the soup.

Not only is this a breakfast staple, but it is eaten when you are not feeling well, to tidy a hangover or for a late-night snack. This is Thai comfort food. It is often made with leftover cooked rice. A poached egg can also be added. While this version contains ground chicken or pork as an option, some omit it entirely or substitute thinly sliced white fish fillets.

This soup is best served soon after making, as it thickens on standing.

Ginger, Fish and Vegetable Soup

Makes 6 servings

Lom Fang, a restaurant at a Cha Am resort that overlooks Lom Fang Lake, is a peaceful and tranquil setting — a good place to linger, day or night, in a hot, sultry environment. This is a version of one of their soups, with soothing ginger undertones.

3	shallots, peeled	3
2 tbsp	coarsely chopped fresh gingerroot	25 mL
3	cloves garlic, peeled	3
1 1⁄2 tsp	chopped fresh red chilies	7 mL
2 tbsp	vegetable oil	25 mL
6 cups	chicken or fish stock	1.5 L
3	stalks lemongrass, white part only, cut in 1-inch (2.5 cm) lengths	3
1 cup	sliced green beans	250 mL
1 cup	chopped Chinese or Napa cabbage	250 mL
1 cup	sliced fresh shiitake mushrooms	250 mL
2	tomatoes, cut in 1⁄2-inch (1 cm) chunks	2
1 lb	white fish fillets (e.g., cod, snapper, tilapia), cut in 1-inch (2.5 cm) pieces	500 g
3 tbsp	lime juice	45 mL
3 tbsp	fish sauce	45 mL
3	green onions, chopped	3
2 tbsp	fresh cilantro leaves	25 mL

1. In a food processor or using a mortar and pestle, combine shallots, ginger, garlic and chilies to make a paste.
2. In a saucepan, heat oil over medium-high heat. Add paste and cook for 1 minute, stirring, until soft and fragrant.
3. Add stock and lemongrass. Bring to a gentle boil, cover, reduce heat and simmer for 20 minutes.
4. Add beans, cabbage and mushrooms and cook for 4 to 5 minutes, or until vegetables are just tender.
5. Add tomatoes and fish and cook, without boiling, for 2 minutes, or until fish is just cooked. Remove from heat.
6. Stir in lime juice, fish sauce, green onions and cilantro.

Pipith's Hot Fish Soup

Makes 3 to 4 servings

Pipith has been our guide on several visits to Thailand. His smile is as welcoming in the middle of the night when we have an early-morning departure as it is on our arrival after a thirty-hour journey. His charm and versatility have endeared him to many visitors. He loves his country, and he is as much at home guiding groups through the jungle as he is on the streets and canals of Bangkok. This clear, hot and spicy soup is his comfort food, and his remedy for offsetting the onset of a cold.

5 cups	water	1.25 L
6	thin slices galangal	6
3	stalks lemongrass, white part only, cut in 1-inch (2.5 cm) lengths	3
4	shallots, peeled and smashed	4
3	cloves garlic, peeled and smashed	3
4	fresh cilantro roots	4
3 tbsp	lime juice	45 mL
2 tbsp	fish sauce	25 mL
3	green onions, cut in pieces	3
1/4 cup	fresh sweet Thai basil leaves	50 mL
4	lime leaves	4
1 tbsp	coarsely chopped fresh red chilies	15 mL
12 oz	sea bass or snapper fillets, cut in 1/2-inch (1 cm) pieces	375 g
2 tbsp	fresh cilantro leaves	25 mL

1. In a large saucepan, combine water, galangal, lemongrass, shallots, garlic and cilantro roots. Bring to a boil. Reduce heat to a medium boil and cook for 15 minutes. Strain and return stock to saucepan.
2. Add lime juice, fish sauce, green onions, basil, lime leaves, chilies and fish. Cook, without boiling, for 2 minutes, or until fish is just cooked.
3. Remove from heat and stir in cilantro leaves.

Make Ahead

Stock can be made ahead, strained and refrigerated for 2 days or frozen for 4 weeks.

Tamarind Seafood Soup

Makes 5 to 6 servings

This is a version of a seafood soup that we had at the seaside restaurant Itsara in Hua Hin. We were also served a crispy taro root basket filled with shrimp, squid and quail eggs. We tried, guided by the always smiling cooks, to assemble these baskets ourselves, but the result was a sad reproduction. They also showed us how to fillet a fish using a cleaver!

Do not let the long list of ingredients stop you from making this soup. There are just a few easy steps.

Frozen squid rings are available in many supermarkets.

3	cloves garlic, peeled	3
3	shallots, peeled	3
1 tbsp	coarsely chopped fresh gingerroot	15 mL
1 1/2 tsp	chopped fresh green chilies	7 mL
3 tbsp	chopped fresh cilantro roots or stems	45 mL
1 tbsp	vegetable oil	15 mL
1/2 tsp	ground turmeric	2 mL
5 cups	fish or chicken stock	1.25 L
2	stalks lemongrass, white part only, cut in 1-inch (2.5 cm) lengths	2
1 tbsp	tamarind paste	15 mL
2 tsp	palm or brown sugar	10 mL
3	tomatoes, chopped	3
12	large shrimp, peeled and deveined	12
16	mussels, scrubbed	16
8 oz	white fish fillets, cut in 1 1/2-inch (4 cm) strips	250 g
8 oz	thin squid rings	250 g
1/2 cup	fresh sweet Thai basil leaves	125 mL
2	small fresh red chilies, seeded and chopped	2
2 tbsp	lime juice	25 mL

1. In a food processor or using a mortar and pestle, combine garlic, shallots, ginger, chilies and cilantro into a paste.
2. In a saucepan or wok, heat oil over medium-high heat. Add paste and turmeric and cook for 2 minutes, or until fragrant.
3. Add stock, lemongrass, tamarind paste and sugar. Bring to a boil. Reduce heat, cover and simmer for 10 minutes. Remove lemongrass if desired.
4. Increase heat to medium. Add tomatoes, shrimp, mussels, fish and squid and cook, without boiling, for 4 to 6 minutes, or until fish and shellfish are just cooked. Stir gently occasionally, but do not break up fish.
5. Garnish with basil, chilies and lime juice.

Stuffed Cucumber Soup

4 cups	chicken stock	1 L
2 tbsp	lime juice	25 mL
1 tbsp	fish sauce	15 mL
2 tsp	soy sauce	10 mL
1 tsp	palm or brown sugar	5 mL
4 oz	shrimp, peeled and deveined	125 g
1 tbsp	chopped fresh cilantro roots or stems	15 mL
1	clove garlic, coarsely chopped	1
1⁄4 tsp	black pepper	1 mL
2 tsp	cornstarch	10 mL
1	long (about 12 inches/30 cm) English cucumber, peeled	1
2 tbsp	fresh cilantro leaves	25 mL

1. In a large saucepan, combine stock, lime juice, fish sauce, soy sauce and sugar. Bring to a simmer over medium heat.
2. Meanwhile, pat shrimp dry and chop coarsely in a food processor. Add cilantro roots, garlic, pepper and cornstarch and process just until combined.
3. Cut cucumber into 1-inch (2.5 cm) rounds to make 12 pieces. Remove seeds with an apple corer or small spoon. Stuff each cucumber slice with filling.
4. Gently add stuffed cucumbers to stock and simmer over medium heat, below boiling, for 6 to 8 minutes, or until filling is set.
5. Serve garnished with cilantro leaves.

Makes 4 to 6 servings

This is a classic soup often associated with "palace" cuisine. The cucumber — refreshing in a hot climate — is stuffed with a shrimp mixture. Sometimes a combination of shrimp and pork is used, and even ground chicken can replace the shrimp. This soup tastes and looks delicate, and it is not spicy.

Meatball Noodle Soup

Makes 5 to 6 servings

As with many Thai dishes, variations of this soup depend on the season, the region and the cook. This perfect winter soup is standard fare in many small restaurants. Some versions contain very thin slices of poached beef, ground beef, small meatballs or dumplings. Wide fresh or dried noodles are normally used, but rice vermicelli noodles can be substituted. Dry noodles will require soaking in warm water for 15 minutes before being added to the soup. A typical condiment is chili vinegar.

Meatballs

12 oz	lean ground beef	375 g
1	egg white	1
2 tbsp	fish sauce	25 mL
2 tbsp	chopped fresh cilantro leaves	25 mL
1	green onion, finely chopped	1
1/4 tsp	black pepper	1 mL

Soup

5 cups	beef stock	1.25 L
2	cloves garlic, minced	2
3	shallots, chopped	3
1	stalk celery, thinly sliced	1
2 tbsp	fish sauce	25 mL
2 oz	dried rice vermicelli noodles, soaked	60 g
3/4 cup	bean sprouts	175 mL
2 tbsp	fresh cilantro leaves (optional)	25 mL

1. To prepare meatballs, in a bowl, combine beef, egg white, fish sauce, chopped cilantro, green onion and pepper. Mix thoroughly. With dampened hands, shape into small balls about 3/4 inch (2 cm) in diameter (about 30).
2. To prepare soup, in a saucepan, combine stock, garlic, shallots, celery and fish sauce. Bring to a boil, reduce heat and simmer for 4 minutes.
3. Carefully add meatballs and cook, stirring occasionally, for 5 minutes, or until meatballs are cooked.
4. Add noodles and simmer for 2 minutes, or until noodles are tender but not mushy.
5. Remove from heat and stir in bean sprouts and cilantro leaves, if using.

Chili Vinegar

In a small bowl, combine 1 tbsp (15 mL) hot pepper flakes, 1 minced clove garlic (optional) and 1/4 cup (50 mL) rice vinegar. Let stand for 30 minutes.

Makes about 1/4 cup (50 mL).

Vegetable and Lemongrass Soup

Makes 6 servings

Lemongrass adds a fresh sparkle to a vegetable soup. Some Thai vegetable soups include shrimp paste, but it has been omitted for this simple vegetarian soup. You could also omit the tofu and add shrimp.

6 cups	vegetable or chicken stock	1.5 L
3	stalks lemongrass, white part only, cut in 1-inch (2.5 cm) lengths	3
4	thin slices galangal	4
6	lime leaves	6
1 cup	shredded bok choy or Chinese cabbage	250 mL
1 cup	quartered fresh button mushrooms	250 mL
1	medium zucchini (about 8 oz/250 g), sliced	1
1 cup	cauliflower florets	250 mL
1/2 cup	corn kernels	125 mL
1/2 cup	sliced green beans	125 mL
6 oz	firm tofu, cut in 1/2-inch (1 cm) pieces (optional)	175 g
3 tbsp	soy sauce or fish sauce	45 mL
2 tbsp	lime juice	25 mL
1/2 tsp	hot chili sauce or roasted chili paste (page 48)	2 mL
2 tbsp	chopped fresh sweet Thai basil or cilantro leaves	25 mL

1. In a saucepan, combine stock, lemongrass, galangal and lime leaves. Bring to a boil, cover, reduce heat and simmer for 20 minutes.
2. Add bok choy, mushrooms, zucchini, cauliflower, corn and beans. Bring to a low boil, cover and cook for 4 to 5 minutes, or until vegetables are just tender. Reduce heat to low.
3. Stir in tofu, if using. Add soy sauce, lime juice and chili sauce and heat for 1 minute.
4. Serve garnished with basil.

Bean Thread Noodle Soup

Makes 5 to 6 servings

Soups like this are sold day and night in Thailand. Customers select their choice of noodle and in the north of Thailand the soup is served with rice as well. Pork is often the protein, and in this version both ground and sliced pork are used. Sometimes tofu is added or used instead of pork. Serve this as soon as the noodles are added, otherwise too much stock is absorbed and the soup becomes thick. This is not a spicy soup.

2 oz	bean thread (cellophane) noodles (page 111)	60 g
2 tbsp	vegetable oil	25 mL
6	cloves garlic, thinly sliced	6
5 cups	chicken stock	1.25 L
4 oz	lean ground pork	125 g
2 tbsp	chopped fresh cilantro roots or stems	25 mL
2 tbsp	fish sauce	25 mL
1/4 tsp	black pepper	1 mL
1 cup	thinly sliced fresh shiitake mushrooms	250 mL
1 cup	thinly sliced Chinese or Napa cabbage	250 mL
8 oz	cooked pork tenderloin (page 271) or pork loin, thinly sliced	250 g
2	green onions, thinly sliced	2

1. In a bowl, cover noodles with warm water and let soften for 20 minutes. Drain and cut into 3-inch (7.5 cm) lengths.
2. In a saucepan, heat oil over medium-high heat. Add garlic and cook, stirring, until golden, about 4 minutes. Remove garlic and drain on paper towels.
3. Add stock to saucepan. Stir in ground pork, cilantro, fish sauce and pepper and cook for 3 to 4 minutes, or until pork is cooked.
4. Add mushrooms and cabbage and cook for 3 minutes.
5. Stir in pork slices, softened noodles and green onions. Sprinkle with fried garlic and serve immediately.

Variation

Bean Thread Noodle Soup with Chicken: Replace ground pork and cooked sliced pork with ground chicken or turkey and cooked sliced chicken or turkey.

Pork and Cabbage Soup

3 cups	chicken stock	750 mL
8 oz	lean ground pork	250 g
1/2 cup	sliced fresh shiitake mushrooms	125 mL
1/2 cup	chopped cabbage	125 mL
4 oz	firm tofu, cut in 1/2-inch (1 cm) pieces	125 g
1/4 cup	coarsely chopped celery leaves	50 mL
3/4 cup	chopped spinach	175 mL
2 tbsp	fish sauce	25 mL
2 tbsp	fried garlic (optional)	25 mL

1. In a saucepan, heat chicken stock to just below boiling. Crumble in pork. Stir in mushrooms and cabbage and cook for 5 to 7 minutes, or until pork is cooked.
2. Add tofu, celery leaves, spinach and fish sauce and simmer for 3 minutes, or until soup is hot.
3. Sprinkle with fried garlic, if using.

Variations

Pork and Cabbage Soup with Bean Thread Noodles: Add 1/2 cup (125 mL) softened bean thread noodles (page 111) along with the tofu. Serve as soon as soup is hot, as noodles will absorb liquid.

Pork and Cabbage Soup with Rice: Add 1/2 cup (125 mL) cooked rice along with tofu.

Chicken and Cabbage Soup: Replace ground pork with ground chicken.

Makes 4 servings

Although the day was very warm, this steaming-hot soup cooled us down. It was brought to the table in a metal pot set over a warming candle. This is another dish adapted from the restaurant Thong Yowd, which sits on the edge of the Chao Phraya River. Start with a full-flavored chicken stock. Diners can stir in fried garlic (page 146), hot sauce or other seasoning condiments to taste.

Chiang Mai Noodle Soup

Makes 6 servings

Sompon and Elizabeth Nabnian, owners of the Chiang Mai Thai Cookery School, conduct exciting cooking classes for people visiting Thailand. After a market tour, we were escorted to their open-air school, where each student had an individual cooking station. Sompon's gentle teaching guided us through many of Thailand's famous dishes. From there, we walked a few steps to the open-air dining room overlooking the family garden, where we savored the fruits of our labor.

This recipe is from the class. Noodles are used both in the soup and as a garnish. For a less rich soup, replace half the coconut milk with chicken stock. Beef or pork can be substituted for the chicken.

2 tbsp	vegetable oil	25 mL
3	shallots, chopped	3
3	cloves garlic, finely chopped	3
1 tbsp	red curry paste	15 mL
4 cups	coconut milk	1 L
8 oz	boneless, skinless chicken breasts and/or thighs, cut in 1⁄2-inch (1 cm) pieces	250 g
3 tbsp	fish sauce	45 mL
1 tbsp	palm or brown sugar	15 mL
1 tsp	ground turmeric	5 mL
1 tbsp	lime juice	15 mL
3 cups	water	750 mL
8 oz	fresh egg noodles	250 g
2	green onions, thinly sliced	2
2 tbsp	coarsely chopped fresh cilantro leaves	25 mL
1 cup	chow mein noodles (optional)	250 mL

1. In a saucepan, heat oil over medium-high heat. Add shallots and garlic and cook, stirring, for 30 seconds. Add curry paste and cook, stirring, for 2 minutes.
2. Add coconut milk and bring to a low boil. Add chicken, reduce heat and simmer for 20 minutes, or until tender.
3. Add fish sauce, sugar, turmeric and lime juice. Stir to combine and simmer for 10 minutes.
4. Meanwhile, in a separate saucepan, bring water to a boil.
5. Just before serving soup, add fresh egg noodles to water and cook for 1 minute. Drain and add noodles to serving bowls.
6. Spoon soup over noodles. Garnish with green onions, cilantro and chow mein noodles, if using.

Salads

Green Papaya Salad

Makes 4 servings

This salad (Som Tam) is originally from northeastern Thailand, but it is popular everywhere. Green papaya has little flavor on its own, but it provides crunch and a background for other ingredients. This salad alone makes purchasing a good-size mortar and pestle worthwhile (page 15), but you can also just combine the chopped garlic, chilies, green beans and shredded papaya without pounding.

To prepare the shrimp floss, process 2 tbsp (25 mL) dried shrimp (page 22) in a small food processor.

If green papaya is unavailable, use a combination of cabbage and carrots.

3	cloves garlic, peeled	3
1 1/2 tsp	chopped fresh red chilies	7 mL
1/2 cup	sliced green beans	125 mL
1	green papaya, peeled, seeded and shredded (about 2 cups/500 mL)	1
2 tbsp	fish sauce	25 mL
2 tbsp	lime juice	25 mL
1 tbsp	palm or brown sugar	15 mL
1	tomato, cut in wedges	1
2 tbsp	chopped roasted peanuts or cashews	25 mL
1 tbsp	shrimp floss (optional)	15 mL

1. Using a mortar and pestle or in a small food processor, finely chop garlic and chilies to form a coarse paste.
2. Add beans and pound to bruise. Add papaya and pound again to bruise papaya shreds, about 2 to 3 minutes, scraping down sides with a spoon.
3. Add fish sauce, lime juice and sugar and pound while scraping sides of bowl with a spoon, turning ingredients. Taste and adjust seasonings if necessary.
4. Stir in tomato, peanuts and shrimp floss, if using. Serve with some of the juices.

Green Papaya

Green papaya is often sold in halves, cut open to expose the white seeds. To shred it, peel and thinly shred by hand with a coarse grater or on a mandolin. Remove the seeds with a spoon. Since papaya is sticky, you may want to wear a glove.

Royal Project Salad

1/2	head iceberg lettuce, broken in bite-size pieces	1/2
2	carrots, cut in matchstick pieces	2
2	cooked beets, peeled and sliced	2
1 cup	diced cooked squash, pumpkin or sweet potato	250 mL
1 cup	cooked corn kernels	250 mL
1/2 cup	baby cherry tomatoes	125 mL
2	green onions, chopped	2
	Fresh cilantro leaves (optional)	

Dressing

2 tbsp	lemon or lime juice	25 mL
1 tbsp	fish sauce	15 mL
1 tsp	liquid honey or maple syrup	5 mL
1	clove garlic, minced	1
1	shallot, chopped	1
1/4 tsp	black pepper	1 mL
1/4 cup	vegetable or olive oil	50 mL

1. Arrange lettuce in a large shallow bowl or platter. Top with carrots, beets, squash, corn, tomatoes, green onions and cilantro, if using.
2. To prepare dressing, in a bowl, whisk together lemon juice, fish sauce, honey, garlic, shallot and pepper. Gradually whisk in oil. Pour dressing over salad just before serving.

Makes 4 servings

At the Chiang Mai airport, I browsed through a store featuring handsomely packaged "Royal Project" products of vegetables, fruit, cakes, vegetable chips, coffee and preserves. Our flight did not include lunch, so in keeping with the Thai tradition of snacking, I bought some items for "research" purposes. I noticed several airline attendants purchasing the vegetable salad, so I bought that, too.

The Royal Project was established in the late sixties to encourage the development of crops to replace opium poppies in northern Thailand. Farmers now produce a variety of fruits and vegetables that supply families, the Royal Project (Doi Kham) shops and restaurants that use Royal Project ingredients.

This is a version of the salad I purchased at the airport.

Crispy Cucumber Salad

Makes 4 servings

Thais use lots of cucumbers — in salads, soups, and stuffed with assorted ingredients. Intricately carved, they also appear as garnishes.
This salad provides a refreshing contrast to grilled and fried foods. It helps to cleanse the palate.

Make Ahead
Salad can be covered and refrigerated for up to 6 hours before garnishing, but for best results, serve it the day it is made.

3 tbsp	lime juice or rice vinegar	45 mL
2 tbsp	water	25 mL
1 tbsp	fish sauce	15 mL
2 tsp	granulated sugar	10 mL
1	large English cucumber, thinly sliced	1
2	shallots, thinly sliced	2
1 1/2 tsp	chopped fresh red chilies	7 mL
2 tbsp	chopped roasted peanuts	25 mL
2 tbsp	fresh mint leaves	25 mL
2 tbsp	fresh cilantro leaves	25 mL

1. In a large bowl, whisk together lime juice, water, fish sauce and sugar until sugar dissolves.
2. Add cucumber, shallots and chilies. Toss together and let stand for 30 minutes.
3. Sprinkle with peanuts, mint and cilantro.

Wing Bean Salad

Makes 4 servings

Wing beans are a delicate-looking vegetable with four frilly edges. Unfortunately, very fresh ones are hard to find, so this recipe uses long or regular green beans. (If you do find wing beans, use them right away.) As in many Thai salads, small quantities of meat and fish add flavor and texture. Two thinly sliced fresh shallots can replace the fried shallots.

8 oz	wing or green beans, cut in 1-inch (2.5 cm) pieces	250 g
4 oz	cooked chicken, shredded	125 g
4 oz	cooked shrimp, peeled and halved lengthwise	125 g
2 tbsp	chopped roasted peanuts	25 mL
1 tsp	chopped fresh red or green chilies	5 mL
1⁄3 cup	coconut milk	75 mL
3 tbsp	lime juice	45 mL
2 tbsp	fish sauce	25 mL
1 tsp	granulated sugar	5 mL
3 tbsp	fried shallots (page 147)	45 mL
2 tbsp	shredded coconut, toasted (page 245)	25 mL

1. In a saucepan of boiling salted water, blanch beans for 30 to 60 seconds, or until tender-crisp. Cool in ice water. Drain well and pat dry.
2. In a large bowl, combine chicken, shrimp, peanuts and chilies.
3. In a small bowl, stir together coconut milk, lime juice, fish sauce and sugar. Add to chicken along with beans and toss to combine.
4. Garnish with shallots and coconut.

Cabbage Salad with Coconut

3 cups	roughly chopped Savoy cabbage	750 mL
2 tbsp	vegetable oil	25 mL
6	cloves garlic, thinly sliced	6
6	shallots, thinly sliced	6
2 tsp	chopped fresh red chilies	10 mL
1⁄3 cup	coconut milk	75 mL
2 tbsp	fish sauce	25 mL
2 tbsp	lime juice	25 mL
2 tbsp	chopped roasted peanuts	25 mL

1. Bring a saucepan of salted water to a boil. Add cabbage and blanch for 3 minutes. Drain.
2. In a wok or skillet, heat oil over medium-high heat. Add garlic, shallots and chilies. Cook, stirring often, for 4 to 6 minutes, or until garlic and shallots are crisp. Remove and drain on paper towels.
3. In a large bowl, whisk together coconut milk, fish sauce and lime juice. Add cabbage and toss.
4. Garnish with garlic mixture and peanuts.

Makes 5 to 6 servings

Occasionally salads in Thailand are served with coconut dressing, a Malaysian influence. For a more substantial dish, cooked ground pork and chopped shrimp are sometimes added.

Eggplant Salad

Makes 4 to 6 servings

Eggplants are used in Thai soups, curries, stir-fries and dipping sauces. They come in many shapes and colors — long green, white or purple; tomato-size green, yellow or white; and small green pea eggplants that are crunchy on the outside and bitter inside.

If you can't find Thai eggplants, Asian eggplants are a good substitute.

4	Asian eggplants	4
3 tbsp	lime juice	45 mL
1 tbsp	fish sauce	15 mL
1 tbsp	soy sauce	15 mL
1 tsp	sesame oil	5 mL
2 tsp	granulated sugar	10 mL
2	shallots, chopped	2
2	green onions, chopped	2
1/2 tsp	chopped fresh green chilies	2 mL
2 tbsp	coarsely chopped fresh cilantro	25 mL

1. Place eggplants on a foil-lined baking sheet and broil on both sides until charred and soft (8 to 10 minutes in total). Cool. Peel eggplants and cut into 1-inch (2.5 cm) pieces. Place in a serving dish.
2. In a bowl, combine lime juice, fish sauce, soy sauce, sesame oil, sugar, shallots, green onions and chilies. Spoon over eggplant and toss lightly.
3. Garnish with cilantro.

Quick Spicy Cashew Salad

In a bowl, toss 2 cups (500 mL) warm deep-fried cashews (page 225) with 1 tbsp (15 mL) lime juice, 2 thinly sliced green onions and 1 tsp (5 mL) hot pepper flakes. Taste and adjust seasonings if necessary. Serve as a small side salad or as a snack with drinks.

Makes about 2 cups (500 mL).

Pomelo Salad

3 tbsp	lime juice	45 mL
2 tbsp	fish sauce	25 mL
2 tsp	palm or brown sugar	10 mL
1	large (3½ lbs/1.5 kg) pomelo	1
2	shallots, thinly sliced	2
2 tbsp	coarsely chopped fresh cilantro leaves	25 mL
2 tbsp	shredded fresh mint leaves	25 mL
1 tsp	thinly sliced fresh red chilies	5 mL
8 oz	small cooked shrimp (optional)	250 g
1 tbsp	shredded coconut, toasted (page 245)	15 mL

1. In a large bowl, combine lime juice, fish sauce and sugar. Stir to dissolve sugar.
2. Peel pomelo with a sharp knife to remove pith. Separate sections and then peel off white membrane and break fruit into bite-size pieces.
3. Add pomelo, shallots, cilantro, mint, chilies and shrimp, if using, to dressing and toss to combine.
4. Sprinkle with coconut.

Weekend Brunch

Pomelo Salad (page 77)
Glass Noodle and Shrimp Casserole (page 111)
Quick Asparagus Stir-fry (page 220)
Mini Banana Pancakes (page 252) with Coconut Ice Cream (page 238)
Samui Seabreeze (page 255)

Makes 4 to 6 servings

Pomelo is a large citrus fruit that resembles grapefruit. The skin is much thicker, but the pulp separates easily once the white membrane has been removed. It makes a refreshing salad perked up with shallots and chilies. Some versions contain chopped dried shrimp or cooked whole shrimp, and at a restaurant in southern Thailand the dressing also contained a small amount of coconut milk. If you can't find pomelo, use three or four large pink or yellow grapefruit.

Make Ahead

Prepare dressing and ingredients up to 4 hours ahead. Cover and refrigerate. Salad can be assembled up to an hour before serving.

Fresh Fruit Salad

Makes 6 servings

On my first visit to Thailand, I took classes directed by Chalie Amatyakul at the famed Oriental Hotel. We smelled, touched, cooked, toured and had a very full and inspiring introduction to Thai cooking.

It is common to find fruit salads that combine sweet and savory, and many include grilled seafood. This one includes a contrast of textures and tastes — soft and crisp, sweet and sour. It is similar to the salad we made in class. It was served in hollowed-out oranges, but a bed of crisp shredded lettuce works, too.

Crispy fried garlic and shallots are available packaged at Asian markets if you don't want to make your own.

Make Ahead

Fried garlic and shallot mixture can be cooled, transferred to in an airtight container and refrigerated for up to a week.

1/4 cup	vegetable oil	50 mL
1/4 cup	thinly sliced garlic cloves	50 mL
1/4 cup	thinly sliced shallots	50 mL
1/4 cup	lime juice	50 mL
1 tsp	brown or granulated sugar	5 mL
1/4 tsp	salt	1 mL
2	oranges, peel and pith removed and separated in sections	2
1 cup	halved green grapes	250 mL
1 cup	halved red grapes	250 mL
1/2 cup	lychee fruit, pitted and sliced	125 mL
1	apple, cut in small pieces	1
1/2 cup	sliced strawberries	125 mL
8 oz	small cooked shrimp or diced cooked chicken	250 g
1/2 cup	water chestnuts, sliced (optional)	125 mL
1/4 cup	chopped roasted peanuts, divided	50 mL
2 tsp	thinly sliced fresh red chilies	10 mL
1 tbsp	fresh cilantro leaves	15 mL

1. In a small skillet, heat oil over medium-high heat. Add garlic and shallots and cook for 4 to 6 minutes, stirring occasionally, until golden and crisp. Remove from pan and drain on paper towels.
2. In a large bowl, combine lime juice, sugar and salt. Add oranges, grapes, lychee fruit, apple, strawberries, shrimp and water chestnuts, if using. Add half the fried garlic and shallots and half the peanuts. Toss gently to combine.
3. Sprinkle with remaining garlic and shallots, remaining peanuts, chilies and cilantro.

Green Mango Salad

3	green mangoes, peeled and cut in matchstick pieces	3
5 tbsp	lime juice, divided	70 mL
1/2 tsp	salt	2 mL
2 tbsp	vegetable oil	25 mL
3	cloves garlic, chopped	3
6	green onions, thinly sliced	6
8 oz	ground chicken or lean ground pork	250 g
1 1/2 tsp	chopped fresh red chilies	7 mL
2 tbsp	fish sauce	25 mL
2 tbsp	palm or brown sugar	25 mL
1/3 cup	coconut milk	75 mL
1/4 cup	coarsely chopped roasted cashews or peanuts	50 mL
6	lettuce leaves	6

1. In a large bowl, combine mangoes, 2 tbsp (25 mL) lime juice and salt.
2. In a wok or skillet, heat oil over medium-high heat. Add garlic and green onions and cook for 1 minute, or until softened.
3. Add chicken and cook for 4 to 5 minutes, or until pinkness disappears, breaking meat up as necessary.
4. Add chilies, remaining lime juice, fish sauce, sugar and coconut milk. Cook, stirring, for 3 minutes. Remove from heat and stir in cashews.
5. Cool for 20 minutes. Add to mango. Stir to combine. Refrigerate.
6. To serve, arrange lettuce leaves on a serving dish and spoon salad on lettuce.

Variation

Simple Mango Salad: Cut 3 green or slightly underripe mangoes into matchstick pieces. In a large bowl, combine mango, 3 tbsp (45 mL) lime juice, 2 tbsp (25 mL) fish sauce, 1 tbsp (15 mL) palm or brown sugar, 2 thinly sliced shallots, 1 tsp (5 mL) chopped fresh red chilies and 2 tbsp (25 mL) chopped roasted cashews or peanuts.

Makes 4 servings.

Makes 6 servings

There are several versions of this recipe. Some contain peanut butter, others include ground dried shrimp (page 22) and some are made without meat. Minh Van, owner of Minh's grocery shop in Peterborough, Ontario, adds some green papaya to his green mango salad, as he says it cuts the tartness of the mango.

Cut the mango by hand or with the shredding blade of a mandolin. If green mangoes are not available, use underripe regular mangoes or tart green apples.

Make Ahead

Salad can be prepared, covered and refrigerated for up to 4 hours.

Glass Noodle Salad with Chicken and Shrimp

Makes 4 to 5 servings

Glass (also called bean thread or cellophane) noodle salads can be very simple or adorned with a variety of vegetables and seasonings. They can be gentle or quite spicy. The protein portion can be chicken, pork, beef, shrimp or mixed seafood, depending on the area of the country and the chef. You can also use all chicken in this recipe.

3/4 cup	dried wood fungus strips	175 mL
4 oz	dried bean thread (cellophane) noodles (page 111)	125 g
2 tbsp	vegetable oil	25 mL
2	cloves garlic, chopped	2
1 tbsp	chopped fresh gingerroot	15 mL
8 oz	boneless, skinless chicken breasts, cut in small pieces	250 g
4 oz	peeled and deveined shrimp, finely chopped	125 g
1 tbsp	soy sauce	15 mL
2 tsp	sesame oil	10 mL
1/4 cup	lime juice	50 mL
2 tbsp	fish sauce	25 mL
1 tbsp	brown sugar	15 mL
1 tsp	hot chili sauce	5 mL
1/2	red bell pepper, seeded and thinly sliced	1/2
1/2 cup	thinly sliced celery	125 mL
1/2	red onion, thinly sliced	1/2
2	green onions, chopped	2
2 tbsp	chopped roasted peanuts	25 mL
	Fresh cilantro sprigs	
	Fresh red chili strips	

1. In a bowl, cover fungus strips with warm water and let soften for 20 minutes. Drain.
2. Meanwhile, in a separate bowl, cover noodles with warm water and let stand for 5 minutes, or until softened. Drain, then cook noodles in a large amount of boiling water for 1 minute. Drain, rinse well with cold water, cut into 6-inch (15 cm) lengths and place in a large bowl. (If noodles dry out, rinse again with cold water and drain well before using.)
3. Heat a wok over medium-high heat and add vegetable oil. Add garlic and ginger and stir-fry for 30 seconds, or until fragrant.
4. Add chicken, shrimp, soy sauce and sesame oil and cook for 2 minutes, or until just cooked. Stir in softened fungus strips. Remove from heat, cool for 15 minutes and add to softened noodles.
5. Meanwhile, in a small bowl, stir together lime juice, fish sauce, sugar and chili sauce. Add to noodles with bell pepper, celery, red onion and green onions. Toss to combine ingredients, trying not to break noodles.
6. Garnish with peanuts, cilantro and chilies.

Squid Salad

Makes 4 servings

On my first visit to Thailand, I had a squid salad that was silk-like in texture and tossed with a zesty dressing. I have been making it ever since.

It is much easier to prepare squid dishes now that it is available fresh or frozen and already cleaned. Try to find very thin squid rings; otherwise slice the tubes thinly.

Squid requires either a brief cooking time or long simmering. In this recipe, the squid is basically blanched, just until firm, then enhanced with a full-flavored dressing.

Chop the lemongrass finely, otherwise it will be too chewy. (Some chefs slice it finely with a mandolin.)

3 tbsp	lime juice	45 mL
1 tbsp	fish sauce	15 mL
1 1/2 tsp	hot chili sauce	7 mL
1 tsp	brown or granulated sugar	5 mL
12 oz	squid rings	375 g
4	green onions, thinly sliced	4
1 tbsp	finely chopped lemongrass, white part only	15 mL
1/4 cup	shredded fresh mint leaves	50 mL

1. In a large bowl, whisk together lime juice, fish sauce, chili sauce and sugar.
2. Bring a pot of water to a boil and add squid. Return to a boil, stir, strain and rinse under cold water. Drain well.
3. Add squid, green onions and lemongrass to dressing and toss.
4. Garnish with mint leaves.

Catfish Salad

1 lb	catfish fillets (or other white fish, such as tilapia)	500 g
2 tbsp	lime juice	25 mL
1 tbsp	fish sauce	15 mL
1 tbsp	granulated sugar	15 mL
1 tsp	chopped fresh red or green chilies	5 mL
2	cloves garlic, minced	2
1/4 cup	vegetable oil	50 mL
Salad		
2 tbsp	lime juice	25 mL
1 tbsp	fish sauce	15 mL
1 tbsp	palm or brown sugar	15 mL
2 tsp	chopped fresh green chilies	10 mL
3	shallots, thinly sliced	3
1	large green mango, shredded	1
2 tbsp	chopped fresh mint leaves	25 mL
2 tbsp	chopped fresh cilantro leaves	25 mL
6	large lettuce leaves	6
2 tbsp	chopped roasted peanuts	25 mL

1. To cook fish, arrange fillets on a parchment-lined baking sheet. In a bowl, combine lime juice, fish sauce, sugar, chilies and garlic. Spoon over fillets and turn to coat all sides.
2. Bake in a preheated 400°F (200°C) oven for 8 to 10 minutes, or until fish flakes easily. Transfer fish to a rack to let excess moisture drain off. Pat fish dry and flake.
3. In a large nonstick skillet, heat oil over medium-high heat. Add flaked fish and cook, stirring, for 3 to 4 minutes, or until brown and crisp. Remove with a slotted spoon and drain on paper towels.
4. To prepare salad, in a bowl, combine lime juice, fish sauce, sugar, chilies, shallots, mango, mint and cilantro.
5. Arrange lettuce leaves on a serving platter. Spoon salad on lettuce and scatter with fish and peanuts.

Makes 4 to 6 servings

Catfish is one of the most popular freshwater fishes in Thailand. It is a firm-fleshed fish sold fresh at markets and may be poached, baked, deep-fried, grilled or smoked. For salads it is often grilled or baked and then broken into tiny pieces and deep-fried (it looks like floss, not like fish at all), but in this recipe the cooked fish is lightly pan-fried. (You can also simply skip the frying step.) Many Thai salads are arranged on a bed of lettuce.

Tuna Salad with Shallots and Lemongrass

Makes 4 servings

One of our most enjoyable experiences in Chiang Mai was attending the Sunday jazz brunch at the Chedi Chiang Mai — a modern, stylish hotel located in the former British consulate beside the Mae Ping River. This is a variation of a salad from Michael Gaehler and Marcel Huser. Be sure to use very fresh lemongrass that is soft enough to be finely sliced. (Even then it might be too chewy for some. Grated lemon zest can be used as an alternative in this recipe.)

1 lb	tuna fillet, about 1 inch (2.5 cm) thick, skin removed	500 g
1 tbsp	lime juice	15 mL
1 tbsp	fish sauce	15 mL
1 tbsp	vegetable oil, divided	15 mL
Salad		
3	shallots, thinly sliced	3
2	stalks lemongrass, white part only, thinly sliced, or 2 tsp (10 mL) grated lemon zest	2
1/2	red bell pepper, seeded and cut in matchstick pieces	1/2
1 tsp	chopped fresh red chilies	5 mL
1/4 cup	lime juice	50 mL
2 tbsp	vegetable oil	25 mL
1 tbsp	fish sauce	15 mL
3	lime leaves, center vein removed, shredded	3
3 tbsp	shredded fresh sweet Thai basil leaves	45 mL
2 tbsp	fresh mint leaves (optional)	25 mL

1. Pat tuna dry and rub with lime juice, fish sauce and 2 tsp (10 mL) oil.
2. Heat remaining oil in a nonstick skillet over medium heat. Add tuna and cook for 2 minutes per side. Cool and break into small chunks.
3. To prepare salad, in a large bowl, combine shallots, lemongrass, red pepper, chilies, lime juice, oil, fish sauce and lime leaves.
4. Add tuna, basil and mint, if using, and toss gently.

Shredding Lime Leaves

Remove the coarse vein running the length of the leaf. Roll up the leaf tightly lengthwise and cut into very fine shreds (the finer the better) using kitchen shears or a very sharp knife. This makes a delicate garnish and makes the leaves easy to eat, as they are chewy.

Cucumber Boats

1	small English cucumber	1
8 oz	cooked beef, cut in thin bite-size pieces	250 g
1/4 cup	shredded fresh mint leaves	50 mL
2 tbsp	chopped fresh cilantro leaves	25 mL
3	green onions, finely chopped	3
2	shallots, chopped	2
1 tsp	chopped fresh red chilies	5 mL
2 tbsp	lime juice	25 mL
1 tbsp	fish sauce	15 mL
1 tsp	granulated sugar	5 mL

1. Cut cucumber in half lengthwise, then cut each half crosswise to make 4 "boats." With a grapefruit spoon or metal measuring spoon, scrape out seeds. Place on a serving platter. (Cut a narrow slice from base of cucumber if necessary.)
2. In a bowl, combine beef, mint, cilantro, green onions, shallots, chilies, lime juice, fish sauce and sugar. Toss to combine.
3. Spoon mixture into cucumber boats.

Makes 4 servings

In Thailand, the waterways are always busy, with heavily loaded barges sharing the rivers with long-tail boats and other craft. At some banquets or buffets, cucumber "barges" are loaded with tasty freight, which might include a beef salad or even hard-cooked eggs.

Any grilled or roasted beef works well in this recipe. You can also use cooked chicken instead of beef. For smaller boats, cut the cucumber into shorter pieces.

Make Ahead

Cucumbers can be seeded and refrigerated 4 hours ahead, but blot off any moisture before filling.

Beef Salad

Makes 4 to 6 servings

Beef salad is one of the many superstars of Thai cooking. It should be spicy yet refreshing. This is a substantial dish that can be served as a main course. Thais often use a fatty cut of beef, but any marinated steak will work, or you can splurge with beef tenderloin. Roasted rice powder, a specialty of northeast Thailand, adds texture to the salad.

1 lb	boneless ribeye, sirloin, flank or tenderloin steak	500 g
1 tbsp	hoisin sauce	15 mL
1/4 cup	fish sauce, divided	50 mL
1/4 cup	lime juice	50 mL
1 tbsp	palm or brown sugar	15 mL
1 tsp	hot pepper flakes	5 mL
1 tbsp	roasted rice powder, optional	15 mL
1/2	English cucumber, peeled, halved lengthwise and thinly sliced	1/2
1 cup	halved cherry tomatoes	250 mL
3	green onions, chopped	3
1/3 cup	coarsely chopped fresh mint leaves	75 mL
1/4 cup	coarsely chopped fresh cilantro leaves	50 mL

1. Place steak on a plate and spoon on hoisin sauce and 1 tbsp (15 mL) fish sauce. Rub seasoning onto both sides of steak.
2. Grill steak for 3 to 4 minutes per side, or until medium-rare. Let stand for 15 minutes, then slice thinly against grain.
3. In a large bowl, combine remaining fish sauce, lime juice, sugar, hot pepper flakes and rice powder, if using.
4. Add cucumber, tomatoes, green onions, mint, cilantro and beef and toss gently.

Roasted Rice Powder

Heat a dry skillet over medium heat. Add 2 tbsp (25 mL) jasmine or glutinous rice and cook, shaking frequently, for 3 to 4 minutes, or until golden. Slide rice onto a plate and cool. When cool, grind with a mortar and pestle or in a spice grinder. This is best when made fresh; otherwise cool rice grains, store in a dry container and grind as needed.

Makes about 3 tbsp (45 mL).

Spicy Ground Beef Salad

Makes 6 servings

This spicy beef salad, a specialty of the Northeast, is known as Laab Nua or Laab Issan. It is a Thai version of steak tartare, although the beef is blanched. Hot chili sauce is the dip of choice, and the salad is often served with sticky rice (page 117). To eat, rice is shaped into a ball and dipped into the salad.

This salad can also be made using ground pork, chicken and even duck.

1 lb	lean ground beef	500 g
1/4 cup	lime juice	50 mL
2 tbsp	fish sauce	25 mL
3	stalks lemongrass, white part only, chopped	3
1 1/2 tsp	chopped fresh red or green chilies	7 mL
6	shallots, thinly sliced	6
2	green onions, chopped	2
2 tbsp	roasted rice powder (page 87), optional	25 mL
2	tomatoes, cut in wedges	2
1/4	English cucumber, sliced	1/4
4 oz	long green beans, cut in 1-inch (2.5 cm) pieces (about 1 1/2 cups/375 mL)	125 g
1/2 cup	fresh mint leaves	125 mL

1. Bring a saucepan of water to a boil. Add beef and stir to separate. Cook for 2 to 3 minutes, or until beef is just cooked. Drain well.
2. In a bowl, combine beef, lime juice, fish sauce, lemongrass, chilies, shallots, green onions and rice powder, if using. Toss together well.
3. Mound beef on a serving platter, and arrange tomatoes, cucumber and beans around meat.
4. Garnish with mint leaves.

Sausage Salad

12 oz	cooked sausage, thinly sliced	375 g
4	shallots, thinly sliced	4
2	green onions, chopped	2
1/4 cup	coarsely chopped fresh mint leaves	50 mL
1/4 cup	coarsely chopped fresh cilantro leaves	50 mL
1/2	English cucumber, halved and thinly sliced	1/2
2 tbsp	lime juice	25 mL
2 tbsp	fish sauce	25 mL
1/2 tsp	granulated sugar	2 mL
1 tsp	chopped fresh green chilies	5 mL
1	tomato, cut in wedges	1

1. In a large bowl, combine sausage, shallots, green onions, mint, cilantro and cucumber.
2. In a small bowl, stir together lime juice, fish sauce, sugar and chilies. Add to salad and toss.
3. Garnish with tomato wedges.

Snack, Soup and Salad

Chicken Tidbits (page 264)

Corn and Crabmeat Soup (page 56)

Spicy Ground Beef Salad (page 88) or Sausage Salad (page 89)

Makes 4 servings

You will find several varieties of sausages at Thai food stands. A northern specialty is fermented sausage (a process started by the inclusion of rice). Depending on the area, sausages are made from pork or beef and may include liver. Homemade sausage patties (page 139) could also be used in this recipe. (I have even made versions of this with "gourmet" wieners.) Chinese sausages are also found in many food courts and stalls. They are a popular ingredient in spring rolls, rice dishes, stir-fries and salads. If you are using them, cook them in boiling water for 4 minutes. You can also use leftover cooked chicken or turkey instead of the sausage.

Thai Chef's Salad

Makes 6 servings

Refreshing and inviting, this salad can be adapted according to the creativeness of the cook. Crisp cooked vegetables such as broccoli or beans make colorful additions. Although duck is popular in Thailand (cooked duck is available at many food courts and stores), any cooked meat, seafood or tofu can be used instead.

To cook quail eggs, place them in a small saucepan and cover with cold water. Bring to a simmer, cover and cook for 5 minutes. Cool eggs under cold running water and peel while they are still warm.

Make Ahead

Assemble salad, cover and refrigerate for up to 4 hours. Add dressing and garnishes just before serving.

6	Boston or leaf lettuce leaves	6
1/3	English cucumber, thinly sliced	1/3
1/2 cup	thinly sliced celery	125 mL
1/2	red bell pepper, seeded and thinly sliced	1/2
1/2 cup	grated carrot	125 mL
2 cups	thinly sliced cooked duck or chicken	500 mL
6	hard-cooked quail eggs, halved, or 3 regular eggs, sliced or quartered	6

Dressing

3 tbsp	lime juice	45 mL
2 tbsp	fish sauce	25 mL
1 tbsp	granulated or brown sugar	15 mL
1	clove garlic, minced	1
1 tsp	hot chili sauce	5 mL
2 tbsp	shredded fresh mint leaves	25 mL
2 tbsp	chopped fresh cilantro leaves	25 mL
1/4 cup	roasted cashews	50 mL

1. Arrange lettuce, cucumber, celery, red pepper and carrot on a large platter. Top with duck and eggs.
2. To prepare dressing, in a bowl, whisk together lime juice, fish sauce, sugar, garlic and chili sauce.
3. Drizzle dressing over salad and garnish with mint, cilantro and cashews.

Noodles

Pad Thai

Makes 4 servings

Pad Thai is one of the best-known dishes of Thailand. It is a meal on its own, but it is often served with other dishes. Sweet, sour and salty are balanced by the blandness of the noodles. This dish varies enormously but the following version is one that my students and family particularly like. Do not oversoften the noodles, since they will soften further when cooked.

Eggs are an important ingredient in Pad Thai. At the Mandarin Oriental Dhara Devi in Chiang Mai, our Pad Thai was garnished with an omelet spiral (thin egg omelets rolled and then cut diagonally into spirals).

8 oz	dried medium rice noodles	250 g
3 tbsp	chicken stock, ketchup or tomato sauce	45 mL
3 tbsp	lime juice or tamarind paste	45 mL
2 tbsp	fish sauce	25 mL
2 tbsp	palm or brown sugar	25 mL
1/2 tsp	hot chili sauce	2 mL
3 tbsp	vegetable oil, divided	45 mL
2	eggs, beaten	2
3	cloves garlic, chopped	3
4 oz	shrimp, peeled and deveined, cut in small pieces	125 g
4 oz	boneless chicken or pork, cut in small pieces	125 g
2 cups	bean sprouts, divided	500 mL
2	green onions, chopped	2
1/4 cup	chopped peanuts	50 mL
1/4 cup	chopped fresh cilantro leaves	50 mL
	Fresh red chilies, cut in strips (optional)	
1	lime, cut in wedges	1

1. To soften noodles, place in a large bowl. Cover with very hot water and let stand for 10 to 12 minutes, or until softened but still firm (pinch them to check). Rinse well with cold water and drain.
2. In a small bowl or measuring cup, combine stock, lime juice, fish sauce, sugar and chili sauce.
3. Heat a wok or large skillet over medium-high heat and add 1 tbsp (25 mL) oil. Add beaten eggs to hot pan and swirl to coat bottom of pan. Cook until starting to set, then stir to break into pieces. Remove from wok and reserve.
4. Add remaining oil to wok. When hot, add garlic, shrimp and chicken and stir-fry for 2 minutes, or until shrimp and chicken are just cooked. Stir in noodles and reserved sauce mixture and cook for 1 to 2 minutes, or until noodles are soft but not mushy.
5. Add 1 cup (250 mL) bean sprouts and cooked eggs and toss to combine.
6. Turn noodles onto a serving platter. Sprinkle with remaining bean sprouts, green onions, peanuts, cilantro and chilies, if using. Garnish with lime wedges.

Stir-fried Pad Thai

1 tbsp	vegetable oil	15 mL
1½ cups	cold Pad Thai	375 mL
1	egg	1
	Sweet chili sauce (page 45) to taste	

Makes 1 serving

Sometimes I have leftover Pad Thai. If there ever is such a thing, do not send it home with guests or even just warm it up the next day. Instead, make this delicious stir-fry for breakfast or as a snack, adding condiments of your choice.

1. Heat oil in a small nonstick skillet over medium-high heat. Add Pad Thai. Stir-fry for 2 minutes, or until noodles start getting a bit crispy.
2. Break egg over top of Pad Thai. Let set for 1 minute.
3. Stir egg into noodles and cook for 1 minute, or until set and scrambled.
4. Add chili sauce to taste.

Omelet Spirals

In a bowl, beat 2 eggs with 2 tsp (10 mL) water. Heat 1 tsp (5 mL) vegetable oil in an 8-inch (20 cm) nonstick skillet over medium-high heat. Add half the egg mixture and swirl around pan. Cook for 2 minutes, or until set. Slide omelet onto a pan or plate. Repeat with remaining egg. When cool enough to handle, roll up omelets and slice diagonally into spirals ½ inch (1 cm) thick. Use as a garnish on rice and noodle dishes.

Vegetarian Pad Thai

Makes 4 servings

A vegetarian version of the popular noodle dish, with tofu replacing the chicken and shrimp. Omit the egg if desired. You can also add extra vegetables such as thinly sliced asparagus, beans or shredded cabbage.

8 oz	dried medium or wide rice noodles	250 g
1⁄4 cup	soy sauce	50 mL
1⁄4 cup	ketchup	50 mL
2 tbsp	lime juice	25 mL
1 tbsp	palm or brown sugar	15 mL
1⁄4 cup	vegetable oil, divided	50 mL
8 oz	firm tofu, cut in 1⁄4-inch (5 mm) cubes	250 g
1⁄2	red bell pepper, seeded and thinly sliced	1⁄2
2	eggs, beaten	2
3	cloves garlic, chopped	3
2 cups	bean sprouts, divided	500 mL
3	green onions, chopped	3
1 tsp	thinly sliced fresh red chilies	5 mL
1⁄4 cup	chopped peanuts	50 mL
2 tbsp	chopped fresh cilantro leaves	25 mL
1	lime, cut in wedges	1

1. Place noodles in a large bowl. Cover with very hot water and let stand for 10 to 12 minutes, or until softened but firm. Rinse well with cold water and drain.
2. In a small bowl or measuring cup, combine soy sauce, ketchup, lime juice and sugar.
3. Heat a wok or large skillet over medium-high heat and add 2 tbsp (25 mL) oil. Add tofu and red pepper and stir-fry for 3 minutes. Remove and reserve.
4. Add remaining oil to wok and heat. Add eggs and garlic and stir-fry to scramble eggs.
5. Add soy sauce mixture and noodles and toss to combine for 2 minutes, or until noodles are softened but not mushy (if mixture becomes dry add a few spoonfuls of water or stock to prevent scorching).
6. Add tofu, red pepper and 1 3⁄4 cups (425 mL) bean sprouts and toss for 1 minute, or until hot.
7. Transfer to a serving platter and top with remaining bean sprouts, green onions, chilies, peanuts and cilantro. Garnish with lime wedges.

Drunkard's Noodles

Makes 4 servings

This is just one version of the famed hot and spicy dish that is rumored to cure a hangover. It is supposedly eaten after an evening spent visiting bars, but you can enjoy it any time. Some versions include more vegetables, some omit the meat. For a really spicy dish, add more chilies or stir in hot chili sauce.

6 oz	dried wide rice noodles	175 g
1/4 cup	chicken stock or water	50 mL
2 tbsp	oyster sauce	25 mL
2 tbsp	fish sauce	25 mL
1/2 tsp	granulated sugar	2 mL
2 tbsp	vegetable oil	25 mL
4	cloves garlic, chopped	4
3	shallots, chopped	3
1 tbsp	chopped fresh red chilies	15 mL
8 oz	ground chicken or pork	250 g
1	small red bell pepper, seeded and thinly sliced	1
1 cup	sliced green beans	250 mL
1	tomato, cut in thin wedges	1
1/4 cup	shredded fresh sweet Thai basil leaves	50 mL
3	lime leaves, center vein removed, shredded	3

1. In a large bowl, cover noodles with very hot water and let stand for 10 to 12 minutes, or until softened but still firm. Rinse with cold water and drain.
2. In a small bowl, combine stock, oyster sauce, fish sauce and sugar.
3. Heat a wok or large skillet over medium-high heat. Add oil. Add garlic, shallots and chilies and stir-fry for 30 seconds. Add chicken and stir-fry for 2 minutes.
4. Add red pepper and beans and stir-fry for 2 to 3 minutes, or until tender-crisp.
5. Stir in reserved sauce mixture, noodles and tomato and cook for 3 to 4 minutes, or until noodles are soft but not mushy.
6. Garnish with basil and lime leaves.

Wide Rice Noodles with Scallops and Asparagus

Makes 4 to 6 servings

Seafood dishes are especially luscious when they feature fresh local seafood. Dishes like this are popular at resort restaurants and markets on the southern coast of Thailand. The sweetness of scallops is offset by the addition of hot chili sauce.

8 oz	dried wide rice noodles	250 g
2 tbsp	fish sauce	25 mL
2 tbsp	lime juice	25 mL
1 tbsp	soy sauce	15 mL
1 tsp	granulated sugar	5 mL
1/2 tsp	hot chili sauce	2 mL
1 tbsp	vegetable oil	15 mL
1 lb	scallops, patted dry	500 g
8 oz	asparagus, trimmed and cut in 1-inch (2.5 cm) lengths	250 g
1/3 cup	fresh sweet Thai basil leaves	75 mL

1. In a large bowl, cover noodles with very hot water and let stand for 10 to 12 minutes, or until softened but still firm. Rinse well with cold water and drain.
2. In a small bowl or measuring cup, combine fish sauce, lime juice, soy sauce, sugar and chili sauce.
3. Heat a wok or large skillet over medium-high heat and add oil. Add scallops and stir-fry for 3 minutes, or until opaque. Remove scallops and reserve.
4. Add asparagus to pan juices and stir-fry for 2 to 3 minutes, or until tender-crisp. Remove and reserve with scallops.
5. Add softened noodles and reserved sauce to pan. Toss noodles with sauce and cook for 3 minutes, or until noodles are soft but not mushy.
6. Return scallops and asparagus to pan with basil and toss to heat through.

Bean Thread Noodles with Chicken

Makes 4 servings

Since bean thread noodles are bland, dishes containing them should be full flavored. Once the noodles have been softened, this is a quick dish to cook. Some cooks scramble eggs and toss them with the noodles.

6 oz	dried bean thread (cellophane) noodles (page 111)	175 g
2 tbsp	fish sauce	25 mL
2 tbsp	lime juice	25 mL
1 tbsp	soy sauce	15 mL
2 tsp	granulated sugar	10 mL
1 tsp	hot pepper flakes	5 mL
2 tbsp	vegetable oil	25 mL
1	onion, thinly sliced	1
4	cloves garlic, chopped	4
8 oz	lean ground chicken, pork or diced shrimp	250 g
2	stalks celery, thinly sliced	2
2	green onions, chopped	2
2 tbsp	chopped fresh cilantro leaves	25 mL
1 tbsp	chopped roasted peanuts (optional)	15 mL

1. Bring a saucepan of water to a boil. Add noodles and cook for 1 minute, or until noodles are softened and turn clear. Drain and rinse well with cold water. Cut noodles into 3-inch (7.5 cm) lengths.
2. In a small bowl or measuring cup, combine fish sauce, lime juice, soy sauce, sugar and hot pepper flakes.
3. Heat a wok or large skillet over medium-high heat and add oil. Add onion and garlic and cook for 1 to 2 minutes, or until onion is soft.
4. Add chicken and stir-fry for 2 minutes, or until pinkness disappears.
5. Add celery and cook for 2 minutes. Add reserved sauce and noodles. Toss mixture well until heated through.
6. Garnish with green onions, cilantro and peanuts, if using.

Hot and Sour Rice Flakes

Makes 4 servings

Rice flakes can be square or triangular; they add variety to noodle, salad and soup dishes. Make this salad-like dish for your vegetarian friends. Other vegetables can be added or substituted. Fried tofu can be found in Asian markets, or you can make your own (page 232). It has more flavor than plain tofu, but if you can't find it, just use regular firm tofu.

8 oz	dried rice flakes	250 g
3 tbsp	soy sauce	45 mL
3 tbsp	lime juice	45 mL
1 tbsp	granulated sugar	15 mL
1/2 tsp	chopped fresh red chilies	2 mL
2 tbsp	vegetable oil	25 mL
3	cloves garlic, chopped	3
4 oz	fried tofu, cut in small pieces	125 g
1 cup	sliced green beans	250 mL
1 cup	small cauliflower florets	250 mL
1	carrot, cut in matchstick pieces	1
2	shallots, thinly sliced	2
3	green onions, chopped	3
1 tbsp	chopped fresh cilantro or mint leaves	15 mL
1	tomato, cut in wedges	1
12	English cucumber slices	12

1. Bring a saucepan of water to a boil. Add rice flakes and cook for 5 to 6 minutes, or until softened. Rinse under cold water, drain well and place in a large bowl.
2. In a small bowl or measuring cup, combine soy sauce, lime juice, sugar and chilies.
3. Heat a wok or large skillet over medium-high heat and add oil. Add garlic and tofu and stir-fry for 1 minute.
4. Add beans, cauliflower and carrot and stir-fry for 3 minutes, or until vegetables are tender-crisp. Stir into cooked rice flakes along with reserved sauce mixture, shallots, green onions and cilantro.
5. Garnish with tomato wedges and cucumber slices.

Egg Noodles with Vegetables

Makes 4 servings

Noodle dishes are sold everywhere in Thailand — from three-wheeled noodle carts, at streetside stands, in restaurants and even from boats. Although especially popular at lunchtime, noodles are eaten any time of the day or night. This recipe uses fresh egg noodles, but softened rice noodles can be substituted. For a vegetarian version, replace the oyster sauce with vegetarian (mushroom) oyster sauce.

1/4 cup	chicken stock or water	50 mL
2 tbsp	oyster sauce	25 mL
1 tbsp	soy sauce	15 mL
1 tbsp	lime juice	15 mL
1 tsp	granulated sugar	5 mL
1/4 tsp	black pepper	1 mL
2 tbsp	vegetable oil	25 mL
4	cloves garlic, chopped	4
1/2	bunch broccoli (about 8 oz/250 g), cut in florets, stems peeled and sliced	1/2
1	red bell pepper, seeded and cut in 1-inch (2.5 cm) pieces	1
2	stalks celery, sliced	2
4 oz	snow peas, trimmed (about 1 cup/250 mL)	125 g
8 oz	fresh egg noodles, rinsed under hot water and loosened	250 g
1 cup	bean sprouts	250 mL
3	green onions, thinly sliced	3
1	small fresh red chili, seeded and thinly sliced	1
2 tbsp	fresh cilantro leaves	25 mL

1. In a small bowl or measuring cup, combine stock, oyster sauce, soy sauce, lime juice, sugar and pepper.
2. Heat a wok or large skillet over medium-high heat and add oil. Add garlic and stir-fry for 30 seconds.
3. Add broccoli, red pepper, celery and snow peas. Increase heat to high and stir-fry for 3 minutes, or until crisp.
4. Add noodles and reserved sauce, tossing to combine with vegetables. Cook for 3 to 4 minutes, or until noodles are tender but not mushy.
5. Add bean sprouts and green onions and toss with noodles.
6. Garnish with chili slices and cilantro.

Rice Noodles with Shrimp and Basil

Makes 4 servings

Shrimp and aromatic Thai basil combine in this simple noodle dish (use regular basil if you can't find Thai). If fresh rice noodles are available, use them. Since they come with a thin coating of oil to keep them separate, rinse gently with warm water before using.

8 oz	dried medium rice noodles	250 g
2 tbsp	fish sauce	25 mL
1 tbsp	soy sauce	15 mL
1 tbsp	lime juice	15 mL
1/2 tsp	hot chili sauce	2 mL
1/4 cup	water	50 mL
2 tbsp	vegetable oil	25 mL
4	cloves garlic, chopped	4
12 oz	shrimp, peeled and deveined	375 g
1/3 cup	fresh sweet Thai basil leaves	75 mL

1. Place noodles in a large bowl. Cover with very hot water and let stand for 10 to 12 minutes, or until softened but still firm. Rinse well with cold water and drain.
2. In a small bowl or measuring cup, combine fish sauce, soy sauce, lime juice, chili sauce and water.
3. Heat a wok or large skillet over medium-high heat and add oil. Add garlic and cook for 30 seconds.
4. Add shrimp and stir-fry for 3 minutes, or until shrimp are just pink. Stir in reserved sauce and heat through.
5. Add noodles and toss to separate and coat with sauce, cooking for 2 to 3 minutes, or until soft but not mushy. Stir in basil.

Rice Noodles

In North America, fresh rice noodles are usually only available in Asian groceries. They are sold already cut or in a large sheet (which can be cut to the desired width). Since they are quite perishable, they should be used shortly after purchase. They can be used directly from the package or cooked briefly.

Dried rice noodles come in various widths and shapes. The names vary, depending on the manufacturer. Most dried rice noodles need to be softened in hot water before being used (see each recipe for directions). When softening noodles that require further cooking, leave some texture, as they will continue to cook.

A small amount of liquid may need to be added to rice noodle dishes toward the end of the cooking time (especially if you are using wide noodles).

Crispy Fried Noodles

6 oz	dried rice vermicelli noodles	175 g
4 cups	vegetable oil	1 L
3 tbsp	fish sauce	45 mL
2 tbsp	soy sauce	25 mL
1/4 cup	plum sauce or ketchup	50 mL
1/4 cup	palm or brown sugar	50 mL
1 tsp	hot pepper flakes	5 mL
1 tbsp	yellow bean or hoisin sauce (optional)	15 mL
4	cloves garlic, chopped	4
2	shallots, thinly sliced	2
8 oz	finely chopped or ground pork, chicken or shrimp	250 g
3 tbsp	lime juice	45 mL
1 1/2 cups	bean sprouts	375 mL
4	green onions, sliced diagonally	4

1. Place noodles in a large plastic or paper bag and break apart in small bunches. Heat oil in a deep saucepan or wok to 325°F (160°C). To see whether oil is hot enough, add a couple of strands of noodles and if they puff, then start cooking.
2. Add noodles a couple of bunches at a time and cook until they puff and are light golden. (This only takes moments.) Lift from oil with a slotted spoon or wire strainer and drain on paper towels. Pour off all but 2 tbsp (25 mL) oil from wok.
3. In a bowl or measuring cup, combine fish sauce, soy sauce, plum sauce, sugar, hot pepper flakes and bean sauce, if using.
4. Reheat wok over medium-high heat. Add garlic and shallots and cook for 30 seconds, or until fragrant. Add pork and cook for 2 to 3 minutes, or until pinkness disappears.
5. Add reserved sauce and cook for 4 to 5 minutes, or until sauce is syrupy. Add lime juice.
6. Layer sauce and noodles in a large shallow serving dish and garnish with bean sprouts and green onions.

Makes 4 to 6 servings

There are many variations of Mee Krob, but basically it is a crispy dish of fried fine noodles topped or lightly tossed with a sweet and sour sauce. Some versions contain small pieces of pork, chicken, shrimp and/or tofu. Eggs might be part of the sauce, or sometimes the dish is garnished with deep-fried egg whites or shredded omelet (page 93).

This is an abbreviated version. Some cooks toss the fried noodles in the sauce, but for more crispiness, I prefer to alternate layers of noodles and sauce in a shallow serving dish. Pickled garlic (available in jars at Asian stores) and thinly sliced fresh red chilies are often used as garnishes.

Make Ahead

Noodles can be fried up to an hour ahead and kept uncovered in a dry place (e.g., a turned-off oven) before using.

Rice Noodles with Chicken and Gravy

Makes 4 servings

In Thailand, when customers order noodles, they specify the type of noodle, their preferred meat and/or vegetable and whether the dish is to be served like a soup, with sauce, or dry. Customers also season the dish to their liking with a variety of condiments such as fish sauce, vinegars, sugar, chilies and other mixtures. The noodles are often served in large bowls and eaten with chopsticks. Use the following recipe as a base for your own house noodles.

8 oz	dried medium or wide rice noodles	250 g
2 tbsp	oyster or soy sauce	25 mL
2 tbsp	vegetable oil	25 mL
4	cloves garlic, chopped	4
3 cups	chicken stock	750 mL
1 1/2 cups	diced cooked chicken or pork	375 mL
1	tomato, chopped	1
2 tbsp	cornstarch	25 mL
3 tbsp	water	45 mL
2 tbsp	fish sauce	25 mL
2	green onions, chopped	2
1 tbsp	chopped fresh cilantro leaves	15 mL

1. Place noodles in a large bowl. Cover with boiling water and let stand for 6 to 8 minutes, or until fairly soft. Rinse well with cold water and drain. Place in a bowl and toss with oyster sauce.
2. Heat oil in a saucepan over medium-high heat. Add garlic and cook for 30 seconds, or until fragrant. Add stock and bring to a low boil.
3. Add chicken and heat through. Stir in tomato.
4. In a small bowl, combine cornstarch and water. Stir into stock and cook, stirring, for 3 minutes, or until thickened.
5. Stir in noodles, fish sauce and green onions and heat through.
6. Garnish with cilantro.

Egg Noodles with Chinese Sausage

8 oz	fresh egg noodles	250 g
1 tsp	sesame oil	5 mL
2 tbsp	chicken stock or water	25 mL
2 tbsp	lime juice	25 mL
1 tbsp	black bean sauce	15 mL
1/2 tsp	granulated sugar	2 mL
2 tbsp	vegetable oil	25 mL
1	onion, thinly sliced	1
3	cloves garlic, chopped	3
1/2 tsp	chopped fresh red chilies	2 mL
6 oz	Chinese sausage, rinsed and thinly sliced, or 1 1/4 cups (300 mL) finely diced ham	175 g
1/3 cup	chopped fresh garlic chives or green onions	75 mL
1 tbsp	coarsely chopped fresh cilantro leaves	15 mL

1. Cook noodles in a saucepan of boiling water for 2 minutes. Rinse with cold water and drain. Place in a bowl and toss with sesame oil.
2. In a small bowl or measuring cup, combine stock, lime juice, black bean sauce and sugar.
3. Heat a wok or large skillet over medium-high heat and add oil. Add onion and garlic and stir-fry for 2 minutes, or until onion is softened.
4. Add chilies and sausage and stir-fry for 2 minutes, or until sausage has softened and is warm.
5. Add noodles and sauce, tossing to combine for 3 minutes, or until noodles are soft but not mushy.
6. Add chives and cilantro and toss to combine.

Makes 3 to 4 servings

Bangkok's Chinatown bustles with activity and noise. It is a maze of narrow alleys lined with stalls overflowing with fresh and preserved foods, decorations, medicines, herbs and much more. Pungent smells just add to the mix, along with tuk-tuk, bus, motorbike and car traffic.

Many dishes combine the Chinese influence of noodles with distinctly Thai flavors. This recipe is just one example.

Chiang Mai Curry Noodles

Makes 4 servings

The city of Chiang Mai in northern Thailand offers ancient temples, designer shops, deluxe hotels and resorts, a myriad of cooking schools, plain and high-end restaurants and the famous night market. There are many handicraft shops featuring silver, wood, ceramics, lacquerware, silk and umbrella painting. Beyond the city you'll find elephant camps, river rafting, trekking and traditional hilltribe villages. Shops in Chiang Mai specialize in this famous noodle dish which has several variations, but generally features a coconut milk-based sauce.

8 oz	fresh egg noodles	250 g
1 1/2 cups	coconut milk, divided	375 mL
6	cloves garlic, chopped	6
4	shallots, chopped	4
1 tbsp	red curry paste	15 mL
1/4 tsp	ground turmeric	1 mL
8 oz	lean beef, thinly sliced	250 g
2 tbsp	fish sauce	25 mL
1 tbsp	soy sauce	15 mL
2 tsp	granulated sugar	10 mL
2 tbsp	lime juice	25 mL
1/2 cup	thinly sliced green onions	125 mL
1	lime, cut in wedges	1

1. Bring a saucepan of water to a boil. Add noodles and cook for 2 minutes. Rinse with cold water and drain.
2. In a wok or saucepan, heat 1/2 cup (125 mL) coconut milk over medium heat and boil gently until oil droplets appear.
3. Add garlic and shallots and cook for 2 minutes. Add curry paste and turmeric and cook, stirring, for 2 minutes, or until fragrant.
4. Add beef and cook, stirring, for 2 minutes, or until meat is just cooked.
5. Add remaining coconut milk, fish sauce, soy sauce and sugar. Bring to a boil, reduce heat and simmer for 4 minutes.
6. Add noodles and toss to coat with sauce. Cook for 2 to 3 minutes, or until noodles are soft but not mushy. Remove from heat.
7. Stir in lime juice and garnish with green onions and lime wedges.

Stir-fried Noodles with Ground Beef and Spinach

Makes 4 to 6 servings

This dish sometimes includes eggs that are added and scrambled near the end of the cooking time. If you cook lots of Thai dishes, try to find yellow bean sauce (also called brown bean sauce) made from yellow fermented soy beans. It adds a full, salty flavor to dishes.

8 oz	dried medium or wide rice noodles	250 g
1/4 cup	water	50 mL
2 tbsp	soy sauce	25 mL
1 tbsp	fish sauce	15 mL
1 tbsp	yellow bean or hoisin sauce	15 mL
1 tsp	sesame oil	5 mL
2 tbsp	vegetable oil	25 mL
3	cloves garlic, chopped	3
2	shallots, chopped	2
8 oz	lean ground beef	250 g
4 cups	loosely packed baby spinach leaves	1 L
2	green onions, chopped	2

1. Place noodles in a large bowl. Cover with very hot water and let stand for 10 to 12 minutes, or until softened but still firm. Rinse with cold water and drain.
2. In a small bowl or measuring cup, combine water, soy sauce, fish sauce, bean sauce and sesame oil.
3. Heat a wok or large skillet over medium-high heat and add vegetable oil. Add garlic and shallots and cook for 1 minute, or until softened.
4. Add beef and stir-fry for 3 to 4 minutes, or until pinkness disappears. Add spinach and stir-fry for 1 minute, until spinach is just wilted.
5. Add noodles and sauce and cook for 3 to 4 minutes, or until noodles are soft but not mushy.
6. Garnish with green onions.

Wide Noodles with Broccoli

Makes 4 to 6 servings

Use fresh noodles in this dish if they are available. The cooked noodle dish can be used as a base for any stir-fry. Blanching the broccoli ensures that it will be cooked to the correct tenderness, but you can also skip this step.

If fresh noodles are not available, use 8 oz (250 g) dried wide rice noodles. Cover with very hot water and soften for 10 to 12 minutes. Rinse with cold water and drain well before using.

1/2	bunch broccoli (about 8 oz/250 g), cut in small florets, stems peeled and sliced	1/2
1 lb	fresh wide rice noodles	500 g
3 tbsp	vegetable oil, divided	45 mL
2	eggs, beaten	2
2 tbsp	sweet soy sauce (page 22) or oyster sauce	25 mL
3	cloves garlic, chopped	3
2 tbsp	oyster sauce	25 mL
1 tbsp	fish sauce	15 mL
1/2 tsp	granulated sugar	2 mL
1/4 tsp	black pepper	1 mL

1. Bring a large pot of water to a boil. Add broccoli and blanch for 2 to 3 minutes, or until just tender crisp. Cool under cold water and drain well.
2. Place noodles in a colander. Pour enough hot water over noodles to soften and separate strands.
3. In a wok or large skillet, heat 2 tbsp (25 mL) oil over medium-high heat. Add eggs and stir to scramble. Add noodles and toss to heat through and separate. Add soy sauce and mix well. Transfer to a serving dish.
4. Return wok to heat and add remaining oil. Add garlic and stir-fry for 1 minute, or until just golden. Add broccoli and stir-fry for 1 minute.
5. Add oyster sauce, fish sauce, sugar and pepper and toss until broccoli is coated with sauce.
6. Spoon broccoli over noodles.

Glass Noodle and Shrimp Casserole

Makes 4 servings

On our return to Bangkok from the Bang Sai Folk Arts and Crafts Center (where villagers are trained in making exquisite folk art and crafts such as basketry, dolls, silks, garments and more), we stopped for a late lunch at Thong Yowd, a family-owned restaurant. Overlooking the Chao Praya River, the open air decor included giant fans, arborite tables, a painted orange floor, royal-blue plastic chairs and light-blue plastic dishes. While we enjoyed a cold beer, we watched barges holding as much cargo as eighty large trucks heading south to deep-sea ports, carrying lumber, rice and other farm products.

6 oz	dried bean thread (cellophane) noodles	175 g
2 tbsp	vegetable oil	25 mL
2 tbsp	chopped fresh gingerroot	25 mL
3	cloves garlic, chopped	3
2 tbsp	chopped fresh cilantro stems or roots	25 mL
4	green onions, coarsely chopped	4
12 oz	shrimp, peeled and deveined	375 g
2 tbsp	oyster sauce	25 mL
1 tbsp	soy sauce	15 mL
1 tbsp	fish sauce	15 mL
2 tsp	sesame oil	10 mL
1/2 cup	chicken stock	125 mL
2 tsp	palm or brown sugar	10 mL
1/4 tsp	black pepper	1 mL
	Fresh cilantro leaves	

1. Bring a saucepan of water to a boil. Add noodles and cook for 1 minute, or until noodles are softened and turn clear. Rinse with cold water, drain and place in a large bowl.
2. Meanwhile, in a 6-cup (1.5 L) saucepan or casserole, heat oil over medium heat. Add ginger, garlic, cilantro stems and green onions and stir-fry for 2 minutes. Remove from heat and arrange shrimp on top.
3. Add oyster sauce, soy sauce, fish sauce, sesame oil, chicken stock, sugar and pepper to noodles. Toss to combine.
4. Spoon noodle mixture over shrimp. Cover and bring to a boil. Reduce heat to medium-low and cook, uncovered, for 8 to 10 minutes, or until noodles have absorbed sauce. Do not stir during cooking.
5. Garnish with cilantro leaves.

Bean Thread Noodles

Bean thread noodles (also called cellophane or glass noodles) are made from mung bean flour. They are very tough when dry and require soaking. Cut them to the desired length after softening. These noodles really absorb the flavorings of a dish. Use them in spring rolls, soups, salads and stir-fries.

Breakfast Noodles with Seafood

Makes 4 servings

Although these noodles are eaten for breakfast, they are also served day and night at noodle stalls. Dried egg noodles can be substituted. Cook in boiling water for 2 to 5 minutes, depending on the thickness of the noodles, until soft but still slightly firm. Drain and rinse with cold water if not using immediately.

Use regular broccoli or asparagus as a substitute for Chinese broccoli.

8 oz	fresh egg noodles	250 g
1 tbsp	oyster sauce	15 mL
1 tbsp	fish sauce	15 mL
2 tsp	hot chili sauce or roasted chili paste (page 48)	10 mL
1 tsp	granulated sugar	5 mL
1/4 cup	water	50 mL
2 tbsp	vegetable oil	25 mL
3	cloves garlic, chopped	3
4 oz	scallops, quartered	125 g
4 oz	shrimp, peeled and deveined, cut in 1/2-inch (1 cm) pieces	125 g
4 oz	firm white fish fillets, cut in 1/2-inch (1 cm) pieces	125 g
1 cup	Chinese broccoli, cut in 1-inch (2.5 cm) lengths	250 mL
1/4 cup	fresh sweet Thai basil leaves	50 mL

1. Bring a large saucepan of water to a boil. Add noodles and cook for 2 minutes. Rinse with cold water and drain.
2. In a bowl or measuring cup, combine oyster sauce, fish sauce, chili sauce, sugar and water.
3. Heat a wok or large skillet over medium-high heat and add oil. Add garlic and cook for 15 seconds. Add scallops, shrimp, fish and broccoli and stir-fry for 1 minute.
4. Add sauce and stir-fry for 1 minute.
5. Add noodles and stir-fry for 2 minutes, tossing to coat ingredients with sauce.
6. Stir in basil.

Rice

Jasmine Rice

Makes 5 cups (1.25 L)

I once read that Thailand was known as the rice bowl of Asia, and after visiting the country I understood why. Rice is the mainstay of the Thai diet, and Thailand is a major producer and exporter of top-quality rices. Jasmine rice, an aromatic long-grain rice grown predominantly in the fertile ricelands of central Thailand, is most commonly used. Rice cookers are popular (follow the manufacturer's directions), but here is a simple stovetop technique for steaming rice. It specifies precise quantities of rice and water, though many cooks simply cover the washed and drained rice with water by approximately 1/2 inch (1 cm), or until the water comes barely to the first joint of the index finger.

1 1/2 cups	jasmine rice	375 mL
2 cups	water	500 mL

1. Rinse rice several times until water runs clear. (Rice can be rinsed in a sieve under cold running water or in a saucepan. Swirl rice with your hand and pour off water.) Drain rice and place in a heavy saucepan.
2. Add water. Bring to a boil over medium heat and boil, uncovered, for 5 to 6 minutes, or until surface water appears to have evaporated and small craters appear.
3. Cover with a tight-fitting lid. Reduce heat to very low for 15 minutes, not removing lid.
4. Remove from heat and let stand, covered, for 10 minutes. Fluff gently with a fork.

Vegetarian Dinner

Vegetable Curry Rolls (page 260)

Tofu with Red Curry and Peanut Sauce (page 202) or Vegetables and Tofu in Green Curry (page 210)

Jasmine Rice (page 114)

Roasted Pineapple (page 245)

Coconut Rice

Makes 6 servings

Plain steamed rice is the norm at most Thai meals, but occasionally coconut milk is used as part of the steaming liquid. This makes a richer dish, but because of the coconut milk and sugar, it can scorch easily, so watch it carefully.

1¾ cups	jasmine rice	425 mL
1¾ cups	coconut milk	425 mL
1 cup	water	250 mL
2 tsp	granulated sugar (optional)	10 mL
½ tsp	salt (optional)	2 mL

1. Wash rice in several changes of cold water until water runs clear. Drain rice.
2. In a saucepan, combine rice, coconut milk and water. Add sugar and salt, if using. Bring to a boil over medium-low heat and cook, uncovered, for 5 minutes, or until surface liquid appears to have evaporated and small craters appear.
3. Cover tightly. Reduce heat to very low and cook for 15 minutes.
4. Remove from heat and let stand, covered, for 10 minutes.

Red Rice

Makes 6 cups (1.5 L)

Jasmine and sticky rice are the most popular rices in Thailand, but red rice is starting to make an appearance. It is a firm-textured rice with a nutty flavor and is becoming more popular in North America as it is not processed or milled. Look for it in Asian stores and in bulk food stores that carry many types of rice.

2 cups	red rice	500 mL
2¾ cups	water	675 mL

1. Rinse rice in cold water until water runs clear. Drain well and place in a saucepan with water.
2. Bring rice to a boil. Boil, uncovered, for 2 minutes. Cover and reduce heat to very low. Cook for 30 minutes.
3. Remove from heat and let stand for 15 minutes. Fluff gently with a fork.

Sticky Rice

2 cups	white glutinous (sticky) rice	500 mL

1. In a bowl, cover rice with at least 2 inches (5 cm) cold water and soak at room temperature for several hours or overnight. To speed up this process, soak in warm water (100°F/38°C) for 2 hours.
2. Drain rice and place in a bamboo basket steamer or in a cheesecloth-lined flat bamboo basket or sieve. Place over (not in) boiling water. Cover with a lid and steam for 35 to 40 minutes, or until rice is shiny and tender. (Check often to make sure there is enough boiling water.)
3. Turn rice onto a tray and gently stir with a wet spoon to release steam and prevent rice from becoming soggy.

Thai Dinner Party

Crispy Wontons with Tamarind Sauce (page 42)
Spicy Shrimp Soup (page 51)
Steamed Fish with Chili Lime Sauce (page 174)
Stir-fried Chicken with Cashews (page 152)
Glazed Spareribs (page 145)
Coconut Rice (page 115) or Red Rice (page 115)
Tofu with Red Curry and Peanut Sauce (page 202)
Cauliflower and Beans with Turmeric (page 222)
Crisp Red Rubies (page 239)

Makes about 5 cups (1.25 L)

Sticky rice, also known as glutinous rice, is the mainstay of northern Thailand. It is traditionally served on a plate or in hand-woven baskets. Since it magically adheres to itself and not to your fingers when cooked, it can be shaped into balls and dipped in sauces or topped with a piece of meat, fish or other foods and eaten by hand. It is delicious hot, warm or even at room temperature. It is also used in desserts (page 236). Sticky rice is usually soaked overnight before being steamed in a conical bamboo steaming basket or in a sieve lined with cheesecloth (page 15). In some homes and markets, it is cooked in banana or lotus leaves or pushed into bamboo stalks and grilled over coals.

Make Ahead

Make rice ahead, cover and serve warm or at room temperature.

Yellow Rice

Makes 4 servings

On my last trip to Thailand, I noticed many Thais wearing yellow shirts, especially on Mondays. I've since learned that this was the color chosen by the king to celebrate his sixtieth anniversary on the throne, and Monday is the day he was born. In this simple rice dish, turmeric provides the yellow color. Serve it with chicken or fish. For a less rich dish, replace the coconut milk with stock or water.

2 tbsp	vegetable oil	25 mL
3	shallots, chopped	3
2	cloves garlic, chopped	2
1 1/2 cups	jasmine rice, rinsed	375 mL
2 cups	chicken stock, vegetable stock or water	500 mL
1/2 cup	coconut milk	125 mL
1 tbsp	fish or soy sauce	15 mL
1/2 tsp	ground turmeric	2 mL
2	stalks lemongrass, white part only, cut in half crosswise	2

1. In a saucepan, heat oil over medium-high heat. Add shallots and garlic and stir-fry for 2 minutes, or until just starting to color.
2. Add rice, stock, coconut milk, fish sauce and turmeric. Bring to a boil. Place lemongrass on rice.
3. Reduce heat to low. Cover and cook for 18 minutes, or until liquid is just absorbed.
4. Remove from heat and let stand for 5 minutes. Remove lemongrass and fluff rice with a fork.

Cozy Winter Supper

Fish Cakes with Green Beans (page 29)
Mussaman Lamb Curry with Potatoes (page 213)
Yellow Rice (page 118)
Thai Chef's Salad (page 90)
Caramel Lime Bananas (page 240)

Vegetable Fried Rice

2 tbsp	vegetable oil	25 mL
4	cloves garlic, chopped	4
1	onion, chopped	1
1 cup	sliced fresh mushrooms	250 mL
1 cup	chopped Napa or Savoy cabbage	250 mL
1/2 cup	chopped carrots	125 mL
1/2 cup	thinly sliced green beans	125 mL
1/2 cup	corn kernels	125 mL
1/4 cup	green peas	50 mL
2	eggs, beaten (optional)	2
3 cups	cooked rice	750 mL
2 tbsp	soy sauce	25 mL
1	tomato, cut in wedges	1
12	English cucumber slices	12

1. Heat a wok or large skillet over medium-high heat and add oil. Add garlic and onion and stir-fry for 1 minute.
2. Add mushrooms, cabbage, carrots, beans, corn and peas. Stir-fry for 3 to 4 minutes, or until just tender.
3. Add eggs, if using, and cook, stirring, for 2 minutes, or until set. Stir in rice and toss to combine rice with all ingredients for 3 minutes, or until heated through.
4. Add soy sauce and toss to combine for 2 minutes, or until hot.
5. Serve garnished with tomato wedges and cucumber slices.

Makes 4 servings

To adapt recipes to vegetarian cooking, fish sauce can be replaced with soy sauce, chicken stock with vegetable stock, and any shrimp or fish products can be left out of pastes. Sometimes tofu will be added.

Cooking Fried Rice

Many cooks prefer to use cold rice when making fried rice. Plan ahead and cook rice the day before or even several hours ahead of time. After fluffing cooked rice gently with a fork, turn onto a baking sheet or shallow dish. Cool and refrigerate without covering until very cold, then cover. Before cooking, break up large clumps before adding it to the pan.

Thai Fried Rice

Makes 4 servings

Although this often contains pork, chicken or shrimp can also be used. For breakfast, a simple fried egg can top each serving. For a simple fried rice, omit the pork and egg, or use 2 cups (500 mL) sliced mushrooms instead of the pork.

2 tbsp	vegetable oil	25 mL
1	onion, chopped	1
6	cloves garlic, chopped	6
4 oz	thinly sliced pork	125 g
3	eggs, beaten	3
4 cups	cooked rice	1 L
2 tbsp	fish sauce	25 mL
1 tbsp	oyster sauce	15 mL
4	green onions, chopped	4

Garnish

1	lime, cut in wedges	1
1/4	English cucumber, sliced (optional)	1/4
1/4 cup	fish sauce	50 mL
2 tsp	chopped fresh red or green chilies	10 mL

1. Heat a wok or large skillet over medium-high heat and add oil. Add onion and garlic and stir-fry for 1 minute. Add pork and stir-fry for 2 minutes, or until pork is cooked.
2. Add eggs and cook, stirring, until eggs are just set.
3. Add rice, fish sauce, oyster sauce and green onions. Cook, tossing rice to incorporate ingredients and heat through. Garnish with lime wedges and cucumber, if using.
4. In a small bowl, combine fish sauce and chilies. Serve alongside rice.

Pineapple Fried Rice

Makes 5 to 6 servings

For an attractive presentation, serve this in hollowed-out pineapple shells, or carefully cut a pineapple into six or eight wedges that include the leaves. (For a less bulky appearance, just trim the leaves so they do not take up too much space.) Select ripe golden pineapples for the best flavor. Chinese sausage is available in Asian stores.

2 tbsp	vegetable oil	25 mL
5	shallots, thinly sliced	5
5	cloves garlic, thinly sliced	5
1/2 tsp	curry powder (optional)	2 mL
1/2 cup	chopped Chinese sausage, cooked chicken or cooked shrimp (optional)	125 mL
2	eggs, beaten	2
4 cups	cooked rice	1 L
2 cups	diced pineapple	500 mL
3 tbsp	fish sauce	45 mL
2 tbsp	soy sauce	25 mL
2	green onions, thinly sliced	2
3 tbsp	chopped fresh cilantro leaves	45 mL
1/4 cup	chopped roasted cashews	50 mL
2	small fresh red chilies, seeded and thinly sliced	2

1. Heat a wok or large skillet over medium-high heat and add oil. Add shallots and garlic and stir-fry for 30 seconds, or until light golden. Add curry powder and sausage (if using) and cook for 30 seconds.
2. Add eggs and stir-fry for 30 seconds.
3. Add rice, pineapple, fish sauce and soy sauce and cook for 3 to 4 minutes, or until rice has separated and ingredients are mixed and heated through.
4. Garnish with green onions, cilantro, cashews and sliced chilies.

Pineapple Boats

Cut a fresh pineapple in half lengthwise through leaves and fruit. Using a sharp knife, hollow out fruit and discard hard core.

Fried Rice with Crabmeat

2 tbsp	vegetable oil	25 mL
4	cloves garlic, chopped	4
4 cups	cooked rice	1 L
1 cup	cooked crabmeat or shrimp, broken up	250 mL
1/2 cup	chopped water chestnuts (optional)	125 mL
2	eggs, beaten	2
2 tbsp	fish sauce	25 mL
2 tbsp	lime juice	25 mL
1 tsp	granulated sugar	5 mL
2	green onions, chopped	2
	Cucumber slices	
	Lime wedges	
	Thinly sliced fresh red or green chilies	

1. Heat a wok or large skillet over medium-high heat and add oil. Add garlic and stir-fry for 30 seconds.
2. Add rice and stir-fry for 3 minutes, breaking up any clumps. Add crabmeat and water chestnuts, if using. Toss together to combine.
3. Clear an area on one side of wok and add eggs. Let set slightly, then stir into rice and toss.
4. Add fish sauce, lime juice, sugar and green onions. Stir to combine ingredients.
5. Serve garnished with cucumber slices, lime wedges and chilies.

Makes 4 servings

Crab appears in Thai appetizers, soups and in curries. It can be fried, steamed or stir-fried. In Thailand, fresh crab is available in many markets, but at home you could use frozen and defrosted or canned. Drain well but do not squeeze too much or you will lose all the crab flavor.

This dish was featured at a restaurant built on stilts overlooking the Gulf of Thailand. It is an easy and inexpensive way to incorporate crab into a dish.

In Thailand, this dish is sometimes garnished with small steamed crab claws.

Fried Rice with Curry

Makes 4 servings

Most fried rice dishes are gently seasoned, but this version has added curry and pepper. On its own it makes a good accompaniment for grilled fish or meat, but you can also add eggs and chicken for a more substantial dish. At markets, rice is often sold wrapped in banana leaves as a take-out dish, especially for breakfast.

2 tbsp	vegetable oil	25 mL
1	onion, chopped	1
4	cloves garlic, chopped	4
1 tbsp	chopped fresh gingerroot	15 mL
1 1/2 cups	sliced fresh mushrooms	375 mL
2 tsp	red curry paste	10 mL
1 tsp	granulated sugar	5 mL
1/4 tsp	ground turmeric	1 mL
1/4 tsp	black pepper	1 mL
1/2 cup	finely sliced green beans	125 mL
4 cups	cooked rice	1 L
2 tbsp	fish sauce	25 mL
2 tbsp	chopped fresh cilantro leaves	25 mL
2	green onions, chopped	2

1. Heat a wok or large skillet over medium-high heat and add oil. Add onion, garlic and ginger and stir-fry for 1 minute, or until soft and fragrant.
2. Add mushrooms and stir-fry for 2 minutes. Add curry paste, sugar, turmeric and pepper and stir-fry for 30 seconds.
3. Add beans and rice and toss for 3 to 4 minutes, or until heated through.
4. Add fish sauce, cilantro and green onions and toss to combine.

Steamed Chicken Fried Rice

Makes 6 servings

This simple dish is basically rice cooked with chicken and stock. It reminds me of a comfy dish that I ordered from room service during my first visit to Thailand, when I had a touch of Thai tummy. Some restaurants serve extra stock on the side, so you can eat it like a soup.

Make Ahead

Chicken and stock can be prepared ahead and refrigerated overnight.

2 lbs	chicken thighs or legs	1 kg
6 cups	cold water	1.5 L
2	cloves garlic, peeled	2
6	sprigs fresh cilantro, including stems and roots	6
1 tsp	salt	5 mL
Rice		
2 tbsp	vegetable oil	25 mL
3	cloves garlic, chopped	3
2 cups	jasmine rice, rinsed	500 mL
3 cups	chicken stock	750 mL
Sauce		
3 tbsp	yellow bean sauce	45 mL
2 tbsp	rice vinegar	25 mL
1 tbsp	soy sauce	15 mL
2 tsp	palm or brown sugar	10 mL
2 tsp	chopped fresh gingerroot	10 mL
1/2 tsp	chopped fresh red chilies	2 mL
Garnish		
	Cucumber slices	
	Fresh cilantro sprigs	

1. To prepare chicken, in a large saucepan, combine chicken, water, whole garlic, cilantro and salt. Bring to a boil. Reduce heat to medium-low. Cover and simmer for 45 minutes, or until chicken is very tender. Remove from heat. Let stand for 10 minutes, skimming surface. Strain stock (some stock is used to cook rice and any extra can be warmed and passed at serving time). When chicken is cool enough to handle, remove meat from bones and shred coarsely.
2. To prepare rice, in the same saucepan, heat oil over medium heat. Add chopped garlic and cook for 1 minute, or until softened. Add rice and stir to coat.
3. Add stock and bring to a boil over high heat. Cook, uncovered, for 5 to 6 minutes, or until small craters appear on surface. Cover, reduce heat to very low and steam for 20 minutes, without removing cover. Remove from heat and let stand for 10 minutes.
4. Meanwhile, to prepare sauce, in a bowl, combine bean sauce, vinegar, soy sauce, sugar, ginger and chilies.
5. To serve, top rice with chicken pieces and garnish with cucumber and cilantro. Pass sauce and extra warmed chicken stock.

Fried Rice with Chicken, Basil and Cilantro

Makes 4 servings

Thai basil and cilantro add a definite Thai flavor to this fried rice. A popular everyday meal, this may contain eggs or not. If the basil leaves are very large, tear them into smaller pieces.

2 tbsp	vegetable oil	25 mL
6 oz	chicken, finely diced	175 g
3	cloves garlic, chopped	3
3	shallots, chopped	3
1 tbsp	chopped fresh gingerroot	15 mL
1 tsp	chopped fresh red chilies	5 mL
3 cups	cooked rice	750 mL
1 tbsp	fish sauce	15 mL
1 tbsp	soy sauce	15 mL
2 tsp	palm or brown sugar	10 mL
1/4 tsp	black pepper	1 mL
1/2 cup	fresh sweet Thai basil leaves	125 mL
2 tbsp	chopped fresh cilantro leaves	25 mL
2	green onions, chopped	2

1. Heat a wok or large skillet over medium-high heat and add oil. Add chicken and stir-fry for 2 minutes, or until just cooked.
2. Add garlic, shallots, ginger and chilies and stir-fry for 1 minute.
3. Add rice and cook for 3 minutes, tossing to break up rice. Add fish sauce, soy sauce, sugar and pepper. Cook for 1 minute.
4. Add basil, cilantro and green onions. Cook for 1 minute and toss to incorporate ingredients.

Duck Fried Rice

Makes 6 servings

Roast duck adds a rich, full flavor to an otherwise gentle dish. The sweet soy sauce enhances the flavor of the duck, but if you can't find it, use two parts soy sauce and one part molasses.

2 tbsp	vegetable oil	25 mL
1	onion, chopped	1
2	cloves garlic, chopped	2
1 tbsp	chopped fresh gingerroot	15 mL
1/2 cup	diced celery	125 mL
1/2 cup	slivered carrots	125 mL
1/4 cup	diced red bell pepper	50 mL
1/2 cup	thinly sliced snow peas	125 mL
1	small tomato, chopped	1
1 1/2 cups	diced cooked duck	375 mL
3 cups	cooked rice	750 mL
2 tbsp	sweet soy sauce (page 22)	25 mL
2 tbsp	fish sauce	25 mL
1/2 tsp	black pepper	2 mL
2	green onions, thinly sliced	2
2 tbsp	chopped fresh cilantro leaves	25 mL
	Lime wedges	

1. Heat a wok or large skillet over medium-high heat and add oil. Add onion, garlic and ginger and stir-fry for 1 minute.
2. Add celery, carrots, red pepper, snow peas and tomato and stir-fry for 2 minutes.
3. Add duck and rice and stir-fry for 3 minutes, or until rice is hot.
4. Add soy sauce, fish sauce, pepper and green onions and toss to combine.
5. Serve garnished with cilantro and lime wedges.

Beef and Pork

Meatballs in Peanut Curry Sauce

Makes 4 to 6 servings

On my first visit to Bangkok, I was invited to a cocktail reception at the Oriental Hotel. It was such a lavish presentation of food, flowers, fruits and vegetables that I stared in awe. Later that week we learned how to make some of the foods, but after I returned home, I realized that it was the brigade of Thai assistants that made it all seem so simple. Tiny meatballs wrapped in a delicate strand of rice noodles and deep-fried proved to be too frustrating to reproduce for catering, so I eventually opted for this modified version similar to those sold on skewers by street vendors.

Make Ahead

Cooked dish can be covered and refrigerated a day ahead. Reheat in a preheated 325°F (160°C) oven for 25 minutes, or until hot, stirring occasionally.

8 oz	lean ground beef	250 g
8 oz	ground pork	250 g
3	cloves garlic, minced	3
2	shallots, finely chopped	2
1/4 cup	chopped fresh cilantro leaves	50 mL
1 tbsp	finely chopped fresh gingerroot	15 mL
1 tbsp	fish sauce	15 mL
1/2 tsp	hot chili sauce	2 mL
1 tsp	cornstarch	5 mL
2 tbsp	vegetable oil, divided	25 mL
1 tbsp	red curry paste	15 mL
1 1/2 cups	coconut milk	375 mL
3 tbsp	finely chopped peanuts or chunky peanut butter	45 mL
2 tbsp	fish sauce	25 mL
2 tbsp	lime juice or tamarind paste	25 mL
2 tbsp	palm or brown sugar	25 mL
2 tbsp	chopped fresh mint or cilantro leaves	25 mL

1. To prepare meatballs, in a bowl, combine beef, pork, garlic, shallots, cilantro, ginger, fish sauce, chili sauce and cornstarch. Mix thoroughly. Shape into about 24 meatballs (about 1 tbsp/ 15 mL each).
2. In a large nonstick skillet, heat 1 tbsp (15 mL) oil over medium-high heat. Add meatballs, in batches if necessary, and brown on all sides. Remove from skillet and reserve.
3. If necessary, add remaining oil to same skillet. Add curry paste and cook, stirring, for 1 minute.
4. Add coconut milk, peanuts, fish sauce, lime juice and sugar. Stir to combine all ingredients.
5. Return meatballs to skillet and cook, without boiling, for 12 to 15 minutes, stirring occasionally, until meatballs are cooked and coated with sauce.
6. Serve meatballs garnished with mint.

Beef with Mushrooms and Oyster Sauce

Makes 4 to 6 servings

Oyster sauce, an integral part of Chinese cooking, is used in many Thai dishes, especially stir-fries. Fresh straw mushrooms are popular in Thailand, but they are not readily available in Western supermarkets. For the best flavor and texture, use a variety of fresh mushrooms such as shiitake and oyster.

2 tbsp	vegetable oil, divided	25 mL
4	cloves garlic, chopped	4
1 tbsp	chopped fresh gingerroot	15 mL
8 oz	lean beef, thinly sliced and cut in 2-inch (5 cm) lengths	250 g
8 oz	fresh mushrooms (about 4 cups/1 L), sliced	250 g
2 tbsp	oyster sauce	25 mL
2 tbsp	fish sauce	25 mL
1 tsp	granulated sugar	5 mL
1/2 tsp	black pepper	2 mL
3	green onions, cut in 1-inch (2.5 cm) lengths	3
	Fresh red chili strips (optional)	

1. Heat a wok or large skillet over medium-high heat and add 1 tbsp (15 mL) oil. Add garlic and ginger and stir-fry for 30 seconds.
2. Add beef and stir-fry for 1 to 2 minutes, or until meat is browned. Remove from pan.
3. Return wok to heat and add remaining 1 tbsp (15 mL) oil. Add mushrooms and stir-fry for 2 minutes, or until golden. Return meat to pan.
4. Add oyster sauce, fish sauce, sugar and pepper. Toss to combine and stir in green onions.
5. Serve sprinkled with chilies, if using.

Beef with Sweet Thai Basil

Makes 4 servings

The Thai basil most commonly found in Western supermarkets is sweet Thai basil (bai horapah). It has purplish stems, large green leaves and lovely purple flowers. It imparts a gentle licorice/anise flavor to dishes and is used in stir-fries, soups and curries. Seeds are now more available, and this basil grows well in North American gardens and patio pots. Thinly sliced beef can be used in place of ground beef.

1/2 cup	chicken stock or water	125 mL
2 tbsp	oyster sauce	25 mL
1 tbsp	fish sauce	15 mL
1 tsp	granulated sugar	5 mL
1 tsp	cornstarch	5 mL
2 tbsp	vegetable oil	25 mL
4	cloves garlic, chopped	4
1 tsp	chopped fresh red chilies	5 mL
12 oz	lean ground beef	375 g
1	onion, thinly sliced	1
1/2 cup	fresh sweet Thai basil leaves	125 mL

1. In a small bowl or measuring cup, combine stock, oyster sauce, fish sauce, sugar and cornstarch.
2. Heat a wok or large skillet over medium-high heat and add oil. Add garlic and chilies and stir-fry for 30 seconds. Add beef and stir-fry for 2 to 3 minutes, or until pinkness disappears.
3. Stir in reserved sauce and onion and stir-fry for 1 to 2 minutes.
4. Stir in basil.

Grilled Beef

1 lb	steak (boneless ribeye, flank or striploin)	500 g
2 tbsp	fish sauce	25 mL
2 tbsp	soy sauce	25 mL
1 tsp	granulated sugar	5 mL
Sauce		
2 tbsp	fish sauce	25 mL
3 tbsp	lime juice	45 mL
2 tsp	palm or brown sugar	10 mL
2 tsp	chopped fresh red chilies	10 mL
2	green onions, finely chopped	2
1/2 cup	chopped tomato	125 mL
2 tsp	chopped fresh cilantro leaves	10 mL
1 tbsp	roasted rice powder (page 87), optional	15 mL

1. Place steak in a shallow dish. In a small bowl or measuring cup, combine fish sauce, soy sauce and sugar. Pour over steak and turn to coat. Marinate, refrigerated, for 30 to 60 minutes.
2. Meanwhile, to prepare sauce, in a bowl, combine fish sauce, lime juice, sugar, chilies, green onions, tomato, cilantro and rice powder, if using.
3. Grill steak for 3 to 4 minutes per side, or until caramelized and brown but still rare.
4. Let stand for 5 minutes before carving against grain into thin slices. Serve with sauce.

Roasted Tomato Sauce

In a bowl, combine 2 cups (500 mL) chopped tomatoes (preferably plum), 3 chopped cloves garlic, 2 chopped shallots, 1 tbsp (15 mL) coarsely chopped fresh red or green chilies and 1 tbsp (15 mL) granulated or brown sugar. Spoon into an ovenproof baking dish. Roast in a preheated 400°F (200°C) oven for 30 minutes, or until tomatoes are very soft. Stir occasionally.

Transfer to a blender or food processor. Add 2 tbsp (25 mL) fish sauce and 2 tbsp (25 mL) lime juice. Pulse to chop coarsely. Taste and adjust seasonings if necessary. Serve at room temperature or cover and refrigerate for up to 3 days. Sauce can also be frozen.

Makes 1 3/4 cups (425 mL).

Makes 4 servings

When we were in Thailand, we kept seeing recipes for Waterfall Beef (named for the sound of dripping juices splashing onto the hot fire) or Crying Tiger (because tigers cried while trying to chew tough meat, because the hot sauce brought tears to their eyes or because the dripping juices are like tiger's tears!). This is a simplified adaptation that is delicious with or without the sauce. Since this dish hails from the Northeast, it is often accompanied by sticky rice (page 117) and raw vegetables (carrots, cucumbers, etc.) to dip into the sauce. The sliced steak can also be served with roasted tomato sauce. Leftover steak is great in salads or sandwiches.

Chili Beef with Peppers

Makes 5 or 6 servings

Colorful and spicy, this Chinese-influenced dish can be served with steamed rice and a pomelo (page 77) or bean salad (page 74). The beef can be replaced with thinly sliced pork tenderloin or chicken thighs.

1 tbsp	cornstarch	15 mL
1 cup	beef or chicken stock	250 mL
2 tbsp	soy sauce	25 mL
2 tbsp	lime juice	25 mL
1 tbsp	fish sauce	15 mL
1 tsp	sesame oil	5 mL
2 tbsp	vegetable oil, divided	25 mL
1	onion, thinly sliced	1
2	cloves garlic, chopped	2
1 tbsp	chopped fresh gingerroot	15 mL
1	red bell pepper, seeded and thinly sliced	1
1	green bell pepper, seeded and thinly sliced	1
2 tsp	thinly sliced fresh red chilies	10 mL
8 oz	lean beef, thinly sliced and cut in 2-inch (5 cm) lengths	250 g

1. In a small bowl or measuring cup, combine cornstarch, stock, soy sauce, lime juice, fish sauce and sesame oil.
2. Heat a wok or large skillet over medium-high heat and add 1 tbsp (15 mL) oil. Add onion, garlic and ginger and stir-fry for 1 minute, or until slightly softened and fragrant.
3. Add red pepper, green pepper and chilies. Stir-fry for 3 to 4 minutes, or until tender-crisp. Remove vegetables to a dish.
4. Return pan to high heat and heat remaining oil. Add beef and stir-fry for 1 to 2 minutes, or until pinkness almost disappears.
5. Stir reserved sauce and add to beef. Cook, stirring, for 2 minutes, or until sauce boils and thickens slightly.
6. Return reserved vegetables to pan and heat through.

Stir-fried Beef with Broccoli

Makes 4 servings

Use Chinese broccoli if it is available; it is sturdier than regular broccoli, with more stem and less flower. You could also substitute rapini, bok choy, green beans or even spinach as long as it is added at the end of the cooking time. This is not a spicy dish.

2 tbsp	oyster sauce	25 mL
1 tbsp	fish sauce	15 mL
1 tbsp	lime juice	15 mL
1/2 tsp	granulated sugar	2 mL
1/2 tsp	cornstarch	2 mL
1/4 cup	water	50 mL
2 tbsp	vegetable oil	25 mL
4	cloves garlic, chopped	4
8 oz	lean beef, thinly sliced and cut in 2-inch (5 cm) lengths	250 g
1	bunch broccoli (about 1 lb/500 g), cut in 1-inch (2.5 cm) pieces	1

1. In a small bowl or measuring cup, combine oyster sauce, fish sauce, lime juice, sugar, cornstarch and water.
2. Heat a wok or large skillet over medium-high heat and add oil. Add garlic and stir-fry for 30 seconds.
3. Add beef and stir-fry for 1 minute. Add broccoli and stir-fry for 1 minute.
4. Add sauce, toss and cook for 3 minutes, or until broccoli is just tender.

Beef with Ginger and Green Beans

Makes 4 to 5 servings

Look for young ginger with smooth, thin skin; older ginger has thicker skin and can be fibrous. In Thailand, several gingers are used, including a popular variety called lesser ginger or krachai, which looks like a bunch of fingers and has a flavor of ginger and pepper. Use long green beans if available. You could also use thinly sliced chicken breasts instead of the beef.

2 tbsp	vegetable oil	25 mL
2 tbsp	chopped fresh gingerroot	25 mL
3	shallots, chopped	3
1	stalk lemongrass, white part only, thinly sliced	1
1 tsp	chopped fresh red chilies	5 mL
8 oz	lean beef, thinly sliced and cut in 2-inch (5 cm) lengths	250 g
2 cups	sliced green beans	500 mL
1/2 cup	coconut milk	125 mL
2 tbsp	fish sauce	25 mL
1/4 cup	fresh sweet Thai basil leaves	50 mL

1. Heat a wok or large skillet over medium-high heat and add oil. Add ginger, shallots, lemongrass and chilies and stir-fry for 30 seconds.
2. Add beef, beans, coconut milk and fish sauce and cook, stirring, for 4 minutes, or until beef is cooked.
3. Stir in basil before serving.

Dried Beef

Makes 6 servings

This is sometimes called Salty Sun-dried Beef — thinly sliced beef marinated and dried in the sun. It might then be deep-fried until crispy. It is a favorite in the Northeast and in Laos. To simulate the sun-drying, the beef is oven-dried until it resembles dried beef jerky. I slice the beef paper thin and omit the deep frying, and it is delicious as a snack, topping or garnish for sticky rice (page 117).

Make Ahead

Once cooled, dried beef can be covered and refrigerated for 3 to 4 days, or frozen for up to 2 weeks. If beef has softened, place in a 350°F (180°C) oven for 5 minutes to dry slightly.

1 lb	flank or sirloin steak	500 g
3 tbsp	fish sauce	45 mL
2	cloves garlic, minced	2
1 tbsp	granulated sugar	15 mL
2 tsp	ground coriander	10 mL
1/2 tsp	black pepper	2 mL

1. Cut steak across grain into very thin slices 2 to 3 inches (5 to 7.5 cm) long. (Freeze meat for 25 to 30 minutes to make it easier to slice thinly.) Place in a shallow dish.
2. In a small bowl or measuring cup, combine fish sauce, garlic, sugar, coriander and pepper. Add to beef slices and toss to coat. Cover and refrigerate for at least an hour or overnight.
3. Arrange slices in a single layer on foil- or parchment-lined baking sheets. Bake in a preheated 200°F (95°C) oven for 2 to 3 hours, turning occasionally, until dry and almost crispy. Timing will depend on how thinly meat is sliced.

Chiang Mai Sausage Patties

1 lb	lean ground pork	500 g
3 tbsp	lime juice	45 mL
3 tbsp	chopped fresh cilantro leaves	45 mL
4	cloves garlic, minced	4
1	shallot, finely chopped	1
2 tsp	finely chopped lemongrass, white part only	10 mL
1 tsp	chopped fresh gingerroot	5 mL
1 tsp	chopped fresh red chilies	5 mL
3/4 tsp	salt	4 mL
1/2 tsp	black pepper	2 mL
1/4 cup	dry bread crumbs	50 mL
2 tbsp	vegetable oil	25 mL

1. In a large bowl, combine pork, lime juice, cilantro, garlic, shallot, lemongrass, ginger, chilies, salt, pepper and bread crumbs. Mix together very well.
2. Shape mixture into 16 patties (about 2 tbsp/25 mL each).
3. In a large skillet, heat oil over medium-high heat. Cook patties for 10 minutes, turning once or twice, until golden brown and center temperature registers 170°F (77°C).

Easy Breakfast

Pineapple Fried Rice (page 122)

Chiang Mai Sausage Patties (page 139)

Iced Coffee (page 258)

Makes 6 to 8 servings

Northern Thailand is famous for its many kinds of sausages — from sweet-sour to chili-hot. Street vendors often sell them on a stick so the customer can snack while strolling.

Most sausages in Thailand are now commercially made, but some are still made by home cooks. The original recipe for this mixture was given to me by Sompon Nabnian of Chiang Mai. Although he makes his sausages in casings, not everyone has the equipment for doing this, so in this version the mixture is shaped into patties.

Make Ahead

Thais often refrigerate sausages overnight before cooking, to let the flavors blend. Patties can be shaped, covered and refrigerated 6 hours earlier or overnight.

Pork with Ginger and Mushrooms

Makes 4 servings

Fresh young ginger is the key to this recipe. In many markets and supermarkets in Thailand, the ginger is sold already finely cut. Beef, chicken or shrimp can also be used instead of pork.

2 tbsp	vegetable oil	25 mL
4	cloves garlic, chopped	4
8 oz	lean pork, thinly sliced	250 g
1/4 cup	slivered fresh gingerroot	50 mL
1 1/2 cups	thinly sliced fresh oyster or shiitake mushrooms (about 4 oz/125 g)	375 mL
4	green onions, sliced	4
2 tbsp	fish sauce	25 mL
1 tbsp	oyster sauce	15 mL
1 tsp	granulated sugar	5 mL
2 tsp	sliced fresh red chilies	10 mL

1. Heat a wok or large skillet over medium-high heat and add oil. Add garlic and pork and stir-fry for 2 minutes.
2. Add ginger and stir-fry for 1 minute.
3. Add mushrooms and stir-fry for 1 minute, or until just softened.
4. Add green onions, fish sauce, oyster sauce, sugar and chilies. Cook for 1 minute, tossing to combine.

Stir-fried Pork with Long Beans

2 tbsp	vegetable oil	25 mL
6	cloves garlic, thinly sliced	6
8 oz	lean pork, thinly sliced	250 g
8 oz	long or regular green beans, cut in 2-inch (5 cm) lengths (about 3 cups/750 mL)	250 g
2 tbsp	fish sauce	25 mL
1 tbsp	oyster sauce	15 mL
2 tsp	palm or brown sugar	10 mL
1/4 tsp	black pepper	1 mL
2 tbsp	fresh cilantro or sweet Thai basil leaves	25 mL
1/4 cup	coarsely chopped peanuts (optional)	50 mL

1. Heat a wok or large skillet over medium-high heat and add oil. Add garlic and pork and stir fry for 2 to 3 minutes, or until pork is just cooked.
2. Add beans, fish sauce, oyster sauce, sugar and pepper and cook, stirring, for 3 to 4 minutes, or until beans are tender.
3. Serve garnished with cilantro and peanuts, if using.

Stir-frying Tips

- Have all the ingredients prepared and assembled ahead of time, so the food does not sit in the wok or skillet, becoming waterlogged and overcooked.
- For the fastest cooking, the pan should be hot before you add the oil, but not so hot that the first ingredients added (often garlic and seasonings) color too quickly.
- Using thinly sliced meat will shorten the cooking time. Freeze meat or poultry until it is firm but not frozen, then slice thinly with a sharp knife. Some supermarkets now sell paper-thin slices of meat ready for stir-frying. Look for it in the frozen section.
- If your sauce is too thin, stir together 2 tbsp (10 mL) cornstarch and 3 tbsp (45 mL) cold water. Gradually add to wok and cook for a few minutes, or until sauce thickens slightly and is translucent.

Makes 4 to 6 servings

Pork is the meat of choice in Thailand. It is extremely versatile and Thais use most parts of the pig. It is sometimes referred to as the "red" meat. The meat is mostly ground, diced or thinly sliced and used in combination with vegetables, fruits, rice and noodles. The Chinese influence is evident in many Thai pork dishes. It is also common to find crispy pork skin used as a garnish or ingredient or sold as a snack.

If long beans are not available, use regular green beans. Beef, chicken or shrimp can be used instead of the pork.

Barbecued Lemongrass Pork

Makes 4 servings

In this recipe, the marinating ingredients can be blended together in a blender or food processor, but Thais would probably use a mortar and pestle. Serve this with Red Rice Salad (page 268).

3 tbsp	coconut milk	45 mL
3 tbsp	finely chopped lemongrass, white part only	45 mL
2	cloves garlic, minced	2
1	green onion, finely chopped	1
2 tbsp	fish sauce	25 mL
1 tbsp	soy sauce	15 mL
1 tbsp	granulated sugar	15 mL
2 tsp	sesame oil	10 mL
1/2 tsp	coarsely chopped fresh red chilies	2 mL
1/2 tsp	black pepper	2 mL
1	pork tenderloin (about 12 oz/375 g), trimmed and cut crosswise in 1/2-inch (1 cm) slices	1

1. In a bowl, combine coconut milk, lemongrass, garlic, green onion, fish sauce, soy sauce, sugar, sesame oil, chilies and pepper.
2. Arrange pork slices in a shallow dish. Pour marinade over meat and turn pork to coat all sides. Cover and marinate, refrigerated, for several hours.
3. Grill pork for 4 to 6 minutes per side, or until no longer pink.

Salads and a Barbecue

Red Rice Salad (page 268)

Crispy Cucumber Salad (page 72)

Green Papaya Salad (page 70)

Smoked Mackerel Salad (page 182)

Barbecued Chicken Thighs (page 160)

Barbecued Lemongrass Pork (page 142)

Sweet and Sour Pork

Makes 5 to 6 servings

Versions of this dish are a mainstay of Chinese cooking, but the Thais have added their own touch. This is not a spicy dish; serve it with rice. You can also use chicken or shrimp instead of pork.

2 tbsp	vegetable oil	25 mL
8 oz	pork tenderloin, thinly sliced	250 g
4	cloves garlic, thinly sliced	4
1	onion, thinly sliced	1
1	carrot, thinly sliced	1
$\frac{1}{2}$	red bell pepper, seeded and cut in 1-inch (2.5 cm) pieces	$\frac{1}{2}$
2 tbsp	fish sauce	25 mL
2 tbsp	rice vinegar	25 mL
2 tbsp	granulated sugar	25 mL
$\frac{1}{2}$	English cucumber, halved lengthwise and sliced	$\frac{1}{2}$
2	plum tomatoes, cut in wedges	2
2 tbsp	fresh cilantro leaves (optional)	25 mL

1. Heat a wok or large skillet over medium-high heat and add oil. Add pork and stir-fry for 2 to 3 minutes, or until pinkness disappears. Lift out pork with a slotted spoon and set aside.
2. Add garlic, onion, carrot and red pepper to wok and stir-fry for 3 minutes.
3. Add fish sauce, vinegar and sugar and cook, stirring, for 2 to 3 minutes, or until vegetables are tender-crisp.
4. Return pork and any juices to wok along with cucumber. Toss to combine all ingredients.
5. Add tomatoes and toss just to incorporate.
6. Sprinkle with cilantro, if using.

Glazed Spareribs

4 lbs	back or side spareribs, cut in 2-rib portions	2 kg
6	cloves garlic, peeled	6
2 tbsp	coarsely chopped gingerroot	25 mL
1/4 cup	fresh cilantro roots and leaves	50 mL
2	green onions, cut in 1-inch (2.5 cm) lengths	2
1/4 cup	palm or brown sugar	50 mL
1/4 cup	ketchup	50 mL
1/4 cup	lime juice	50 mL
1/4 cup	coconut milk	50 mL
2 tbsp	fish sauce	25 mL
2 tbsp	oyster sauce	25 mL

1. Place ribs in a shallow baking dish.
2. In a food processor, combine garlic, ginger, cilantro, green onions, sugar, ketchup, lime juice, coconut milk, fish sauce and oyster sauce. Blend until smooth. Pour over ribs and turn to coat in sauce. Cover and refrigerate overnight.
3. Place ribs with marinade, in a single layer, on a foil- and parchment-lined baking sheet and cover with foil. Bake in a preheated 350°F (180°C) oven for 45 minutes. Remove foil and bake for another 45 minutes, basting and turning ribs until tender.
4. To glaze ribs, place meat side up under a preheated broiler for 3 minutes.

Makes 4 to 6 servings

In Thailand, oven cooking/baking is rare. Most dishes are steamed, stewed or grilled. For convenience, though, these ribs are cooked in the oven and then broiled for a final glazing. Combining the marinade ingredients in the food processor instead of using a mortar and pestle makes this an easy dish to assemble.

Garlic Spareribs

Makes 4 servings

These garlicky spareribs are often served with sweet chili sauce (page 45) and garnished with crispy fried garlic. Traditionally deep-fried, in this recipe they are baked and then crisped under the broiler or on the barbecue. Since these are often served as finger food, ask the butcher to cut the rack of ribs in half through the bone to make two mini racks.

2 lbs	back or side spareribs	1 kg
4	cloves garlic, peeled	4
3 tbsp	coarsely chopped fresh cilantro leaves	45 mL
2 tbsp	fish sauce	25 mL
2 tbsp	water	25 mL
1 tsp	granulated sugar	5 mL
1/2 tsp	black pepper	2 mL

1. Cut ribs into single rib pieces and place in a shallow dish.
2. In a food processor, combine garlic, cilantro, fish sauce, water, sugar and pepper. Puree until smooth. Spoon over ribs and rub marinade into ribs. Cover and refrigerate up to overnight.
3. Place ribs in a single layer on a foil- and parchment-lined baking sheet. Bake, uncovered, in a preheated 350°F (180°C) oven for 1 hour, turning 2 or 3 times, until meat is tender.
4. To crisp ribs, grill on a barbecue or under a preheated broiler for 3 to 4 minutes per side, or until crisped.

Crisp Fried Garlic

Fried garlic is sold in jars or bags in Asian supermarkets, but you can also make your own. In a small skillet, heat 1/4 cup (50 mL) vegetable oil over medium-high heat. Add 6 to 8 thinly sliced large garlic cloves and cook for 4 to 6 minutes, stirring occasionally, until golden and crisp. Do not overcook. Remove from pan and drain on paper towels.

Makes about 1/3 cup (75 mL).

Sweet Pork

1 tbsp	vegetable oil	15 mL
1	onion, chopped	1
1 lb	pork shoulder or butt, cut in ½-inch (1 cm) pieces	500 g
¼ cup	palm or brown sugar	50 mL
3 tbsp	fish sauce	45 mL
1 tbsp	soy sauce	15 mL
¼ cup	water	50 mL
	Fried shallots, optional	

1. Heat a wok or skillet over medium-high heat and add oil. Add onion and pork and stir-fry for 2 to 3 minutes, or until browned.
2. Add sugar, fish sauce, soy sauce and water. Bring to a boil. Reduce heat to low. Cover and simmer for 15 to 20 minutes, or until pork is cooked, stirring occasionally.
3. Uncover, bring to a boil and cook, stirring often, for 10 to 15 minutes, or until pork is glazed and sauce becomes thick and syrupy.
4. Sprinkle with fried shallots before serving.

Crisp Fried Shallots

Most Thai cooks deep-fry crisp garlic or shallots, but here is a pan-fried version. (You can also buy fried shallots at Asian grocery stores.)

In a small skillet, heat ¼ cup (50 mL) vegetable oil over medium-high heat. Add 6 to 8 thinly sliced shallots and cook for 6 minutes, stirring occasionally, until golden and crisp. Do not overcook. Remove from pan and drain on paper towels.

Makes about ½ cup (125 mL).

Makes 4 servings

Sometimes referred to as Caramel Pork, this dish might be considered an eastern version of a sugar-glazed ham. While some cooks make a caramel sauce before adding the pork, others simmer the pork in a sugary syrup and reduce the sauce once the pork is cooked. It is common to see Thai cooks use pork belly, but this recipe uses pork shoulder or butt. (Pork loin is too dry.) Serve this hot with rice and hot chili sauce or cold as a snack. It can also be used in fried rice, stir-fried dishes or soups. On its own, it is frequently garnished with fried shallots or garlic, which many Thai home cooks buy already prepared.

Pork Belly with Five Spices

Makes 4 servings

This is a rich dish and is best served with steamed rice. Pork belly is used in many Thai dishes. It is becoming increasingly available in North America and usually comes in a slab. In some supermarkets it might be called side pork. Occasionally it comes with the rind, which can be left on or removed. To firm the meat, it is blanched in boiling water for 4 to 5 minutes, rinsed well and patted dry.

1 1/2 lbs	pork belly or side pork strips	750 g
2 tbsp	vegetable oil	25 mL
2 tsp	green curry paste	10 mL
2	cloves garlic, chopped	2
3/4 tsp	five-spice powder (page 170)	4 mL
3/4 cup	chicken stock	175 mL
2 tbsp	fish sauce	25 mL
2 tbsp	soy sauce	25 mL
2 tbsp	granulated sugar	25 mL
1 tbsp	lime juice	15 mL
	Fresh cilantro leaves	

1. Place pork in a saucepan of boiling water. Blanch for 4 minutes. Rinse with cold water, drain and pat dry. Cut into 1-inch (2.5 cm) pieces.
2. In a wok or large skillet, heat oil over medium-high heat. Add curry paste and garlic and stir-fry for 1 minute.
3. Add pork pieces and stir-fry for 3 to 4 minutes, or until pork is colored (be careful not to burn curry paste).
4. Add five-spice powder, stock, fish sauce, soy sauce and sugar. Stir to coat pork.
5. Cover, reduce heat to medium-low and simmer for 30 minutes, or until pork is tender, stirring occasionally.
6. Uncover, bring to a boil and cook, stirring often, for 6 to 10 minutes, or until sauce thickens and lightly coats meat. (Try not to reduce sauce too much. Leave some sauce for rice to soak up.)
7. Add lime juice and stir to combine. Serve garnished with cilantro.

Variation

Chicken Thighs with Five Spices: Cut 1 1/2 lbs (750 g) boneless, skinless chicken thighs into 1-inch (2.5 cm) pieces. Add to wok in Step 3 and stir-fry. After adding sauce ingredients, simmer for 15 minutes, or until tender. Uncover and cook on high for 8 to 10 minutes, or until chicken is coated with sauce.

Poultry

Chicken with Asparagus and Mint

Makes 4 servings

Although we most commonly associate asparagus with spring, it is really available year round now, and it is a popular ingredient in Thailand. The cooking time will depend on the thickness of the spears. Roasted chili paste provides a zippy background to this colorful dish. You can buy it in jars or make your own (page 48). Start with a small amount to test the heat.

2 tbsp	vegetable oil	25 mL
3	shallots, thinly sliced	3
2	cloves garlic, chopped	2
1 tbsp	roasted chili paste (approx.)	15 mL
1 lb	boneless, skinless chicken breasts, cut in 1-inch (2.5 cm) pieces	500 g
2 tbsp	fish sauce	25 mL
2 tsp	granulated sugar	10 mL
2 cups	asparagus pieces, cut in 1-inch (2.5 cm) pieces (about 8 oz/250 g)	500 mL
$\frac{1}{2}$	red bell pepper, seeded and thinly sliced (optional)	$\frac{1}{2}$
$\frac{1}{3}$ cup	shredded fresh mint leaves	75 mL

1. Heat a wok or large skillet over medium-high heat and add oil. Add shallots and garlic and stir-fry for 30 seconds. Add chili paste and stir-fry for 30 seconds.
2. Add chicken and stir-fry for 3 to 4 minutes, or until almost cooked.
3. Add fish sauce, sugar, asparagus and red pepper, if using. Stir-fry for 3 to 4 minutes, or until chicken is cooked and asparagus is tender-crisp.
4. Remove from heat, add mint and toss to combine.

Braised Lemongrass Chicken

2 tbsp	vegetable oil	25 mL
4	shallots, chopped	4
3	cloves garlic, chopped	3
1 lb	boneless, skinless chicken thighs, cut in 1-inch (2.5 cm) pieces	500 g
4	stalks lemongrass, white part only, cut in 1-inch (2.5 cm) pieces	4
1/4 cup	chicken stock	50 mL
2 tbsp	fish sauce	25 mL
2 tbsp	lemon or lime juice	25 mL
1 tbsp	palm or brown sugar	15 mL
1	red bell pepper, seeded and cut in 1-inch (2.5 cm) pieces	1
2	green onions, chopped	2
2 tbsp	chopped roasted peanuts	25 mL

1. Heat a wok or large skillet over medium-high heat and add oil. Add shallots and garlic and cook for 1 minute, or until light golden.
2. Add chicken and stir-fry until light golden, about 4 minutes.
3. Add lemongrass, stock, fish sauce, lemon juice and sugar. Bring to a boil. Reduce heat to low, cover and simmer for 10 minutes. Add red pepper and cook for 5 minutes, or until chicken is tender.
4. Sprinkle with green onions and peanuts before serving.

Makes 4 servings

Lemongrass adds a fresh flavor to this simple braised chicken dish (diners just push the pieces aside, as they are too chewy to eat). For a spicier version, add 1 tsp (5 mL) or more chopped fresh red chilies along with the lemongrass. Serve with noodles or steamed rice.

Stir-fried Chicken with Cashews

Makes 4 servings

In Thailand, cashews are often deep-fried with chilies and served as a snack with a beer or refreshing lime beverage. We ordered this dish several times. Each time it was different, but always delicious.

Peeled and deveined shrimp can replace the chicken.

2 tbsp	sweet soy sauce (page 22) or oyster sauce	25 mL
2 tbsp	water	25 mL
1 tbsp	fish sauce	15 mL
1 tsp	hot chili sauce	5 mL
1 tsp	cornstarch	5 mL
2 tbsp	vegetable oil	25 mL
3	cloves garlic, chopped	3
1 lb	boneless, skinless chicken breasts, thinly sliced	500 g
1/2	onion, thinly sliced	1/2
1/2	red bell pepper, seeded and thinly sliced	1/2
8	small dried red chilies	8
6	green onions, cut in 1-inch (2.5 cm) lengths	6
1/2 cup	roasted cashews	125 mL

1. In a small bowl or measuring cup, combine soy sauce, water, fish sauce, chili sauce and cornstarch.
2. Heat a wok or large skillet over medium-high heat and add oil. Add garlic and stir-fry for 30 seconds, or until golden. Add chicken and stir-fry for 3 minutes.
3. Add onion, red pepper and dried chilies and stir-fry for 2 minutes.
4. Stir reserved soy mixture and add to wok. Toss to coat all ingredients with sauce and cook for 1 minute.
5. Stir in green onions and cashews.

Chicken and Vegetable Stir-fry

Makes 5 to 6 servings

When I had this stir-fry in New Zealand, it was served with fresh baby corn. This tender vegetable is rarely available fresh in Western markets (though I planted seeds bought in New Zealand in my garden at home and it grew to great heights, producing perfect baby corn cobs). Although canned baby corn is available, fresh or frozen regular corn has a better flavor.

2 tbsp	vegetable oil	25 mL
3	cloves garlic, thinly sliced	3
1 tsp	chopped fresh red chilies	5 mL
1 lb	boneless, skinless chicken thighs, cut in 1/4-inch (5 mm) strips	500 g
1	carrot, cut in matchsticks	1
1 cup	sliced beans, cut in 1/2-inch (1 cm) lengths	250 mL
1/2	red bell pepper, seeded and thinly sliced	1/2
1/2 cup	corn kernels	125 mL
1/3 cup	coconut milk	75 mL
2 tbsp	oyster sauce	25 mL
2 tbsp	lime juice	25 mL
1 tbsp	fish sauce	15 mL

1. Heat a wok or large skillet over medium-high heat and add oil. Add garlic and chilies and stir-fry for 30 seconds. Add chicken and stir-fry for 2 minutes.
2. Increase heat to high. Add carrot, beans, red pepper and corn and stir-fry for 4 minutes, or until vegetables are just tender and chicken is cooked.
3. Add coconut milk, oyster sauce, lime juice and fish sauce. Toss to combine until heated through.

Chicken with Basil and Mint

2 tbsp	fish sauce	25 mL
1 tbsp	water	15 mL
2 tsp	soy sauce	10 mL
2 tsp	granulated sugar	10 mL
1 tsp	cornstarch	5 mL
2 tbsp	vegetable oil	25 mL
3	cloves garlic, chopped	3
1 lb	boneless, skinless chicken thighs, cut in $\frac{1}{2}$-inch (1 cm) pieces	500 g
2 tsp	coarsely chopped fresh red chilies	10 mL
$\frac{1}{2}$ cup	fresh mint leaves	125 mL
$\frac{1}{4}$ cup	fresh sweet Thai basil leaves	50 mL
1 $\frac{1}{2}$ cups	chopped Napa cabbage (optional)	375 mL

1. In a small bowl or measuring cup, combine fish sauce, water, soy sauce, sugar and cornstarch.
2. Heat a wok or large skillet over medium-high heat and add oil. Add garlic and stir-fry for 15 seconds.
3. Add chicken and chilies and stir-fry for 4 to 5 minutes, or until chicken is just cooked.
4. Stir sauce and add to wok. Cook, stirring, for 2 minutes, or until chicken is coated in sauce. Remove from heat and stir in mint and basil.
5. Arrange cabbage, if using, on a serving platter. Spoon chicken over cabbage.

Makes 4 servings

In Thailand, this dish is generally made with holy basil (page 17), which has a pungent, almost spicy taste. Since it is not readily available in Western markets, use the more common sweet Thai basil or regular large leaf basil.

I like to serve this over cabbage to cool the spiciness of the chilies, but you can also serve it with steamed rice.

Grilled Soy-glazed Chicken Breasts

Makes 4 servings

Every time I visit Thailand, I am in awe of the Thai women who create elaborate and precise needlework pieces, some of which depict life in their villages. When I come home I am always inspired to do some quilting or needlework of my own. That leaves less time for cooking, but I can always prepare a dish like this that can be made ahead or cooked at the last minute. Serve it with rice, sweet chili sauce (page 45) and cucumber relish (page 46). Flattening the chicken breasts makes for quick grilling. Do not overcook them.

Make Ahead

Grilled chicken can be cooked, covered and refrigerated a day ahead. This is a good picnic dish.

4	6-oz (175 g) boneless, skinless chicken breasts, or 8 boneless, skinless chicken thighs	4
2 tbsp	sweet soy sauce (page 22)	25 mL
2 tbsp	lime juice	25 mL
1 tbsp	oyster sauce	15 mL
1 tsp	sesame oil	5 mL
1⁄2 tsp	black pepper	2 mL

1. Place a chicken breast between sheets of parchment paper or plastic wrap (or cut open a plastic bag). With a meat pounder or rolling pin, flatten chicken to 1⁄2-inch (1 cm) thickness. Place in a shallow dish. Repeat with remaining chicken breasts.
2. In a bowl, combine soy sauce, lime juice, oyster sauce, sesame oil and pepper. Pour over chicken. Turn chicken pieces to coat. Cover and refrigerate for up to 12 hours.
3. Grill chicken for 6 to 8 minutes, turning once, until no longer pink inside. Cut each breast crosswise into 5 or 6 pieces. Serve hot or warm.

Garlic Chicken

4	cloves garlic, peeled	4
2	shallots, peeled	2
1 cup	packed fresh cilantro leaves, stems and roots	250 mL
3 tbsp	lime or lemon juice	45 mL
2 tsp	fish sauce	10 mL
1 tsp	black pepper	5 mL
4	6-oz (175 g) boneless, skinless chicken breasts	4

1. In a food processor, combine garlic, shallots, cilantro, lime juice, fish sauce and pepper and blend until smooth.
2. Place chicken breasts in a shallow dish. Pour marinade over chicken and turn to coat. Cover and marinate in refrigerator for 2 hours or up to overnight.
3. Grill chicken for 6 minutes per side, or until no longer pink, being careful not to overcook. Serve hot, warm or cold.

Variation

Garlic Tofu: Replace chicken with 12 oz (375 g) firm tofu cut in ½-inch (1 cm) slices. For a vegetarian version, replace fish sauce with soy sauce. Marinate for up to 3 hours. Grill for 3 to 4 minutes per side, or until golden.

Makes 4 servings

After my first trip to Thailand in the early eighties, I wanted to recreate many of the dishes I had eaten there, including this popular street vendor item. At that time indoor barbecues and grills were uncommon, so I prepared dishes like this under the broiler (arrange the chicken on a foil-lined baking sheet to make cleanup easier, and place about 4 inches/10 cm from the element). Whole chicken pieces, with skin, are the norm in Thailand, but this recipe uses boneless, skinless chicken breasts. Serve any leftover chicken in salads or sandwiches.

River Kwai Chicken and Mango Stir-fry

Makes 4 to 6 servings

After a solemn tour of the Jeath Museum and the Chung Kai Cemetery at Kanchanaburi, we ate in an open-air restaurant overlooking the River Kwai. The warmth of the Thai workers, their children and lunch restored our spirits. This is my version of one of the several dishes we were served, accompanied by fried rice.

Peeled and deveined shrimp can replace the chicken.

1 lb	boneless, skinless chicken thighs, cut in 3⁄4-inch (2 cm) pieces	500 g
2	cloves garlic, chopped	2
2 tsp	chopped fresh gingerroot	10 mL
1⁄2 tsp	chopped fresh red chilies	2 mL
2 tbsp	fish sauce	25 mL
2 tbsp	oyster sauce or sweet soy sauce (page 22)	25 mL
1 tsp	sesame oil	5 mL
2 tbsp	vegetable oil	25 mL
1	onion, thinly sliced	1
1	red bell pepper, seeded and cut in thin strips	1
1 1⁄2 cups	snow peas, trimmed (about 6 oz/175 g)	375 mL
1⁄2 cup	corn kernels	125 mL
4	green onions, sliced	4
2	mangoes, peeled and cut in 1-inch (2.5 cm) pieces	2

1. In a bowl, combine chicken, garlic, ginger and chilies.
2. In a small bowl or measuring cup, combine fish sauce, oyster sauce and sesame oil.
3. Heat a wok or large skillet over medium-high heat and add vegetable oil. Add chicken mixture and stir-fry for 3 minutes, or until chicken is almost cooked.
4. Add onion and red pepper and cook for 2 minutes, or until vegetables are tender. Add snow peas and corn and cook for 1 minute.
5. Add reserved sauce mixture, green onions and mangoes and toss to combine.

Barbecued Chicken Thighs

Makes 4 servings

Thais can eat outside at any time of year, so there are charcoal braziers everywhere. Large marinated chicken pieces are skewered with split pieces of bamboo and barbecued. Vendors often sell the chicken with plastic bags of sticky rice (page 117) and small packages of sweet chili sauce (page 45).

8	boneless, skinless chicken thighs	8
4	cloves garlic, minced	4
2 tbsp	chopped fresh cilantro leaves	25 mL
2 tbsp	oyster sauce	25 mL
1 tbsp	granulated sugar	15 mL
1 tsp	red curry paste	5 mL
1/4 cup	coconut milk	50 mL

1. Place chicken thighs in a shallow dish.
2. In a bowl, combine garlic, cilantro, oyster sauce, sugar, curry paste and coconut milk. Pour over chicken and rub into meat. Cover and marinate in refrigerator for 2 hours or up to overnight.
3. Grill chicken for 4 to 5 minutes per side, or until juices run clear.

Variation

Barbecued Lemongrass Chicken Thighs: In a bowl, combine 1/4 cup (50 mL) lime juice, 2 tbsp (25 mL) vegetable oil, 2 tbsp (25 mL) fish sauce, 1 tbsp (15 mL) granulated sugar, 2 chopped shallots, 3 minced garlic cloves, 2 finely chopped stalks lemongrass (white part only), 1/2 tsp (2 mL) hot chili sauce and 1/4 tsp (1 mL) black pepper.

Arrange 8 boneless and skinless chicken thighs in a shallow dish. Pour lemongrass marinade over chicken. Cover and refrigerate up to overnight. Cook chicken as in Step 3.

Chicken Wings with Dry Rub

3 lbs	chicken wings	1.5 kg
1 tbsp	black peppercorns	15 mL
1 tbsp	sesame seeds	15 mL
1 tbsp	coriander seeds	15 mL
1 tsp	whole cloves	5 mL
1 tsp	cumin seeds	5 mL
1 tsp	fennel seeds	5 mL
1/2 tsp	hot pepper flakes	2 mL
1 tsp	ground ginger	5 mL
1 tsp	ground turmeric	5 mL

1. Trim off wing tips (freeze tips and reserve for making stock). Cut each wing into two pieces at the joint. Place in a large bowl.
2. In a small dry skillet, combine peppercorns, sesame seeds, coriander seeds, cloves, cumin, fennel and hot pepper flakes. Heat over medium-low heat, stirring, for 3 to 4 minutes, or until spices are fragrant. Do not brown. Turn mixture onto a plate or paper towel and cool.
3. Grind spice mixture in a spice or coffee grinder to form a powder. Stir in ginger and turmeric.
4. Add spice mixture to wings and toss to coat.
5. Arrange wings skin side up on a wire rack placed over a foil-lined baking sheet. Bake in a preheated 425°F (210°C) oven for 35 to 40 minutes, or until wings are cooked through and crisp.

Makes 4 to 5 servings

With the popularity of Thai food, pubs and restaurants in North America now feature wings with varying degrees of "Thai heat," and many manufacturers have created their own line of rubs. Serve with sweet chili sauce (page 45).

This spice mixture can also be used as a rub on meats and whole chicken, or small amounts can be added to stir-fries as a seasoning.

Make Ahead

Prepare toasted spice mixture and transfer to a jar or container. Store in a dark, dry place for up to 2 months.

Chicken Wings with Plum Ginger Sauce

Makes 4 to 5 servings

When I took cooking classes at the Oriental Hotel in Bangkok many years ago, we prepared stuffed chicken wings. The flavoring paste was prepared using a mortar and pestle and combined with a shrimp/pork mixture. That was the easy part. Then we boned out several chicken wings, being careful not to pierce the skin. The filling was stuffed into the wings (like making sausages), closed, dusted with rice flour and deep-fried a few at a time. The result was impressive and delicious, but when I returned home I could not convince my students to tackle such a labor-intensive recipe. So here is a simple yet tasty adaptation. Mekong whiskey is a spirit produced in Thailand, but you can use bourbon, rice wine or chicken stock. Serve with cucumber slices and raw carrots or cabbage pieces.

3 lbs	chicken wings	1.5 kg
1/3 cup	plum sauce	75 mL
2 tbsp	whiskey, bourbon or rice wine	25 mL
2 tbsp	palm or brown sugar	25 mL
2 tbsp	fish sauce	25 mL
2 tbsp	finely chopped fresh gingerroot	25 mL
3	cloves garlic, chopped	3
1 tsp	hot chili sauce	5 mL

1. Trim off wing tips (freeze tips and reserve for making stock). Cut each wing into two pieces at the joint.
2. In a bowl, combine plum sauce, whiskey, sugar, fish sauce, ginger, garlic and chili sauce. Pour sauce over chicken wings and stir well to coat. Cover and refrigerate for up to 8 hours or overnight.
3. Arrange wings with sauce on a foil- and parchment-lined baking sheet. Bake in a preheated 400°F (200°C) oven for 35 minutes, turning once, until golden.
4. To glaze wings, heat broiler and broil wings for 1 minute, or until crisp and caramelized. Remove from oven and stir wings gently to coat with sauce.

Chicken with Spicy Peanut Sauce

2	cloves garlic, peeled	2
3	shallots, peeled	3
1	stalk lemongrass, white part only, cut in 1/2-inch (1 cm) pieces	1
1/4 cup	roasted peanuts	50 mL
2 tsp	coarsely chopped fresh red chilies	10 mL
2 tbsp	fish sauce	25 mL
2 tsp	granulated sugar	10 mL
1/4 tsp	black pepper	1 mL
2 tbsp	vegetable oil	25 mL
1 lb	boneless, skinless chicken thighs, cut in 1-inch (2.5 cm) pieces	500 g
1 cup	coconut milk	250 mL
2 tbsp	chopped fresh cilantro leaves	25 mL

1. In a food processor, finely chop garlic, shallots, lemongrass and peanuts. Add chilies, fish sauce, sugar and pepper and process until fine.
2. Heat a wok or large skillet over high heat and add oil. Add chicken and stir-fry for 3 minutes. Remove with a slotted spoon. Reduce heat to medium.
3. Add peanut sauce and cook, stirring, for 1 minute. Add coconut milk and simmer for 3 minutes.
4. Return chicken to wok and turn to coat with sauce. Simmer for 4 to 5 minutes, or until chicken is cooked.
5. Serve garnished with cilantro.

Variation

Chicken with Spicy Peanut Sauce and Broccoli: Blanch 8 oz (250 g) broccoli (cut in florets, with stems peeled and sliced diagonally) in boiling water for 3 minutes, or until just tender. Cool under cold water and drain. Stir into chicken with sauce at end of cooking time and combine to heat through.

Makes 4 to 6 servings

Peanuts (sometimes called groundnuts) are found in several forms in Thai cuisine, from raw to peanut butter. Raw peanuts are often deep-fried before using, but roasted peanuts are available everywhere. Chopped peanuts are used as a flavoring, garnish and thickener. For home use, buy unsalted or salted roasted peanuts (adjust the salt in the recipe accordingly) and store them in the freezer.

To adjust the "spiciness" of this dish, increase or reduce the chilies. Serve it with rice and a cooling cucumber salad (page 72).

Chicken with Chili Jam

Makes 4 servings

Chili jam is a condiment that may be used as a seasoning or as an accompaniment. It is often eaten with sticky rice (page 117).

2 tbsp	vegetable oil	25 mL
4	cloves garlic, thinly sliced	4
1 lb	boneless, skinless chicken breasts, thinly sliced	500 g
1	onion, thinly sliced	1
3 tbsp	chili jam	45 mL
1/4 cup	chicken stock, water or coconut milk	50 mL
2 tbsp	oyster sauce	25 mL
2 tsp	soy sauce	10 mL
1/4 cup	sweet Thai basil leaves	50 mL
1 tsp	thinly sliced fresh red chilies	5 mL

1. Heat a wok or large skillet over medium-high heat and add oil. Add garlic and stir-fry for 1 minute. Add chicken and onion and stir-fry for 3 minutes.
2. Add chili jam and stir-fry for 2 minutes, tossing to coat chicken and onion.
3. Add stock, oyster sauce and soy sauce and cook, stirring, for 2 minutes, or until chicken is cooked.
4. Stir in basil and garnish with fresh chilies.

Chili Jam

This is an abbreviated version using easily accessible ingredients. (Authentic recipes often include dried shrimp and shrimp paste.)

In a dry skillet, cook 6 large dried chilies over medium heat for 2 minutes, or until lightly browned. Remove, cool and chop coarsely.

Heat 1/4 cup (50 mL) oil in skillet over medium-high heat. Add 10 sliced shallots and 8 sliced garlic cloves and cook, stirring, for 4 to 5 minutes, or until golden.

Place chilies, garlic, shallots and oil in a blender or food processor and puree.

Return puree to skillet. Add 2 tbsp (25 mL) palm or brown sugar and 2 tbsp (25 mL) tamarind paste. Cook over medium heat, stirring, for 3 minutes, or until all ingredients are combined.

Transfer mixture to a clean jar, cover and refrigerate for up to 2 weeks.

Makes 2/3 cup (150 mL).

Ginger Chicken with Peppers

Makes 3 to 4 servings

A refreshing, colorful stir-fry to serve with steamed rice and cucumber slices.

2 tbsp	vegetable oil	25 mL
12 oz	boneless, skinless chicken breasts, thinly sliced	375 g
2 tbsp	chopped or slivered fresh gingerroot	25 mL
1	onion, thinly sliced	1
1/2 cup	sliced red bell pepper	125 mL
1/2 cup	sliced yellow bell pepper	125 mL
1/2 cup	sliced green bell pepper	125 mL
1/2 cup	chicken stock	125 mL
2 tbsp	oyster sauce	25 mL
1 tbsp	fish sauce	15 mL
1 tsp	granulated sugar	5 mL
4	green onions, cut in 1-inch (2.5 cm) pieces	4
	Fresh cilantro leaves	

1. Heat a wok or large skillet over medium-high heat and add oil. Add chicken and stir-fry for 3 minutes.
2. Add ginger, onion and peppers and stir-fry for 1 minute.
3. Add stock, oyster sauce, fish sauce and sugar and cook, stirring, for 2 minutes, or until chicken is cooked.
4. Add green onions. Toss to combine and garnish with cilantro.

Tamarind Chicken

Makes 4 to 5 servings

Tamarind (page 23) provides the tangy, tart, sour flavor often associated with Thai food. Buy the paste (sometimes called juice) or make your own.

1/3 cup	water	75 mL
3 tbsp	tamarind paste	45 mL
2 tbsp	fish sauce	25 mL
2 tbsp	palm or brown sugar	25 mL
2 tsp	chopped fresh red chilies	10 mL
2 tbsp	vegetable oil	25 mL
1	onion, thinly sliced	1
4	shallots, thinly sliced	4
4	cloves garlic, chopped	4
1 lb	boneless, skinless chicken thighs, cut in 1/2-inch (1 cm) pieces	500 g
1 1/2 cups	snow peas (about 6 oz/175 g), trimmed	375 mL
3	green onions, thinly sliced	3

1. In a small bowl or measuring cup, combine water, tamarind paste, fish sauce, sugar and chilies.
2. Heat a wok or large skillet over medium-high heat and add oil. Add onion, shallots and garlic and stir-fry for 2 minutes, or until very soft and fragrant and starting to color.
3. Add chicken and stir-fry for 5 minutes. Add reserved tamarind mixture and toss with chicken. Reduce heat to medium-high and stir-fry for 4 minutes, or until chicken is cooked and coated with sauce.
4. Add snow peas, toss and cook for 1 to 2 minutes, or until tender-crisp.
5. Serve garnished with green onions.

Tamarind Paste

In a bowl, combine 1/4 cup (50 mL) tamarind pulp with 3/4 cup (175 mL) warm water. Let stand for 20 to 25 minutes, stirring and mashing occasionally to soften. Press mixture through a sieve to remove seeds and fibers (scrape puree from underside of sieve). Stir puree to mix thoroughly.

Transfer to a clean container. Cover and refrigerate for up to a week or freeze for up to 3 weeks. The concentrate becomes more sour as it stands. Add sugar to tone down if necessary.

Makes 3/4 cup (175 mL).

Chicken and Mushroom Casserole

Makes 4 to 6 servings

This bears little resemblance to the Western-style casserole that usually is sauce-based and baked. It is a Chinese-style dish with added Thai flavors. Dried black mushrooms are becoming more available in regular supermarkets, but for the best choice, buy them from an Asian store. They need to be soaked in warm water before being used. Some versions of this casserole include hard-cooked eggs that are added toward the end of cooking time. In this recipe, they are an optional garnish. This is typically not a spicy dish, but thinly sliced fresh red chilies can be added as garnish.

10	large dried black Chinese mushrooms	10
3/4 cup	chicken stock or water	175 mL
2 tsp	cornstarch	10 mL
2 tbsp	palm or brown sugar	25 mL
1 tbsp	fish sauce	15 mL
1 tbsp	soy sauce	15 mL
2 tbsp	chopped fresh cilantro leaves	25 mL
1/4 tsp	black pepper	1 mL
2 tbsp	vegetable oil	25 mL
1	onion, cut in 1/2-inch (1 cm) pieces	1
4	cloves garlic, chopped	4
2 tbsp	chopped fresh gingerroot	25 mL
1 lb	boneless, skinless chicken thighs, cut in 1-inch (2.5 cm) pieces	500 g
2	green onions, thinly sliced	2
4	hard-cooked eggs, peeled and quartered lengthwise (optional)	4

1. In a bowl, soak mushrooms in warm water for 20 minutes, or until softened. Drain. Cut off stems and discard and cut mushrooms into quarters.
2. In a small bowl or measuring cup, combine stock, cornstarch, sugar, fish sauce, soy sauce, cilantro and pepper.
3. Heat a wok or large skillet over medium-high heat and add oil. Add onion, garlic and ginger and stir-fry for 2 minutes, or until golden.
4. Add chicken and stir-fry for 3 minutes. Stir in mushrooms.
5. Add sauce and cook, stirring, for 2 minutes, or until sauce has thickened slightly. Reduce heat and simmer for 8 to 10 minutes, or until chicken is cooked.
6. Garnish with green onions and eggs, if using.

Barbecued Quail

6	quail	6
2	cloves garlic, peeled	2
2	shallots, peeled	2
1 tbsp	coarsely chopped fresh gingerroot	15 mL
1⁄4 cup	hoisin sauce	50 mL
1⁄4 cup	coconut milk	50 mL
2 tbsp	fish sauce	25 mL
2 tbsp	lime juice	25 mL
1 tsp	hot chili sauce	5 mL

1. Use kitchen shears to remove wing tips from quail and cut down both sides of backbone. Open quail and press firmly to flatten. (Quail could also be cut in half.) Place in a shallow dish, in a single layer if possible.
2. In a food processor, combine garlic, shallots, ginger, hoisin, coconut milk, fish sauce, lime juice and chili sauce. Puree until smooth. Pour marinade over quail and rub in. Cover and refrigerate for 2 hours or up to overnight.
3. Remove quail from marinade. Grill for 3 to 4 minutes per side, or until just cooked through. (If you prefer, you can also roast quail in the oven. Arrange in a single layer on a foil- and parchment-lined baking sheet and cook in a preheated 425°F/210°C oven for 10 to 12 minutes.)

Variation

Barbecued Tofu: Instead of quail, use 1 lb (500 g) firm tofu cut in slices 1⁄2 inch (1 cm) thick. Marinate tofu and grill for 3 to 4 minutes per side, or until golden.

Makes 4 to 5 servings.

Makes 6 servings

The mild yet rich flavor of quail adapts well to Thai seasonings. In Thailand, it may be deep-fried or roasted, but most often it is grilled over hot coals. This marinade can also be used on chicken, pork or shrimp.

Roast Duck

Makes 4 to 5 servings

Fresh roast duck is a main ingredient in Thai curries, salads, stir-fries and soups. In Thailand it can be prepared at home or purchased from Chinese shops and markets. When roast duck is served on its own it is cut into small pieces using a cleaver.

1	4-lb (2 kg) duck	1
1/4 cup	loosely packed fresh cilantro roots, stems and leaves	50 mL
4	cloves garlic, peeled	4
2 tbsp	coarsely chopped fresh gingerroot	25 mL
1/4 cup	sweet soy sauce (page 22) or oyster sauce	50 mL
2 tbsp	lime juice	25 mL
1 tsp	hot chili sauce	5 mL
1/2 tsp	five-spice powder	2 mL

1. Pat duck dry inside and out and pierce skin all over with a fork.
2. In a food processor or blender, combine cilantro, garlic, ginger, soy sauce, lime juice, chili sauce and five-spice powder. Puree until smooth.
3. Rub paste all over outside and inside of duck. Loosely tie legs together. Place duck, breast side up, on a wire rack set over a roasting pan. Pour about 3/4 cup (175 mL) water into bottom of pan.
4. Roast in a preheated 425°F (210°C) oven for 30 minutes. Carefully pour off any accumulated fat. Reduce temperature to 350°F (180°C) and roast for 50 to 60 minutes, or until juices run clear, skin is crisp and a meat thermometer inserted in thigh registers 180°F (82°C). If duck is browning too much, cover loosely with foil.
5. Remove from oven and let stand for 15 minutes before cutting into serving pieces.

Five-spice Powder

Five-spice powder is an aromatic mixture of ground spices (usually more than five) which might include cinnamon, star anise, fennel, ginger, cloves, licorice, Szechuan peppercorns and white pepper. Popular in Chinese and Vietnamese cuisine, Thais also use it. Although flavorful, it should be used sparingly so it does not overwhelm a dish.

Fish and Seafood

Whole Sea Bass with Tamarind Sauce

Makes 3 to 4 servings

One is never far from fresh fish or seafood in Thailand. Cheerful open-air restaurants often have open kitchens where you can watch the cooks as they "dance" back and forth between the woks and charcoal fires. Fortunately, cooking fish for one table at home is much easier. I use wild striped or black sea bass in this dish. Have your fishmonger clean and scale the fish. Serving whole fish is common in Thailand, but you can have the head removed if you prefer.

1	whole sea bass, cleaned and scaled (about 2 lbs/1 kg)	1
3	cloves garlic, minced	3
2 tbsp	fish sauce	25 mL
1 tsp	granulated sugar	5 mL
1/2 tsp	ground turmeric	2 mL
1/2 tsp	black pepper	2 mL

Tamarind Sauce

2 tbsp	fish sauce	25 mL
1 tbsp	lime juice	15 mL
1 tbsp	tamarind paste	15 mL
1 1/2 tbsp	granulated sugar	22 mL
1 tsp	chopped fresh red chilies	5 mL

1. Rinse fish with cold water and dry with paper towels. With a sharp knife, score fish diagonally 3 or 4 times on each side. Place in a shallow dish.
2. In a small bowl, stir together garlic, fish sauce, sugar, turmeric and pepper. Rub mixture all over fish. Cover and refrigerate for 1 hour. Transfer to a parchment-lined baking sheet.
3. Cook fish in a preheated 400°F (200°C) oven for 16 to 20 minutes, or until fish is opaque when flesh is checked next to bone.
4. Meanwhile, to prepare sauce, in a small saucepan, combine fish sauce, lime juice, tamarind paste, sugar and chilies. Bring just to a boil.
5. Pour sauce over baked fish before serving.

Variation

Baked Fish Fillets with Tamarind Sauce: Replace whole fish with 1 1/2 lbs (750 g) boneless fish fillets, such as sea bass, grouper, tilapia, snapper or halibut. Bake for 6 to 8 minutes, or until fish is just opaque.

Salmon and Dill in Banana Leaves

4	pieces banana leaf, about 10 by 12 inches (25 by 30 cm) each	4
4	6-oz (175 g) salmon fillets	4
1 tbsp	tamarind paste	15 mL
1 tbsp	fish sauce	15 mL
1 tsp	chopped fresh red chilies	5 mL
1/4 cup	coarsely chopped fresh dillweed	50 mL

1. Rinse banana leaves and pat dry. Place on a flat surface. Arrange a fillet in center of each leaf.
2. Top each fillet with tamarind paste and fish sauce and sprinkle with chilies and dill.
3. Starting with one corner, wrap leaf over salmon to make a package and fasten with a toothpick. Arrange toothpick-side up on a parchment-lined baking sheet.
4. Bake in a preheated 400°F (200°C) oven for 14 minutes. Remove from oven and let stand for 2 minutes before serving.

Makes 4 servings

Dill is not used in great quantities in Thai cooking, but it is a natural with fish. Banana leaves are a common wrapper for grilled, steamed, baked and roasted foods. They are used in both sweet and savory dishes to add a light flavor and to protect foods from direct heat. Toothpicks are used to hold or pin the leaves. If banana leaves are not available, use heavy foil.

Make Ahead

Salmon packages can be assembled, placed on a baking sheet and refrigerated for 2 hours before cooking.

Steamed Fish with Chili Lime Sauce

Makes 4 servings

This light, healthful dish is very popular throughout Thailand. Usually a whole fish is steamed and presented with the head on, but this recipe uses fish fillets. Instead of steaming you can bake the fish in a shallow baking dish. Cover the fish and lime slices with a piece of parchment paper and bake in a preheated 400°F (200°C) oven for about 8 minutes.

1 ½ lbs	fish fillets (e.g., salmon, sea bass, snapper, halibut, monkfish or cod)	750 g
1	lime, thinly sliced	1

Chili Lime Sauce

2	cloves garlic, minced	2
1 ½ tsp	chopped fresh red chilies	7 mL
2 tbsp	lime juice	25 mL
2 tbsp	fish sauce	25 mL
2 tbsp	palm or brown sugar	25 mL
1 tbsp	chopped fresh cilantro leaves	15 mL
1	green onion, chopped	1
1	lime, thinly sliced	1

1. Place fish fillets in a round shallow dish that will fit in a steamer. Arrange lime slices over fish. Place dish on a steaming rack. Cover, bring to a boil and steam over high heat for 8 to 10 minutes, or until fish is opaque, depending on thickness of fillets.
2. Meanwhile, to prepare sauce, in a bowl, combine garlic, chilies, lime juice, fish sauce, sugar, cilantro and green onion. Stir together until sugar dissolves.
3. Serve fish in baking dish or gently transfer to a platter. Pour sauce over fish and garnish with lime slices.

Steaming Fish

Prepare a steaming unit by placing a small rack or crisscrossed set of chopsticks in the bottom of a wok or large deep skillet. Add hot water to the bottom of the rack. Place dish on rack. Cover, bring to a boil and start timing.

Alternatively, place dish with prepared fish in a bamboo steamer. Place steamer over hot water (at least 2 inches/5 cm) in a wok or large deep skillet. Cover, bring to a boil and start timing. In either case, be careful not to burn yourself on the steam and do not let wok or skillet boil dry.

Fried Fish with Sweet and Sour Chili Sauce

4	cloves garlic, peeled	4
3	shallots, peeled	3
2 tbsp	coarsely chopped fresh cilantro roots or stems	25 mL
1 tbsp	coarsely chopped fresh red chilies	15 mL
1/4 cup	cornstarch or tapioca starch	50 mL
1 lb	fish fillets (e.g., halibut, tilapia, grouper or sea bass)	500 g
1/4 cup	vegetable oil	50 mL
1/4 cup	tamarind paste or rice vinegar	50 mL
3 tbsp	water	45 mL
2 tbsp	fish sauce	25 mL
1 tbsp	palm or brown sugar	15 mL
	Fresh cilantro leaves	
	Thinly sliced fresh red chilies	

1. With a mortar and pestle or in a food processor, combine garlic, shallots, cilantro roots and chilies to a paste.
2. Place cornstarch in a shallow dish. Pat fish dry and coat with starch.
3. In a large skillet, heat oil over medium-high heat. Cook fish for 3 to 4 minutes per side, or until brown and crispy on both sides and cooked through. Transfer to a serving dish. Pour off all but 2 tbsp (25 mL) oil from skillet.
4. Add reserved garlic paste to oil and cook for 2 minutes, or until fragrant. Add tamarind paste, water, fish sauce and sugar. Stir to heat through and thicken slightly.
5. Pour sauce over fish and garnish with cilantro and chilies.

Makes 4 servings

At the Blue Elephant restaurant in Bangkok, the sauce on this fish had just a gentle heat, although we had several hotter variations throughout Thailand. In this recipe, simple pan-frying replaces the usual deep-frying technique. Dipping the fish in tapioca starch or cornstarch helps provide a crisp exterior and absorb surface moisture on the fish. Some cooks use all-purpose flour instead.

This versatile sauce can be served on any roasted, grilled or steamed fish

Oven-steamed Salmon with Chili and Ginger

Makes 4 to 6 servings

Oven steaming is an easy alternative to the traditional steaming method in a wok (page 174). This light, refreshing dish reminds me of the simple fish dishes (using freshly caught local fish) served at seaside resorts and restaurants along the Gulf of Thailand.

4	6-oz (175 g) salmon fillets, skin removed	4
1 tbsp	chopped fresh gingerroot	15 mL
1 tbsp	chopped fresh cilantro stems	15 mL
2	cloves garlic, finely chopped	2
2 tsp	chopped fresh red chilies	10 mL
2 tbsp	lime juice	25 mL
1 tbsp	fish sauce	15 mL
2 tsp	brown or granulated sugar	10 mL
2	green onions, thinly sliced	2
	Fresh cilantro leaves	

1. Arrange salmon in a single layer in a shallow baking dish.
2. In a bowl, combine ginger, cilantro stems, garlic, chilies, lime juice, fish sauce and sugar. Spoon mixture over fillets. Cover dish with foil and seal edges.
3. Bake in a preheated 400°F (200°C) oven for 8 to 10 minutes, or until fish is opaque and flakes easily with a fork.
4. Garnish with green onions and cilantro leaves.

Pan-fried Fish with Tamarind and Ginger

Makes 4 to 5 servings

When I returned from my first visit to Thailand, this dish became one of my many favorites — to teach and to cook at home. I used to deep-fry a whole fish, the same way it had been served in Thailand. Since then I've adapted the recipe and I now use pan-fried fillets.

1/4 cup	vegetable oil, divided	50 mL
3	shallots, thinly sliced	3
3	cloves garlic, thinly sliced	3
2 tbsp	chopped fresh gingerroot	25 mL
1/3 cup	tamarind paste	75 mL
1/4 cup	water	50 mL
2 tbsp	soy sauce	25 mL
1 tbsp	fish sauce	15 mL
1 tbsp	palm or brown sugar	15 mL
1/2 cup	tapioca starch, cornstarch or all-purpose flour	125 mL
1 1/2 lbs	fish fillets (e.g., snapper, tilapia, catfish or sea bass)	750 g
2	green onions, chopped	2
1	fresh red chili, sliced	1
	Fresh cilantro leaves	

1. In a saucepan, heat 2 tbsp (25 mL) vegetable oil over medium heat. Add shallots, garlic and ginger and cook for 2 to 3 minutes, or until softened and fragrant.
2. Add tamarind paste, water, soy sauce, fish sauce and sugar. Bring to a gentle boil and cook for 1 minute. Remove from heat.
3. Spread starch in a shallow pan. Pat fish dry and coat both sides, shaking off excess.
4. In a nonstick skillet, heat remaining oil over medium-high heat. Add fish and pan-fry for 3 minutes. Turn and cook for 2 to 4 minutes, or until golden brown, crispy and cooked through.
5. Serve fish with sauce and garnish with green onions, chilies and cilantro.

Grilled Fish with Spicy Tomato Sauce

Makes 4 servings

One of the most interesting markets we visited in Thailand was at the Maeklong train station in Samut Songkhram, southwest of Bangkok. Some food vendors set up their stalls right on the tracks. A whistle blew whenever a train was about to enter the station, giving them just enough time to remove their wares and awnings. As soon as the train departed, everything went back into place. This happened several times a day.

While meandering back to Bangkok, we stopped for lunch. Of course it was fish, since we were so close to the Gulf.

The seasoned fish can also be placed on a parchment-lined baking sheet and roasted in a preheated 425°F (210°C) oven for 15 minutes.

1	whole fish (e.g., sea bass, snapper or trout), cleaned (about 2 lbs/1 kg)	1
2 tbsp	soy sauce	25 mL
1 tbsp	vegetable oil	15 mL
2	cloves garlic, minced	2
Spicy Tomato Sauce		
2	tomatoes, finely chopped	2
2	shallots, chopped	2
2 tbsp	chopped fresh cilantro leaves	25 mL
2 tsp	chopped fresh red or green chilies	10 mL
2 tbsp	lime juice	25 mL
2 tbsp	fish sauce	25 mL
2 tsp	palm or brown sugar	10 mL

1. Pat fish dry and place in a shallow pan.
2. In a small bowl or measuring cup, combine soy sauce, oil and garlic. Rub into fish.
3. To prepare sauce, in a bowl, combine tomatoes, shallots, cilantro, chilies, lime juice, fish sauce and sugar.
4. Grill fish for 4 to 5 minutes per side, or until flesh is opaque and just flakes easily with a fork. For best results, place on a lightly oiled fish rack, so fish can be easily turned.
5. Serve fish with sauce.

Turmeric Fried Fish

Makes 4 to 5 servings

In southern Thailand, a large segment of the population is Muslim, bringing the influence of India and Malaysia, including spices such as cardamom, cumin and turmeric. Ground turmeric is the substitute when fresh is unavailable. The brilliant color gives many dishes a bright, sunny appearance. When working with turmeric, protect work surfaces and clothing, since it will stain (though it will wash off your hands). For a colorful display, serve the fish surrounded by sliced lettuce, tomatoes and cucumbers.

3	cloves garlic, minced	3
2 tsp	ground turmeric	10 mL
1 tsp	black pepper	5 mL
1 tsp	granulated sugar	5 mL
½ tsp	salt	2 mL
3 tbsp	vegetable oil, divided	45 mL
1 ½ lbs	fish fillets (e.g., tilapia, catfish, grouper or cod)	750 g
¾ cup	tapioca starch, cornstarch or all-purpose flour	175 mL
2 tbsp	fish sauce	25 mL
2 tbsp	rice vinegar	25 mL
½ tsp	hot pepper flakes	2 mL

1. In a bowl, combine garlic, turmeric, pepper, sugar, salt and 1 tbsp (15 mL) oil.
2. Arrange fish fillets in a shallow dish in a single layer. Spoon marinade over fish and rub into surface.
3. Spread tapioca starch in a shallow pan. Coat both sides of fish, shaking off excess.
4. In a nonstick skillet, heat remaining oil over medium-high heat. Add fish and cook for 3 to 4 minutes per side, or until golden and cooked through.
5. In a small bowl, combine fish sauce, vinegar and hot pepper flakes. Serve with fish.

Fish Fillets in Coconut Milk

Makes 4 servings

A comforting dish simply made with coconut milk and a few aromatic seasonings. Fish dishes similar to this are served at restaurants and resorts along the Gulf of Thailand. Pea eggplants or fresh green peppercorns would be a common addition. Serve this as a quick dinner with steamed rice.

1 1/2 cups	coconut milk	375 mL
2	stalks lemongrass, white part only, cut in 1-inch (2.5 cm) lengths	2
3	lime leaves, or 1/2 tsp (2 mL) grated lime zest	3
1/2 tsp	chopped fresh gingerroot	2 mL
1	clove garlic, minced	1
1 tsp	palm or brown sugar	5 mL
1/2 tsp	chopped fresh red chilies	2 mL
1 1/4 lbs	white fish fillets, cut in 2-inch (5 cm) pieces	625 g
1 cup	green peas	250 mL
2 tbsp	lime juice	25 mL
1 tbsp	fish sauce	15 mL
2	green onions, thinly sliced	2

1. In a large, deep skillet, combine coconut milk, lemongrass, lime leaves, ginger, garlic, sugar and chilies. Bring to a gentle boil over medium heat. Reduce heat and simmer for 3 minutes.
2. Add fish pieces and peas. Simmer for 3 to 4 minutes, or until fish is opaque and peas are cooked.
3. Stir in lime juice and fish sauce. Serve garnished with green onions.

Variation

Chicken in Coconut Milk: Replace fish with boneless, skinless chicken breasts cut in 1/2-inch (1 cm) pieces. Simmer for 5 to 6 minutes, or until chicken is cooked.

Smoked Mackerel Salad

Makes 4 servings

Mackerel is a mainstay of the Thai diet. It is sold fresh, salted, smoked and grilled. In many markets, steamed mackerel is artfully displayed in bamboo steamers. Serve this with steamed rice or as an omelet filling. Adding green mango adds texture and cuts the richness of the fish.

Make Ahead

Mackerel salad can be prepared up to 4 hours ahead and refrigerated. Toss before serving and arrange on a serving platter with lettuce, cucumber and cilantro.

12 oz	smoked mackerel, skin and bone removed	375 g
2	green onions, chopped	2
3	shallots, thinly sliced	3
2 tsp	chopped fresh gingerroot	10 mL
1	clove garlic, minced	1
1 tsp	chopped fresh red or green chilies	5 mL
2 tbsp	lime juice	25 mL
1 tsp	granulated sugar	5 mL
1	tomato, finely chopped	1
1 cup	diced English cucumber	250 mL
1	green mango, chopped, or ½ cup (125 mL) chopped green cabbage	1
2 tbsp	chopped roasted peanuts	25 mL
	Lettuce leaves	
	English cucumber slices	
	Fresh cilantro leaves	

1. Break mackerel into small flakes and place in a bowl. Add green onions, shallots, ginger, garlic, chilies, lime juice, sugar, tomato, cucumber, mango and peanuts. Toss to thoroughly combine.
2. Spoon mixture into center of a shallow serving dish. Arrange lettuce leaves and cucumber slices around fish. Top with cilantro.

Last-minute Chili Sauce

In a small bowl or measuring cup, combine 3 tbsp (45 mL) rice vinegar or lime juice, 1 tbsp (15 mL) fish sauce, 1 tsp (5 mL) granulated sugar and 2 tsp (10 mL) chopped fresh red chilies.

Makes ¼ cup (50 mL).

Mussel Pancake

Makes 2 servings

A common street food dish made to order on large flat griddle pans. The cook uses long wooden spatulas to shape and turn the pancakes. At the floating market, vendors take orders for these cakes from customers waiting on shore and those paddling by. The vendors' boats are equipped with charcoal or gas burners. This recipe is an easy version for home cooking. You can cook fresh mussels especially for this recipe, use leftover steamed mussels, or you can use frozen cooked mussels. Serve with Last-minute Chili Sauce (page 182).

1/2 cup	cooked shelled mussels or clams, halved if large	125 mL
2	eggs	2
1/4 cup	all-purpose flour	50 mL
2 tbsp	cornstarch	25 mL
2 tbsp	water	25 mL
2	green onions, chopped	2
2 tsp	fish sauce	10 mL
2 tbsp	vegetable oil	25 mL
2	cloves garlic, chopped	2
1/2 cup	bean sprouts	125 mL
2 tsp	chopped fresh cilantro leaves	10 mL

1. Drain cooked mussels and pat dry.
2. In a large bowl, beat eggs. Add flour, cornstarch and water and mix until no lumps remain. Stir in mussels, green onions and fish sauce.
3. Heat oil in a 10-inch (25 cm) nonstick skillet over medium-high heat. Add garlic and stir-fry for 30 seconds, or until golden.
4. Add mussel batter and cook, swirling pan, for 3 minutes, or until browned on bottom. With a wide spatula, carefully turn pancake and cook for 2 to 3 minutes, or until browned.
5. Slide pancake onto a serving platter and garnish with bean sprouts and cilantro. Cut into wedges.

Oven-cooked Mussels

Place fresh mussels on a baking sheet and cook in a preheated 375°F (190°C) oven for 4 to 6 minutes, or until mussels open. Discard any unopened mussels. Cool mussels until easy to handle (8 oz/250 g fresh mussels in the shell will yield about 1/2 cup/125 mL cooked mussels). Remove from shells and place cooked mussels in a sieve to drain off excess juices. Cover and refrigerate if not using within 30 minutes.

Mussels in Coconut Broth

Makes 4 servings

Thailand has such a bountiful supply of fresh fish and shellfish that a simply prepared dish made with the freshest catch requires little embellishment. Serve this in bowls with spoons, or with steamed rice and a salad.

3⁄4 cup	coconut milk	175 mL
3 tbsp	lime juice	45 mL
1 tbsp	fish sauce	15 mL
2 tsp	granulated sugar	10 mL
1 tsp	thinly sliced fresh red chilies	5 mL
1⁄2 tsp	curry powder	2 mL
2 lbs	mussels, cleaned	1 kg
2 tbsp	fresh cilantro leaves	25 mL

1. In a large saucepan or wok, whisk together coconut milk, lime juice, fish sauce, sugar, chilies and curry powder. Bring to a gentle boil over medium heat.
2. Add mussels, cover and steam over medium heat for 6 to 8 minutes, or until mussels open. Discard any unopened mussels.
3. Serve mussels with juices, and garnish with cilantro.

Variation

Shrimp in Coconut Broth: Replace mussels with 1 lb (500 g) large shelled and deveined shrimp. Simmer for 3 to 4 minutes, or until shrimp are just cooked.

Mussels

Select mussels that are tightly closed. If they are slightly open, press the shells together to see if they close. If they do not close, discard them. Try to use mussels the same day as purchasing. To store at home, place in a strainer over ice and keep refrigerated. Do not let mussels sit in water. Wash mussels well and remove the beards before cooking. Discard any mussels that do not open when cooked.

Clams with Roasted Chili Paste

Makes 4 servings

Small shiny clams with a herringbone pattern are piled high on ice in the many markets throughout Thailand. In several markets we also saw clam-cooking "kits" — plastic bags containing clams, basil and seasonings ready to be cooked at home.

2 tbsp	vegetable oil	25 mL
3	cloves garlic, chopped	3
2	shallots, chopped	2
2 lbs	small clams, well scrubbed	1 kg
2 tbsp	roasted chili paste (page 48)	25 mL
1/3 cup	chicken stock	75 mL
1 tbsp	fish sauce	15 mL
1 tbsp	soy sauce	15 mL
2 tsp	granulated sugar	10 mL
1/2 cup	fresh sweet Thai basil leaves	125 mL
	Thinly sliced fresh red chilies	

1. Heat a wok or large skillet over medium-high heat and add oil. Add garlic, shallots and clams and stir-fry for 2 minutes.
2. Add chili paste, stock, fish sauce, soy sauce and sugar and cook, uncovered, for 8 to 10 minutes, tossing occasionally, until clams open. Discard any clams that do not open.
3. Stir in basil. Serve with juices, garnished with fresh chilies.

Steamed Clams with Ginger

Makes 4 servings

A quick dish that makes the most of Thailand's abundant supply of seafood. When scrubbing clams, discard any uncooked clams that don't close.

3	cloves garlic, chopped	3
3 tbsp	slivered fresh gingerroot	45 mL
1/3 cup	chicken stock or water	75 mL
1 tbsp	oyster sauce	15 mL
1 tbsp	fish sauce	15 mL
2 lbs	small clams, well scrubbed	1 kg
3	green onions, cut in 1-inch (2.5 cm) lengths	3
	Fresh cilantro leaves	

1. Place garlic, ginger, stock, oyster sauce, fish sauce and clams in a wok or saucepan. Toss to combine. Bring to a boil.
2. Reduce heat to medium. Cover and steam for 12 to 14 minutes, or until clams open, tossing occasionally (steaming time will depend on size of clams). Discard any clams that do not open.
3. Serve clams with juices, garnished with cilantro.

Phuket Sweet and Sour Scallops

Makes 4 servings

In the tropical resort area of Phuket (considered the seafood capital of Thailand), this dish is also prepared with shrimp, which are farmed along the coast of southern Thailand (and you can use peeled and deveined shrimp in this recipe instead of scallops). Many fish and shellfish dishes from this region are hot and spicy, but this is an exception.

2 tbsp	vegetable oil	25 mL
12 oz	scallops	375 g
2	cloves garlic, chopped	2
1	onion, chopped	1
1	red bell pepper, seeded and cut in 1-inch (2.5 cm) pieces	1
1/2	English cucumber, peeled and cut in 1/2-inch (1 cm) pieces	1/2
1	tomato, cut in wedges	1
1/4 cup	chicken stock	50 mL
2 tbsp	tomato paste	25 mL
2 tbsp	lime juice	25 mL
2 tbsp	soy sauce	25 mL
1 tbsp	fish sauce	15 mL
1 tbsp	palm or brown sugar	15 mL
1/2 cup	diced pineapple	125 mL
2 tsp	cornstarch	10 mL
2 tbsp	water	25 mL
1 tbsp	chopped fresh cilantro leaves	15 mL

1. Heat a wok or large skillet over medium-high heat and add oil. Add scallops and stir-fry for 2 minutes, or until light golden. Remove with a slotted spoon and reserve.
2. Add garlic and onion to skillet and stir-fry for 1 minute.
3. Add red pepper, cucumber, tomato, chicken stock, tomato paste, lime juice, soy sauce, fish sauce and sugar. Bring to a boil and cook for 3 minutes.
4. Add reserved scallops and pineapple and combine with other ingredients.
5. In a small bowl or measuring cup, stir together cornstarch and water. Add to scallops. Cook, stirring, for 1 minute, or until slightly thickened.
6. Serve garnished with cilantro.

Scallops and Shrimp with Lemongrass and Coconut Milk

Makes 4 to 5 servings

This is a version of a dish I enjoyed at a luncheon buffet at the Oriental Hotel's Thai restaurant, Sala Rim Nam. The combination of sweet scallops and shrimp simmered briefly with lemongrass and coconut milk makes a fast yet elegant dish to serve with steamed rice.

3/4 cup	coconut milk	175 mL
3	stalks lemongrass, white part only, cut in 1-inch (2.5 cm) lengths	3
2	cloves garlic, finely chopped	2
2	shallots, thinly sliced	2
1 1/2 tsp	chopped fresh red chilies	7 mL
2 tbsp	fish sauce	25 mL
2 tsp	granulated sugar	10 mL
8 oz	shrimp, peeled, deveined and halved lengthwise	250 g
8 oz	scallops, quartered	250 g
1 tbsp	lime juice	15 mL
1 tbsp	shredded fresh cilantro or basil leaves	15 mL

1. In a wok or saucepan, combine coconut milk, lemongrass, garlic, shallots, chilies, fish sauce and sugar. Bring to a gentle boil and cook for 4 minutes.
2. Add shrimp and scallops. Reduce heat and simmer for 3 to 4 minutes, or until scallops and shrimp are just cooked.
3. Remove from heat and stir in lime juice and cilantro.

Lemongrass

Fresh lemongrass, readily available in Asian shops, is now being sold more often in supermarkets. To chop it finely, make sure your knife is very sharp. (You can also look for finely chopped frozen lemongrass; defrost the package just until you can measure out the required amount and then return the remainder to the freezer.)

Garlic Shrimp

Makes 4 servings

Garlic, cilantro and black pepper are the trademark seasonings of this extremely popular and quick stir-fried dish. Some cooks add even more garlic. Traditionally, a paste is made with a mortar and pestle, using fresh cilantro root. Serve this hot or cold as a main course or appetizer.

1 lb	shrimp, peeled and deveined	500 g
4	cloves garlic, chopped	4
2 tbsp	chopped fresh cilantro leaves and roots	25 mL
1 tbsp	oyster sauce	15 mL
1 tbsp	soy sauce	15 mL
2 tsp	granulated sugar	10 mL
1/2 tsp	black pepper	2 mL
3 tbsp	vegetable oil	45 mL
	Fresh cilantro leaves	
	Fresh red chili strips	

1. In a large bowl, combine shrimp, garlic, chopped cilantro, oyster sauce, soy sauce, sugar and pepper. Toss to combine.
2. Heat a wok or large skillet over medium-high heat and add oil. Add shrimp and stir-fry for 3 to 4 minutes, or until shrimp are cooked.
3. Serve shrimp garnished with cilantro and chilies.

Variation

Garlic Shrimp with Asparagus or Carrots: Add 1 1/2 cups (375 mL) blanched asparagus pieces or thin carrot slices to shrimp just before they are cooked. Turn to coat vegetables with sauce.

Shrimp Cakes

3	cloves garlic, peeled	3
2	shallots, peeled	2
1 1/2 lbs	shrimp, peeled and deveined	750 g
1 tbsp	chopped fresh cilantro root or stems	15 mL
1 tbsp	fish sauce	15 mL
1 tsp	hot chili sauce	5 mL
1 tsp	grated lime zest	5 mL
1/4 tsp	black pepper	1 mL
1 1/2 cups	dry bread crumbs (preferably panko)	375 mL
1/4 cup	vegetable oil (approx.)	50 mL

1. Chop garlic and shallots in a food processor.
2. Pat shrimp dry and add to food processor. Process until coarsely chopped.
3. Add cilantro, fish sauce, chili sauce, lime zest and pepper. Pulse to combine ingredients, scraping down sides as necessary, to make a coarse paste (do not overprocess). Transfer mixture to a bowl.
4. Spoon mixture in 18 mounds (a heaping tablespoon each) onto a parchment-lined baking sheet. With wet hands, shape each mound into a round cake. Roll cakes in bread crumbs to coat surface. Flatten slightly.
5. In a large nonstick skillet, heat oil over medium-high heat. Cook shrimp cakes, in batches, for 3 to 4 minutes per side, or until golden and crispy.

Makes 6 servings (about 18 cakes)

We ordered shrimp cakes like these at one of the many open-sided restaurants located along the riverside in Thailand. It was another hot and steamy day, but for a cooling effect, water was dripping off the steel roof into the river. We were surprised to see a neighboring table ordering a large basket of bread, which turned out to be for feeding the catfish in the river!

These cakes are often made with a combination of shrimp and ground pork and deep-fried. Serve with homemade (page 45) or storebought sweet chili sauce or cucumber salad (page 72).

Make Ahead

Cakes can be shaped, rolled in breadcrumbs and refrigerated up to 2 hours before cooking. Cooked cakes can be reheated in a preheated 375°F (190°C) oven for 8 minutes, or until hot.

Sweet and Hot Shrimp

Makes 4 servings

On one of our visits to Thailand, our guide arranged for us to visit a small family-owned palm sugar plantation near Phetchaburi, halfway between Bangkok and Hua Hin. It reminded me slightly of making maple syrup at home, but instead of freezing temperatures, the heat was sweltering, and there was absolutely no wind. The son climbed the sugar palms barefoot to tap the trees and would return to collect the sap in large bamboo containers. The sap was poured into a large wok over a roaring fire and reduced until almost sugary. Then the wok was placed on the ground and we all took turns beating the sugar with a huge whisk. At just the right stage, the sugar (which was now fudge-like) was poured into shallow pans and allowed to firm before being packaged. This is a very sweet, almost candy-like dish.

1/2 cup	palm or brown sugar	125 mL
1/4 cup	water	50 mL
2 tbsp	fish sauce	25 mL
2	cloves garlic, chopped	2
2 tbsp	lime juice	25 mL
1 1/2 tsp	chopped fresh red chilies	7 mL
1 lb	shrimp, peeled and deveined	500 g
1 tbsp	chopped fresh cilantro leaves	15 mL

1. In a saucepan, combine sugar, water, fish sauce and garlic. Bring to a boil, reduce heat to medium-low and cook for 8 to 10 minutes, or until syrupy. Do not let sauce burn.
2. Add lime juice and chilies and simmer for 2 minutes. Taste and adjust seasonings, adding more lime juice if necessary.
3. Add shrimp and cilantro and simmer, stirring, for 2 minutes, or until shrimp are just pink. Do not overcook.

Shrimp Omelet

3	eggs	3
2 tbsp	water	25 mL
2 tsp	fish sauce	10 mL
1 tbsp	vegetable oil	15 mL
2	cloves garlic, chopped	2
1	shallot, chopped	1
1	green onion, chopped	1
8 oz	shrimp, diced	250 g

1. In a bowl, beat together eggs, water and fish sauce.
2. Heat oil in an 8- to 10-inch (20 to 25 cm) skillet over medium-high heat. Add garlic, shallot and green onion and stir-fry for 30 seconds.
3. Add shrimp and stir-fry for 1 minute.
4. Add egg mixture. Swirl around shrimp and cook for 2 to 3 minutes, or until eggs are firm and golden brown on bottom. Flip omelet and cook for 2 minutes on second side.

Variation

Oyster Omelet: Replace shrimp with 6 shucked oysters, drained and patted dry. Stir-fry for 1 minute, or until just set, before adding eggs.

Makes 2 servings

During my first trip to Thailand, I stayed at the Oriental Hotel so I could attend their cooking school. Since this was my first time in Asia, I was rather timid about sightseeing and did not venture too far on my own. Fortunately, there were some wonderful guides to show me the highlights. At the same time, I spent many satisfying hours taking classes and trying the various restaurants and simply relaxing at the beautiful hotel. This is a version of a seafood omelet I had at the hotel's fish restaurant. I often make it as a quick supper dish or even for brunch. Serve it with a simple green salad.

Stir-fried Squid with Garlic and Mushrooms

Makes 4 servings

Along the coast of Thailand, squid is sold in several forms — uncleaned or cleaned, whole, dried, cut in tubes or rings. Grilled squid is a popular street snack, and restaurant menus often feature stuffed squid, either cooked in sauces or poached in soups. For last-minute dishes, keep frozen squid rings on hand.

2 tbsp	vegetable oil	25 mL
4	cloves garlic, chopped	4
3	shallots, thinly sliced	3
1 1/2 cups	sliced fresh shiitake mushrooms (about 4 oz/125 g)	375 mL
1 lb	fresh or frozen squid rings	500 g
1 tsp	chopped fresh red chilies	5 mL
2 tbsp	oyster sauce	25 mL
1 tbsp	fish sauce	15 mL
1 tbsp	water	15 mL
1 tbsp	lime juice	15 mL
1 tsp	granulated sugar	5 mL
1/4 cup	fresh sweet Thai basil leaves	50 mL

1. In a wok or large skillet, heat oil over medium-high heat. Add garlic and shallots and stir-fry for 1 minute.
2. Add mushrooms and stir-fry for 3 minutes. Add squid and chilies and stir-fry for 1 minute.
3. Add oyster sauce, fish sauce, water, lime juice and sugar and cook for 2 minutes.
4. Add basil and toss to combine.

Variation

Stir-fried Shrimp and Scallops with Garlic and Mushrooms: Replace squid with 8 oz (250 g) peeled and deveined shrimp and 8 oz (250 g) scallops. Stir-fry for 2 to 3 minutes before adding sauce.

Curries

Red Curry Paste

Makes about ¾ cup (175 mL)

Traditionally, curry pastes are prepared using a mortar and pestle, sometimes requiring 15 to 20 minutes of patient pounding to achieve a pastelike consistency. A blender or a small food processor makes the task easier, with a small amount of liquid added to smooth the paste. Red curry paste is a good all-purpose paste used in many curry dishes as well as a seasoning ingredient in other dishes. There are good-quality commercial pastes, but the flavor changes from brand to brand. If you want to make your own, this is a shortcut version.

Make Ahead

Curry pastes can be covered tightly and refrigerated for up to 3 days or frozen for up to 3 months (page 205).

16	small dried red chilies, seeded	16
2	stalks lemongrass, white part only, coarsely chopped	2
3 tbsp	coarsely chopped fresh red chilies	45 mL
6	cloves garlic, coarsely chopped	6
5	shallots, coarsely chopped	5
1 tbsp	coarsely chopped galangal or fresh gingerroot	15 mL
1 tbsp	coarsely chopped fresh cilantro roots or stems	15 mL
1 tbsp	ground coriander	15 mL
1 tsp	grated lime zest	5 mL
1 tsp	ground cumin	5 mL
½ tsp	black pepper	2 mL
½ tsp	salt, shrimp paste or anchovy paste	2 mL

1. Place dried chilies in a bowl. Cover with hot water and soak for 25 minutes, or until soft. Drain, reserving 3 tbsp (45 mL) soaking water.
2. In a food processor or using a mortar and pestle, combine lemongrass, fresh chilies, garlic, shallots, galangal, cilantro, coriander, lime zest, cumin, pepper, salt and soaking water. Blend to combine.
3. Add softened dried chilies and process until a smooth paste is formed. Add a small amount of water if paste does not come together. Scrape down sides of bowl as necessary. Transfer to a clean container and cover tightly.

Red Beef Curry with Sweet Potato

Makes 4 to 6 servings

2 tbsp	vegetable oil	25 mL
4	shallots, chopped	4
3	cloves garlic, finely chopped	3
1 tbsp	chopped fresh cilantro roots or stems	15 mL
2 tbsp	red curry paste (page 196)	25 mL
12 oz	lean beef, thinly sliced	375 g
1 1/2 cups	cubed sweet potato (1/2-inch/1 cm pieces)	375 mL
2 cups	coconut milk	500 mL
1 cup	beef or chicken stock	250 mL
4	lime leaves	4
2 tbsp	fish sauce	25 mL
1 tbsp	palm or brown sugar	15 mL
1/4 cup	fresh sweet Thai basil leaves	50 mL

1. In a wok or saucepan, heat oil over medium-high heat. Add shallots, garlic, cilantro and curry paste. Cook, stirring, for 2 minutes.
2. Add beef and cook, stirring, for 2 minutes.
3. Add sweet potato, coconut milk, stock, lime leaves, fish sauce and sugar. Bring to a boil, reduce heat and simmer for 10 to 12 minutes, stirring occasionally, until beef is tender and sweet potatoes are just cooked.
4. Stir in basil.

The Blue Elephant restaurant and cooking school are situated in a century-old mansion in the heart of Bangkok. The dining room is furnished with antiques and tables are set with bronze cutlery and unique china. Tropical trees, trickling fountains and plants provide a lush setting. (Blue Elephant restaurants are also located in many major cities around the world.)

This is a version of one of the restaurant's many dishes. They used pumpkin, but sweet potato can be substituted.

Thai curries often begin by reducing a small portion of coconut milk and using it as the frying medium, but some cooks start with vegetable oil, as in this recipe. You could also use thinly sliced chicken or pork, or diced firm tofu or shrimp instead of the beef. (If you use tofu or shrimp, add during the last 4 minutes of the cooking time.)

Chicken with Red Curry, Pineapple and Grapes

Makes 4 to 5 servings

When we stayed at the Jasmine Rice Village resort in Chiang Mai, Rutch, who used to have her own restaurant in Pattaya, prepared this dish for our lunch, which we ate in the open-air dining room overlooking two small rice paddies. Since she was not sure of our "heat" tolerance, she prepared a mild version similar to this one. She also added a few pea eggplants and fresh green peppercorns still on the stem.

1 1/2 cups	coconut milk, divided	375 mL
2 tbsp	red curry paste (page 196)	25 mL
1/2 cup	chicken stock	125 mL
1 1/2 cups	diced eggplant	375 mL
4	lime leaves, center vein removed, shredded	4
12 oz	shredded cooked chicken	375 g
1 cup	diced pineapple	250 mL
1/2 cup	red or green seedless grapes	125 mL
12	small cherry tomatoes	12
1/2 cup	fresh sweet Thai basil leaves	125 mL
2 tsp	sliced fresh red chilies	10 mL
2 tbsp	fish sauce	25 mL
1 tbsp	granulated sugar	15 mL

1. In a wok or saucepan, heat 1/2 cup (125 mL) coconut milk over medium-high heat. Add curry paste and cook, stirring, for 2 to 3 minutes, or until fragrant.
2. Add remaining coconut milk, stock, eggplant and lime leaves. Simmer for 6 to 8 minutes, or until eggplant is almost tender.
3. Add chicken, pineapple, grapes and tomatoes and simmer for 4 minutes, or until hot.
4. Stir in basil, chilies, fish sauce and sugar and heat through.

Chicken in Red Curry with Carrots

Makes 5 to 6 servings

The MBK shopping mall in Bangkok is a multi-floor complex that houses a myriad of stalls, shops, a supermarket, cinemas and food outlets. The fifth floor is mainly devoted to food stations featuring Thai food as well as other international cuisines, including Egyptian, Indian, Vietnamese and Japanese. This is similar to a curry we had there.

Make Ahead

Dish can be made a day ahead, covered and refrigerated. Reheat gently, without boiling, just before serving.

1 ½ cups	coconut milk, divided	375 mL
2 tbsp	red curry paste (page 196)	25 mL
1 lb	boneless, skinless chicken breasts, thinly sliced	500 g
1 cup	thinly sliced carrots, blanched	250 mL
1 cup	canned sliced bamboo shoots, rinsed and drained (optional)	250 mL
½ cup	chicken stock	125 mL
1 tbsp	fish sauce	15 mL
2 tsp	palm or brown sugar	10 mL
2 tsp	lime juice or tamarind paste	10 mL
4	lime leaves, center vein removed, shredded	4
¼ cup	fresh sweet Thai basil leaves	50 mL
2	fresh red chilies, sliced (optional)	2

1. In a wok or saucepan, heat ½ cup (125 mL) coconut milk over medium-high heat. Add curry paste. Cook, stirring, for 2 to 3 minutes, or until fragrant.
2. Add chicken, carrots and bamboo shoots, if using. Stir in stock, fish sauce, sugar, lime juice and remaining coconut milk. Reduce heat to a simmer and cook, stirring frequently, for 6 to 8 minutes, or until chicken is cooked.
3. Stir in lime leaves and basil and serve garnished with chilies, if using.

Jungle Curry with Ground Pork and Vegetables

Makes 5 to 6 servings

Jungle curry is generally hot, without the addition of soothing coconut milk. On a trip north of Chiang Mai, on yet another hot and humid day interspersed with downpours of rain, we had a version of this for lunch, served with lots of rice and cooling sliced cucumbers and cherry tomatoes.

Cooking curry paste in oil or coconut milk brings out the flavor of the curry spices and prevents clumps of paste in the finished dish.

The ground pork can be replaced with ground beef or chicken.

2 tbsp	vegetable oil	25 mL
2 tbsp	red curry paste (page 196)	25 mL
8 oz	lean ground pork	250 g
1 cup	sliced fresh mushrooms	250 mL
1 ½ cups	sliced green beans	375 mL
1	small Asian eggplant, halved lengthwise, cut in ½-inch (1 cm) pieces	1
1 cup	corn kernels	250 mL
4	lime leaves	4
2 cups	chicken or vegetable stock or water	500 mL
2 tbsp	fish sauce	25 mL
1 tbsp	palm or granulated sugar	15 mL
¼ cup	fresh sweet Thai basil or cilantro leaves	50 mL

1. In a wok or large skillet, heat oil over medium-high heat. Add curry paste and cook, stirring, for 1 to 2 minutes, or until fragrant.
2. Add pork and mushrooms and cook, stirring, for 4 minutes.
3. Add beans, eggplant, corn, lime leaves, stock, fish sauce and sugar. Bring to a gentle boil. Cook for 5 to 7 minutes, or until vegetables are tender.
4. Stir in basil.

Variations

Jungle Curry with Shrimp: Omit ground pork. Add 1 lb (500 g) peeled and deveined shrimp for the last 3 minutes of cooking time.

Jungle Curry with Vegetables: Omit ground pork. Add 1 seeded and sliced red bell pepper and 1 sliced medium zucchini along with other vegetables. For a vegetarian version, use curry paste made without shrimp paste and replace fish sauce with soy sauce.

Tofu with Red Curry and Peanut Sauce

Makes 5 to 6 servings

Wherever there are universities and colleges, you'll find an assortment of ethnic restaurants, particularly Thai or a combination of Thai, Cambodian, Laotian, Malaysian and Vietnamese. In Kingston, Ontario, home to Queen's University, there are several to choose from and all have vegetarian selections. This is a version of a vegetarian dish that my editor Shelley Tanaka and I keep reordering whenever we get together for a meeting.

Make Ahead

Sauce can be made 6 to 8 hours earlier and refrigerated. Gently reheat before adding tofu.

2 tbsp	vegetable oil	25 mL
3	shallots, chopped	3
1 1/2 tbsp	red curry paste (page 196)	22 mL
2 cups	coconut milk	500 mL
1/3 cup	chopped peanuts	75 mL
2 tbsp	soy sauce	25 mL
1 tbsp	fish sauce (optional)	15 mL
1 tbsp	tamarind paste or lime juice	15 mL
1 lb	firm tofu, cut in 1/2-inch (1 cm) slices	500 g
	Fresh cilantro leaves	

1. In a shallow saucepan, heat oil over medium heat. Add shallots and curry paste and stir-fry for 2 minutes, or until fragrant.
2. Whisk in coconut milk, peanuts, soy sauce and fish sauce, if using. Bring to a gentle boil. Reduce heat and simmer for 4 minutes. Stir in tamarind paste.
3. Gently add tofu to sauce and spoon sauce over tofu. Simmer for 3 to 5 minutes, without boiling, until heated through.
4. Sprinkle with cilantro.

Variation

Tofu and Green Beans with Red Curry and Peanut Sauce: Add 1 cup (250 mL) blanched green beans with tofu and heat through.

Shrimp and Pineapple Curry

Makes 4 servings

On our way to Mae Sai and the Golden Triangle (where the borders of Myanmar, Laos and Thailand meet), we saw numerous roadside stands featuring lychee fruit and honey pineapple, a regional specialty, but regular pineapple also works well in this dish, and you can substitute thinly sliced chicken breasts for the shrimp. This is a quick dish for entertaining.

2 tbsp	vegetable oil	25 mL
1 tbsp	red curry paste (page 196)	15 mL
1 cup	coconut milk	250 mL
4	lime leaves	4
2 tbsp	tamarind paste	25 mL
12 oz	shrimp, peeled and deveined	375 g
1 1⁄2 cups	cubed pineapple	375 mL
1 tbsp	fish sauce	15 mL
1 tbsp	palm or brown sugar	15 mL
1 tbsp	lime juice	15 mL
1⁄4 cup	chopped cashews (optional)	50 mL

1. In a wok or large saucepan, heat oil over medium heat. Add curry paste and cook for 30 seconds, or until fragrant.
2. Add coconut milk, lime leaves and tamarind paste. Bring to a gentle boil and cook for 3 minutes.
3. Add shrimp and pineapple and cook for 3 minutes, or until shrimp are just cooked.
4. Stir in fish sauce, sugar and lime juice. Cook for 2 minutes.
5. Serve garnished with cashews, if using.

Green Curry Paste

3 tbsp	coarsely chopped fresh green chilies (about 15 bird's eye chilies)	45 mL
1	stalk lemongrass, white part only, coarsely chopped	1
5	shallots, coarsely chopped	5
4	cloves garlic, coarsely chopped	4
1 tbsp	chopped galangal or fresh gingerroot	15 mL
1	lime leaf, center vein removed, torn	1
3 tbsp	chopped fresh cilantro roots or stems	45 mL
1/4 cup	water	50 mL
1/2 tsp	ground coriander	2 mL
1/2 tsp	ground cumin	2 mL
1/2 tsp	black pepper	2 mL
1/2 tsp	shrimp or anchovy paste (optional)	2 mL

1. In a food processor or using a mortar and pestle, combine chilies, lemongrass, shallots, garlic, galangal, lime leaf, cilantro and water. Blend until coarsely chopped.
2. Add coriander, cumin, pepper and shrimp paste, if using. Process until a paste forms, scraping down sides of food processor. Add extra water 1 tsp (5 mL) at a time, if necessary.

Freezing Curry Paste

Transfer curry paste to a small resealable freezer bag and flatten. Freeze.

To use, break off the required amount and seal the remaining paste tightly.

Alternatively, place the paste in mounds (about 1 tbsp/15 mL each) on a parchment-lined baking sheet. Freeze, then wrap each mound tightly and store in a resealable plastic bag.

Makes about 3/4 cup (175 mL)

You can buy a commercial curry paste or make your own. For a milder paste, reduce the number of chilies or scrape out the seeds. Some cooks add a small amount of fresh cilantro, basil or spinach leaves to increase the green color, but this makes the paste more perishable.

This recipe can easily be doubled.

Make Ahead

Cover tightly and refrigerate for up to 3 days or freeze in small portions for up to 3 months.

Grilled Beef Tenderloin with Green Curry Sauce

Makes 4 servings

This recipe is not a typical curry dish, since the meat is not cooked in the sauce. Topping sliced grilled beef with a curry sauce is an easy last-minute dish that is also suitable for entertaining. In Thailand, many curry dishes are served with a side plate of raw vegetables such as green beans, tomato wedges, cabbage pieces, sliced cucumbers, bean sprouts and lettuce leaves.

Other beef steaks can be used, such as ribeye, flank or sirloin. Adjust the grilling time to the thickness of the steak.

4	beef tenderloin steaks (about 6 oz/ 175 g each)	4
1 tbsp	soy sauce	15 mL
1/2 tsp	black pepper	2 mL

Green Curry Sauce

1 cup	coconut milk, divided	250 mL
1 tbsp	green curry paste (page 205)	15 mL
1 tbsp	palm or brown sugar	15 mL
1 tbsp	fish sauce	15 mL
1 tbsp	lime juice	15 mL
2 tbsp	chopped roasted peanuts	25 mL
2 tbsp	fresh cilantro leaves	25 mL

1. Place steaks in a shallow dish. Sprinkle with soy sauce and pepper and rub onto surface of meat.
2. In a saucepan or wok, heat 1/2 cup (125 mL) coconut milk over medium-high heat. Whisk in curry paste and cook for 2 minutes, or until fragrant.
3. Add remaining coconut milk, sugar and fish sauce and bring to a low boil. Reduce heat and cook for 4 to 5 minutes, or until slightly thickened. Remove from heat and stir in lime juice.
4. Grill steaks for 3 to 4 minutes per side, or until medium-rare to medium.
5. Slice steaks and spoon sauce over sliced beef. Garnish with peanuts and cilantro.

Variations

Grilled Chicken with Green Curry Sauce: Replace beef with 4 boneless, skinless chicken breasts (about 6 oz/175 g each). Grill for 3 to 4 minutes per side, or until cooked through.

Grilled Tofu with Green Curry Sauce: Replace beef with 1 lb (500 g) firm tofu, cut in 1/2-inch (1 cm) slices. For a vegetarian dish, replace fish sauce with soy sauce. Grill for 3 to 4 minutes, or until heated through.

Green Curry Chicken with Eggplant

Makes 4 to 6 servings

Probably one of the most popular dishes ordered in Thai restaurants, this silky-smooth curry is quick and easy. Eggplants offset the richness of the coconut milk. If pea eggplants are available, add 1/4 cup (50 mL) with the other eggplants — they'll add a herby flavor to the dish (you could also make this using diced zucchini). Often made with all coconut milk, the chicken stock helps to cut the richness.

1 tbsp	vegetable oil	15 mL
2 tbsp	green curry paste (page 205)	25 mL
1 lb	boneless, skinless chicken breasts, cut in 3/4-inch (2 cm) pieces	500 g
1 cup	coconut milk	250 mL
1/2 cup	chicken stock	125 mL
2 tbsp	fish sauce	25 mL
1 tbsp	palm or brown sugar	15 mL
1 1/2 cups	diced Asian eggplant	375 mL
4	lime leaves	4
1/2 cup	fresh sweet Thai basil leaves	125 mL
1 tbsp	lime juice	15 mL
2 tsp	sliced fresh red chilies (optional)	10 mL

1. In a wok or saucepan, heat oil over medium-high heat. Add curry paste and stir-fry for 1 minute, or until fragrant, but be careful not to burn.
2. Add chicken and stir-fry for 2 minutes.
3. Add coconut milk, stock, fish sauce, sugar, eggplant and lime leaves. Bring to a low boil, reduce heat and simmer for 8 to 10 minutes, or until chicken is cooked and eggplant is just tender. Remove from heat.
4. Stir in basil and lime juice and garnish with chilies, if using.

Variation

Green Curry Chicken with Bok Choy: Omit eggplant. Add 8 halved baby bok choy (about 2 inches/5 cm long) for last few minutes of cooking time.

Salmon with Green Curry Broth

Makes 4 servings

Freshwater fish and seafood are an important part of the Thai diet, but not a lot of salmon is served. This is a variation of a dish that we prepared as a starter course for a Rotary function of 375 guests. We were concerned that some of the guests might balk if we used the word curry, so we called it Salmon with Red Coconut Broth instead, and it was a big hit. Other fish such as halibut, cod or tilapia can be used.

1 tbsp	vegetable oil	15 mL
1 tbsp	chopped fresh gingerroot	15 mL
1	shallot, chopped	1
1	stalk lemongrass, white part only, chopped	1
2 tsp	green curry paste (page 205)	10 mL
1 cup	coconut milk	250 mL
1/2 cup	fresh sweet Thai basil leaves	125 mL
1/4 cup	coarsely chopped fresh cilantro leaves	50 mL
1 tbsp	fish sauce	15 mL
1 tbsp	granulated sugar	15 mL
4	6-oz (175 g) salmon fillets, skin removed	4
1 tbsp	lime juice	15 mL
	Fresh cilantro leaves	

1. In a skillet, heat oil over medium heat. Add ginger, shallot, lemongrass and curry paste and stir-fry for 3 to 4 minutes, or until just fragrant but not browned.
2. Add coconut milk, basil, chopped cilantro, fish sauce and sugar. Bring to a gentle boil and cook for 10 minutes, stirring occasionally. Strain into a shallow saucepan that will hold salmon in a single layer.
3. Arrange salmon in sauce in a single layer. Spoon some sauce over salmon. Cover fish directly with a round of parchment paper. Cook over low heat for 6 to 8 minutes, or until salmon is just cooked. Gently transfer salmon to a serving dish.
4. Stir lime juice into sauce. Pour sauce over salmon.
5. Garnish with fresh cilantro leaves.

Shrimp with Coconut Curry Sauce

2 tbsp	vegetable oil	25 mL
3	cloves garlic, chopped	3
2	shallots, chopped	2
2 tbsp	green curry paste (page 205)	25 mL
1 ½ cups	coconut milk	375 mL
¾ cup	chopped tomato	175 mL
1 lb	shrimp, peeled and deveined	500 g
2 tbsp	fish sauce	25 mL
1 tbsp	palm or brown sugar	15 mL
½ cup	fresh sweet Thai basil leaves	125 mL
2 tsp	grated lime zest	10 mL

1. In a wok or saucepan, heat oil over medium-high heat. Add garlic, shallots and curry paste. Stir-fry for 2 to 3 minutes, or until garlic is softened and curry paste is fragrant.
2. Add coconut milk and tomato and stir to combine with paste mixture. Bring to a gentle boil. Reduce heat to low and cook for 3 minutes.
3. Add shrimp, fish sauce and sugar and cook for 4 to 6 minutes, or until shrimp have just turned opaque.
4. Remove from heat. Stir in basil and lime zest.

Makes 4 servings

A similar dish made with fish balls was one of the many glorious dishes served at the famous Oriental Hotel's lunch buffet. You could also replace the shrimp with white-fleshed fish (skin removed) such as tilapia or snapper, cut in 1-inch (2.5 cm) pieces.

Vegetables and Tofu in Green Curry

Makes 5 servings

To make this a true vegetarian dish, curry paste made without shrimp paste or fish sauce is required. Check the package label or use homemade (page 205).

2 tbsp	vegetable oil	25 mL
1	onion, chopped	1
2 tbsp	green curry paste (page 205)	25 mL
1 cup	coconut milk	250 mL
1 cup	water	250 mL
1	small sweet potato, peeled and cut in 1/2-inch (1 cm) pieces	1
1	carrot, thinly sliced diagonally	1
1 1/2 cups	cauliflower florets	375 mL
1 cup	green beans, cut in 1-inch (2.5 cm) lengths	250 mL
1/2	red bell pepper, seeded and cut in 1/2-inch (1 cm) pieces	1/2
1/2 cup	corn kernels	125 mL
4 oz	firm tofu, cut in 1/2-inch (1 cm) cubes	125 g
1/4 cup	fresh sweet Thai basil leaves	50 mL
2 tbsp	soy sauce	25 mL
1 tbsp	lime juice	15 mL

1. In a wok or large skillet, heat oil over medium-high heat. Add onion and curry paste and stir-fry for 2 minutes, until onion is softened.
2. Add coconut milk and water and bring to a gentle boil.
3. Add sweet potato and carrot and cook for 12 minutes.
4. Add cauliflower and beans and cook for 4 minutes.
5. Add red pepper, corn and tofu and cook for 3 minutes, or until all vegetables are tender.
6. Stir in basil, soy sauce and lime juice.

Variation

Vegetables and Chickpeas in Green Curry: Replace tofu with 3/4 cup (175 mL) cooked chickpeas.

Mussaman Curry Paste

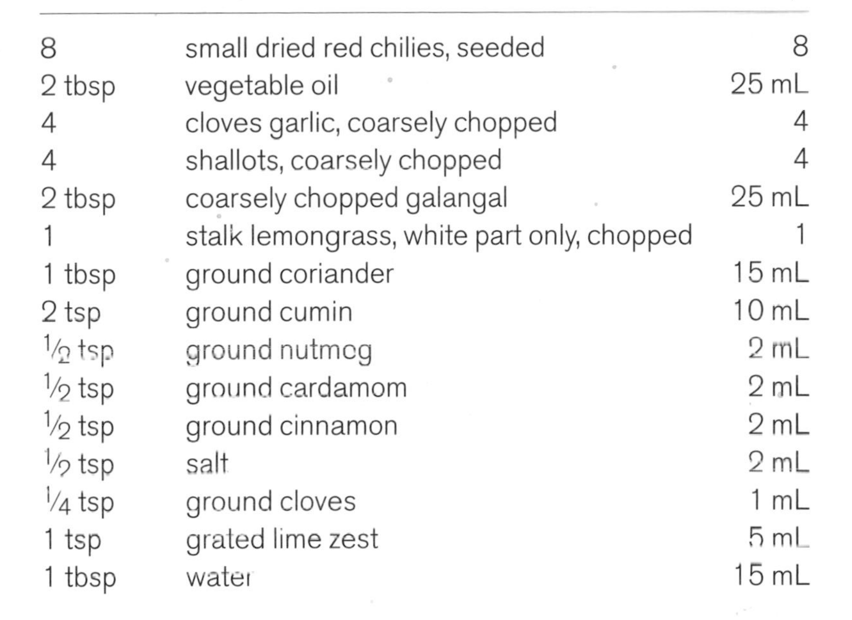

8	small dried red chilies, seeded	8
2 tbsp	vegetable oil	25 mL
4	cloves garlic, coarsely chopped	4
4	shallots, coarsely chopped	4
2 tbsp	coarsely chopped galangal	25 mL
1	stalk lemongrass, white part only, chopped	1
1 tbsp	ground coriander	15 mL
2 tsp	ground cumin	10 mL
1/2 tsp	ground nutmeg	2 mL
1/2 tsp	ground cardamom	2 mL
1/2 tsp	ground cinnamon	2 mL
1/2 tsp	salt	2 mL
1/4 tsp	ground cloves	1 mL
1 tsp	grated lime zest	5 mL
1 tbsp	water	15 mL

1. Place chilies in a small bowl of hot water and let sit for 25 minutes. Drain.
2. In a small skillet, heat oil over medium heat. Add garlic, shallots, galangal and lemongrass. Stir-fry for 4 to 6 minutes, or until golden.
3. Add soaked chilies and cook for 2 minutes. Remove from heat and cool slightly.
4. Place garlic mixture in a blender or food processor. Add coriander, cumin, nutmeg, cardamom, cinnamon, salt, cloves and lime zest. Add water and process until a paste forms, scraping down sides of bowl as necessary.

Makes about 1/2 cup (125 mL)

The aromatic spices in this curry paste reflect the influence of Malaysia and India. The authentic way to prepare curry pastes with spices is to roast them whole, cool and then grind them using a mortar and pestle. Since prepared Mussaman curry paste is difficult to find, this is an easy homemade version. Some cooks use prepared Madras curry paste as a substitute. The aroma of the spices is reminiscent of garam masala.

Make Ahead

Paste can be refrigerated, covered, for up to 3 days or frozen in small portions (page 205) for up to 3 months.

จน เครียด กินเหล้า
ขับ ถูกจับแน่
THAILAND

Mussaman Lamb Curry with Potatoes

Makes 5 to 6 servings

This dish (it is sometimes called Thai Muslim Curry) is generally made with beef or lamb. Chicken and tofu can also be used. It is not overly spicy and is one of the few Thai curry dishes containing potatoes. Although originating in southern Thailand, it is popular throughout the country, especially as a celebration dish.

Make Ahead

Curry can be made ahead, covered and refrigerated a day before serving.

2 tbsp	vegetable oil	25 mL
3 tbsp	Mussaman curry paste (page 211)	45 mL
1	onion, thinly sliced	1
1 $\frac{1}{2}$ lbs	lamb, cut in 1-inch (2.5 cm) pieces	750 g
2 cups	coconut milk	500 mL
2 cups	beef or chicken stock	500 mL
3 tbsp	fish sauce	45 mL
1 tbsp	palm or brown sugar	15 mL
2	medium potatoes, peeled and cut in 1-inch (2.5 cm) pieces	2
2 tbsp	tamarind paste or lime juice	25 mL
$\frac{1}{2}$ cup	coarsely chopped roasted peanuts or cashews	125 mL

1. In a wok or large saucepan, heat oil over medium-high heat. Add curry paste and stir-fry for 1 minute.
2. Add onion and lamb and stir-fry for 3 to 4 minutes, or until lightly browned.
3. Add coconut milk, stock, fish sauce and sugar. Bring to a boil. Reduce heat and simmer for 1 hour, partially covered.
4. Add potatoes and cook for 20 minutes, or until lamb is tender.
5. Stir in tamarind paste and peanuts.

Variation

Mussaman Chicken Curry with Potatoes: Replace lamb with 1 $\frac{1}{4}$ lbs (625 g) diced boneless, skinless chicken thighs. Add to wok with onions. Bring coconut milk mixture to a boil and add potatoes. Cook for 25 minutes, or until chicken is tender.

Yellow Curry Paste

Makes about ½ cup (125 mL)

Unlike some commercial yellow curry pastes, this one is quite gentle. Turmeric is the spice that gives it its lovely color. Fresh yellow (orange) and white turmeric are available in Thai markets (and in some Western Asian stores), but yellow is more popular. It is a small root, similar to ginger, and needs to be peeled before using.

Make Ahead

Paste can be prepared, covered and refrigerated for up to 3 days or frozen in small amounts (page 205) for up to 3 months.

6	small dried red chilies, seeded	6
¼ cup	hot water	50 mL
2	cloves garlic, coarsely chopped	2
2	shallots, coarsely chopped	2
2	stalks lemongrass, white part only, coarsely chopped	2
1 tbsp	coarsely chopped fresh gingerroot	15 mL
2 tsp	ground turmeric	10 mL
1 tsp	ground coriander	5 mL
½ tsp	ground cumin	2 mL
½ tsp	curry powder	2 mL
½ tsp	black pepper	2 mL

1. In a bowl, cover dried chilies with hot water and let stand for 25 minutes, or until softened.
2. In a blender or food processor or using a mortar and pestle, combine soaked chilies, soaking liquid, garlic, shallots, lemongrass, ginger, turmeric, coriander, cumin, curry powder and pepper. Process until a paste forms, scraping down sides of bowl as necessary.

Yellow Curry Chicken with Squash

Makes 5 to 6 servings

While visiting Australia with friend Bonnie Stern (owner of The Bonnie Stern School of Cooking in Toronto), we enjoyed a dish similar to this at Sailor's Thai, a restaurant in Sydney. They used pumpkin, but in this recipe butternut squash has been substituted. In Thailand it is common to see curry powder used in recipes containing curry paste. Commercial yellow curry pastes vary in heat. Increase the amount if you wish.

2 tbsp	vegetable oil	25 mL
1 lb	boneless, skinless chicken thighs, cut in 1-inch (2.5 cm) pieces	500 g
1	onion, thinly sliced	1
1 tbsp	yellow curry paste (page 214)	15 mL
1 tsp	curry powder	5 mL
1 cup	coconut milk	250 mL
1 cup	chicken stock	250 mL
1 1/2 cups	cubed butternut squash (1/2-inch/1 cm pieces)	375 mL
2 tbsp	fish sauce	25 mL
2 tbsp	lime juice	25 mL
1 tbsp	palm or brown sugar	15 mL
	Fried shallots, storebought or homemade (page 147)	

1. In a wok or large saucepan, heat oil over medium-high heat. Add chicken pieces and cook for 6 to 8 minutes, or until golden.
2. Add onion and cook for 2 minutes.
3. Add curry paste and curry powder and mash curry paste to soften, then stir to coat chicken and cook for 2 minutes.
4. Stir in coconut milk and stock. Bring to a gentle boil. Add squash and simmer for 15 to 20 minutes, or until chicken and squash are tender. Stir occasionally.
5. Stir in fish sauce, lime juice and sugar and garnish with fried shallots.

Variation

Yellow Curry Tofu with Vegetables: Omit chicken. Use vegetable stock instead of chicken stock and soy sauce instead of fish sauce. Add 2 thinly sliced carrots, 2 diced potatoes and 1 diced sweet potato to saucepan with squash. Cook in coconut milk and stock for 15 minutes, or until vegetables are almost tender. Add 4 oz (125 g) diced firm tofu, 1/2 cup (125 mL) corn kernels and 1 cup (250 mL) sliced green beans and cook for 3 minutes.

Shrimp in Yellow Curry Sauce

Makes 4 servings

Yellow curry dishes remind you of sunshine — of which there is lots in Thailand. Although often used in chicken dishes, yellow curry paste is also at home with seafood and fish. This can be also be made with frozen king crab legs or small crab claws.

1 tbsp	vegetable oil	15 mL
1 tbsp	yellow curry paste (page 214)	15 mL
1 cup	coconut milk	250 mL
1 cup	diced tomato	250 mL
2 tbsp	fish sauce	25 mL
1 tsp	palm or brown sugar	5 mL
1 lb	peeled and deveined shrimp	500 g
1 tbsp	lime juice, or 1 tsp (5 mL) grated lime zest	15 mL
2	green onions, thinly sliced	2
1	small fresh red chili, thinly sliced	1

1. In a wok or large saucepan, heat oil over medium heat. Add curry paste and stir-fry for 1 minute, or until fragrant.
2. Add coconut milk, tomato, fish sauce and sugar and stir to combine. Bring to a gentle boil.
3. Add shrimp, reduce heat and cook for 5 to 6 minutes, or until shrimp turn opaque and are just cooked.
4. Remove from heat and stir in lime juice and green onions.
5. Garnish with sliced chilies.

Steamed Fish Pudding

Makes 6 servings

While attending an IACP (International Association of Cooking Professionals) conference in Chicago, I enrolled in an inspiring workshop conducted by Arun Sampanthavivat, owner of Arun's Thai Restaurant in Chicago, which has the reputation of being one of the best Thai restaurants in the United States. The focus of the demonstration was the sophistication of Thai curries. This is a shortcut version of one of the dishes. Serve it as a snack or appetizer. In Thailand, a similar dish uses fresh banana leaves (the aluminum foil of Southeast Asia) as a container. The containers are then steamed. Unfortunately, frozen banana leaves do not work as well, so this pudding is made in ramekins and cooked in a water bath.

3/4 cup	coconut milk	175 mL
1 tsp	yellow curry paste (page 214)	5 mL
1 tsp	all-purpose flour	5 mL
1	egg	1
2 tbsp	fish sauce	25 mL
1 tbsp	lime juice	15 mL
1 tbsp	chopped fresh cilantro leaves	15 mL
2 tsp	granulated sugar	10 mL
12 oz	firm white fish fillets, cut in 1/2-inch (1 cm) pieces	375 g
2 tbsp	thick coconut milk (page 18)	25 mL
	Thinly sliced fresh red chilies	
	Fresh cilantro leaves	

1. In a bowl, whisk together coconut milk, curry paste, flour and egg.
2. Add fish sauce, lime juice, cilantro, sugar and fish. Spoon into six 1/2-cup (125 mL) ramekins.
3. Place ramekins in a shallow pan. Fill pan with hot water until it comes part way up sides of ramekins. Bake in a preheated 400°F (200°C) oven for 22 to 25 minutes, or until puddings are set.
4. Remove puddings from water bath. Let stand for 5 minutes before serving.
5. Top each pudding with a small spoonful of thick coconut milk, sliced chilies and cilantro leaves.

Vegetables and Side Dishes

Quick Asparagus Stir-fry

Makes 4 servings

For a richer flavor, some cooks add oyster sauce to this recipe, but simple is also good.

2 tbsp	vegetable oil	25 mL
2	cloves garlic, chopped	2
1 tbsp	chopped fresh gingerroot	15 mL
1 lb	fresh asparagus, trimmed and cut in 2-inch (5 cm) lengths (about 4 cups/1 L)	500 g
½ tsp	chopped fresh red chilies	2 mL
1 tbsp	fish sauce	15 mL
1 tbsp	soy sauce or oyster sauce	15 mL
2 tbsp	water	25 mL
1 tsp	palm or brown sugar	5 mL

1. Heat a wok or large skillet over medium-high heat and add oil. Add garlic and ginger and stir-fry for 30 seconds.
2. Add asparagus and chilies and stir-fry for 1 minute.
3. Add fish sauce, soy sauce, water and sugar and stir-fry for 3 minutes, or until asparagus is tender-crisp.

Variation

Quick Snow Pea Stir-fry: Replace asparagus with trimmed snow peas or sugar snap peas. Cook for 1½ to 3 minutes (snow peas will not take as long to cook), or until just crisp.

Asparagus and Tofu with Roasted Chili Paste

2 tbsp	vegetable oil	25 mL
1 cup	diced firm tofu (about 6 oz/175 g)	250 mL
4	cloves garlic, chopped	4
1 lb	asparagus, trimmed and cut in 2-inch (5 cm) lengths (about 4 cups/1 L)	500 g
2 tbsp	water	25 mL
1 tbsp	roasted chili paste	15 mL
1 tbsp	fish sauce	15 mL
¼ cup	shredded fresh sweet Thai basil leaves	50 mL

1. Heat a wok or large skillet over medium-high heat and add oil. Add tofu and garlic and stir-fry for 1 minute.
2. Add asparagus and stir-fry for 1 minute.
3. Add water, chili paste and fish sauce and toss to coat tofu and asparagus. Cover and cook for 3 minutes, or until asparagus is tender.
4. Remove from heat and stir in basil.

Makes 4 servings

For a true vegetarian dish, use a roasted chili paste (page 48) that does not contain fish sauce or shrimp paste. If you prefer less heat, reduce the amount of chili paste.

Variation

Green Beans and Tofu with Roasted Chili Paste: Replace asparagus with 4 cups (1 L) green beans, cut in 2-inch (5 cm) lengths. In Step 3, cook for 4 to 5 minutes, or until tender.

Asparagus

Asparagus varies in width from pencil thin to chubby stalks. To prepare it for cooking, break off and discard the woody base, leaving the tender stalk. If the asparagus is very thick, some cooks like to peel the bottom half of the stalks. It can also be cut into long diagonal pieces for a more elegant appearance and to shorten the cooking time. Very thin asparagus does not require peeling.

After purchasing asparagus, stand the bunch upright in a container of cold water (like a bouquet of flowers), cover with plastic and refrigerate until using.

Cauliflower and Beans with Turmeric

Makes 4 servings

For a spicier dish, add ½ tsp (2 mL) chopped fresh red or green chilies with the garlic.

2 tbsp	vegetable oil	25 mL
3	cloves garlic, chopped	3
3 cups	small cauliflower florets	750 mL
2 tbsp	chopped fresh cilantro leaves	25 mL
1 tbsp	fish sauce	15 mL
1 tsp	granulated sugar	5 mL
½ tsp	ground turmeric	2 mL
¼ cup	water	50 mL
1 cup	sliced green beans, cut in 1-inch (2.5 cm) lengths	250 mL
4	green onions, sliced	4

1. Heat a wok or large skillet over medium-high heat and add oil. Add garlic and stir-fry for 15 seconds.
2. Add cauliflower and stir-fry for 1 minute.
3. Add cilantro, fish sauce, sugar, turmeric and water. Cover and cook for 3 minutes.
4. Add beans. Cover and cook for 2 to 3 minutes, or until vegetables are tender.
5. Stir in green onions and cook for 1 minute.

Beans and Cabbage with Ginger

Makes 5 to 6 servings

Most Thai vegetable dishes are stir-fried, with seasoning sauces added. This one includes creamy coconut milk and the added freshness of ginger and lemongrass.

2 tbsp	vegetable oil	25 mL
2 tbsp	coarsely chopped fresh gingerroot	25 mL
1 tbsp	chopped fresh lemongrass, white part only	15 mL
1 tsp	chopped fresh red or green chilies	5 mL
2 cups	sliced green beans (about 8 oz/250 g), cut in 2-inch (5 cm) lengths	500 mL
2 cups	chopped cabbage	500 mL
1/2 cup	coconut milk	125 mL
2 tbsp	fish sauce	25 mL
2 tsp	granulated sugar	10 mL
	Fresh sweet Thai basil leaves	

1. Heat a wok or large skillet over medium-high heat and add oil. Add ginger, lemongrass and chilies and stir-fry for 30 seconds.
2. Add beans and cabbage and stir-fry for 2 minutes.
3. Add coconut milk, fish sauce and sugar and combine. Cover and cook for 3 minutes.
4. Remove cover and cook for 1 minute, or until beans and cabbage are just tender.
5. Garnish with basil.

Green Beans with Cashews and Chilies

Makes 4 servings

Cashews are a major crop in southern Thailand. Mostly they are sold raw in Thai markets, but they must be cooked before eating. Raw (uncooked) cashews keep for several months. In Thailand they are usually deep-fried, but you can use salted or unsalted dry roasted cashews instead (hide them if you want to save them for cooking, however, since they are hard to resist). When both yellow and green beans are ready in my garden, I use a combination.

2 tbsp	vegetable oil	25 mL
1	onion, thinly sliced	1
10	small dried red chilies	10
4 cups	sliced green beans (about 1 lb/500 g), cut in 2-inch (5 cm) lengths	1 L
1 tbsp	fish sauce	15 mL
1 tbsp	water	15 mL
1/2 tsp	granulated sugar	2 mL
1/2 cup	roasted cashews	125 mL

1. Heat a wok or large skillet over medium-high heat and add oil. Add onion and stir-fry for 1 minute, or until softened.
2. Add chilies and beans and stir-fry for 2 minutes.
3. Add fish sauce, water and sugar and stir-fry for 2 to 3 minutes, or until beans are tender.
4. Stir in cashews.

Deep-fried Cashews

In a wok or medium saucepan, heat 3 cups (750 mL) vegetable oil over medium heat to about 275 to 300°F (135 to 150°C); cashews need to cook at a lower oil temperature so heat can penetrate to the center. Add 2 cups (500 mL) raw cashews a cup at a time and fry, stirring often, for 2 to 3 minutes, until nuts are a light golden brown. Lift nuts from oil with a wire mesh strainer, shaking off excess oil. Drain on a paper towel-lined tray. Repeat with remaining cashews. Toss with 1/2 tsp (2 mL) salt. Let nuts cool before tasting, because they really hold their heat.

Makes 3 cups (750 mL).

Broccoli with Oyster Sauce

1	large bunch broccoli (about $1\frac{1}{2}$ lbs/750 g)	1
2 tbsp	vegetable oil	25 mL
3	cloves garlic, chopped	3
2 tbsp	oyster sauce	25 mL
1 tsp	fish or soy sauce	5 mL
$\frac{1}{2}$ tsp	black pepper	2 mL

1. Cut broccoli into florets. Discard tough bottom part of stems, then peel stems and cut crosswise into $\frac{1}{4}$-inch (5 mm) slices.
2. Steam or blanch broccoli for 3 minutes. Rinse with cold water and drain.
3. Heat a wok or large skillet over medium high heat and add oil. Add garlic and stir-fry for 30 seconds.
4. Add broccoli, oyster sauce, fish sauce and pepper and stir-fry for 3 minutes, or until broccoli is heated through.

Variation

Broccoli and Mushrooms with Oyster Sauce: Add $1\frac{1}{2}$ cups (375 mL) sliced fresh shiitake or button mushrooms after garlic and stir-fry for 2 minutes before adding broccoli.

Makes 4 servings

Steaming or blanching the broccoli before a quick stir-fry prevents the florets from overcooking, but if you don't want to partially cook the broccoli ahead, stir-fry for 3 to 4 minutes, or until it is tender-crisp. Chinese broccoli can often be found in Asian stores.

For a vegetarian version, use vegetarian oyster sauce, also available in Asian stores.

Asparagus, snow peas, baby bok choy, zucchini or other vegetables can be used instead of broccoli. These more tender vegetables would not require steaming in advance; just add the raw vegetables to the wok.

Make Ahead

Broccoli can be partially cooked, rinsed with cold water and well drained 3 to 4 hours before stir-frying.

Spicy Eggplant with Tofu

Makes 4 servings

In this recipe, the eggplant is double cooked (in Thailand, it would be roasted over charcoal and the paste would be made using a mortar and pestle). This is a good vegetarian dish if you use soy sauce instead of fish sauce.

1 lb	Asian eggplants (about 2 medium), cut in ½-inch (1 cm) slices	500 g
¼ cup	vegetable oil, divided	50 mL
2	cloves garlic, peeled	2
3	shallots, peeled	3
¼ cup	packed fresh cilantro leaves, stems and roots	50 mL
2½ tsp	coarsely chopped fresh red chilies	12 mL
2 tbsp	fish or soy sauce	25 mL
2 tbsp	lime juice	25 mL
1 tbsp	palm or brown sugar	15 mL
8 oz	firm tofu, cut in ½-inch (1 cm) cubes	250 g
¼ cup	fresh sweet Thai basil leaves	50 mL

1. In a bowl, combine eggplant slices with 2 tbsp (25 mL) vegetable oil. Arrange on a parchment-lined baking sheet. Bake in a preheated 400°F (200°C) oven for 12 minutes, or until tender.
2. Meanwhile, in a food processor or using a mortar and pestle, combine garlic, shallots, cilantro, chilies, fish sauce, lime juice and sugar. Process to make a paste.
3. Heat a wok or large skillet over medium-high heat and add remaining oil. Add paste and cook, stirring, for 1 minute, or until light golden.
4. Add eggplant and tofu and combine. Cover and cook for 2 to 3 minutes, or until tender and hot, stirring gently.
5. Stir in basil.

Spinach with Yellow Bean Sauce

Makes 4 servings

In Thailand, water spinach (also known as morning glory or swamp cabbage) is a popular green that consists of arrow-shaped leaves on hollow stems that stay crisp when cooked. In casual restaurants, it is not uncommon to see your cooked water spinach order being tossed into the air by the cook and (hopefully) caught on a plate by a waiter (who often has his back turned!). It's great dinner theater. When water spinach is not available, cooks use spinach or watercress or a combination. (Do not use the flowering garden variety of morning glory.) This dish is cooked very quickly over high heat. Combining the greens with the seasonings before cooking leaves your hands free to stir-fry quickly.

4 cups	spinach, trimmed	1 L
4 cups	watercress, trimmed	1 L
3	cloves garlic, chopped	3
1 tsp	thinly sliced fresh red chilies	5 mL
1 tbsp	water	15 mL
1 tbsp	yellow bean sauce	15 mL
1 tbsp	fish sauce	15 mL
1 tsp	granulated sugar	5 mL
2 tbsp	vegetable oil	25 mL

1. In a large bowl, combine spinach, watercress, garlic, chilies, water, yellow bean sauce, fish sauce and sugar. Toss to coat greens with seasonings.
2. Heat a wok or large skillet over high heat and add oil. Carefully add seasoned greens and stir-fry for 2 to 3 minutes, or until greens have wilted and are just cooked.

Grilled Corn on the Cob

In markets and on the streets of Thailand, it is common to see grilled corn on the cob. The corn is husked and a portion of the stem is left on to act as a handle.

To grill corn, remove husks and corn silk. Place on a preheated grill or barbecue and turn occasionally for 5 minutes, or until kernels turn golden.

Stir-fried Mixed Vegetables

Makes 6 servings

Practically any combination of vegetables can be stir-fried. The longer a vegetable takes to cook, the smaller the pieces should be (e.g., carrots should be cut in matchsticks or very thinly sliced). Try not to overload the wok, otherwise cooking will be slowed and some vegetables will overcook. You can use just one or two different vegetables if you wish.

2 tbsp	vegetable oil	25 mL
3	cloves garlic, chopped	3
1 tbsp	chopped fresh gingerroot	15 mL
1/2	bunch broccoli (about 8 oz/250 g), cut in small florets	1/2
1	carrot, cut in matchstick pieces	1
1/2	red bell pepper, seeded and cut in bite-size pieces	1/2
1 cup	sliced green beans	250 mL
1 cup	sliced asparagus	250 mL
1 cup	snow peas, trimmed	250 mL
1 cup	quartered fresh mushrooms	250 mL
1/4 cup	vegetable stock or water	50 mL
2 tbsp	soy sauce	25 mL
1 tbsp	oyster sauce	15 mL
1 tsp	sesame oil	5 mL
1 tbsp	sesame seeds, toasted	15 mL
	Fresh cilantro leaves	

1. Heat a large wok or skillet over medium-high heat and add oil. Add garlic and ginger and stir-fry for 30 seconds.
2. Add broccoli, carrot, red pepper, beans, asparagus, snow peas and mushrooms and toss to combine.
3. Add stock and bring to a boil. Cover and cook for 2 minutes, or until vegetables are just tender.
4. Add soy sauce, oyster sauce and sesame oil and cook, stirring, for 30 seconds.
5. Garnish with sesame seeds and cilantro.

Toasting Sesame Seeds

Place sesame seeds in a dry skillet. Place over medium heat and cook for 2 to 3 minutes, stirring occasionally, until golden brown. Tip onto a plate and cool completely. Store toasted sesame seeds in a small container and freeze for up to 4 weeks.

Sweet and Sour Vegetables

Makes 6 servings

Another stir-fried vegetable dish with a sweet-and-sour twist. This is a good dish for entertaining, since all the preparation can be done in advance, leaving just a bit of last-minute cooking. Serve it with other dishes that do not require too much last-minute attention or, better yet, have someone cook with you. For a spicy dish, add 2 tsp (10 mL) chopped fresh red chilies with the other vegetables.

1⁄2 cup	vegetable stock or water	125 mL
1⁄4 cup	ketchup	50 mL
3 tbsp	lime juice	45 mL
2 tbsp	fish sauce	25 mL
1 tbsp	granulated sugar	15 mL
2 tsp	cornstarch	10 mL
2 tbsp	vegetable oil	25 mL
1	onion, thinly sliced	1
3	cloves garlic, chopped	3
1	carrot, thinly sliced	1
1 cup	sliced green beans, cut in 2-inch (5 cm) lengths	250 mL
1⁄2	red bell pepper, seeded and cut in bite-size pieces	1⁄2
1⁄2	yellow bell pepper, seeded and cut in bite-size pieces	1⁄2
2	small zucchini (about 8 oz/250 g total), halved lengthwise and cut in 1⁄4-inch (5 mm) slices	2
1	tomato, cut in 8 wedges	1

1. In a small bowl or measuring cup, combine stock, ketchup, lime juice, fish sauce, sugar and cornstarch.
2. Heat a wok or large skillet over medium-high heat and add oil. Add onion and garlic and stir-fry for 1 minute.
3. Add carrot, beans, peppers and zucchini and stir-fry for 2 minutes.
4. Stir up sauce. Add to vegetables and toss to coat vegetables. Cook, stirring, for 4 minutes, or until vegetables are tender.
5. Add tomato, toss to combine and cook for 1 minute.

Variation

Sweet and Sour Vegetables with Pineapple: Replace vegetable stock with pineapple juice and add 3⁄4 cup (175 mL) fresh or canned pineapple chunks with tomato.

Spicy Tofu with Vegetables

Makes 5 to 6 servings

Vegetarian festivals are celebrated in Thailand, with a large one held in Phuket around October. The number of vegetarian restaurants is also increasing, and diners can request vegetarian dishes in non-vegetarian restaurants.

3 tbsp	vegetable oil, divided	45 mL
12 oz	firm tofu, patted dry, cut in ½-inch (1 cm) cubes	375 g
3	shallots, thinly sliced	3
2	cloves garlic, thinly sliced	2
1	carrot, cut in matchstick pieces	1
½	red bell pepper, seeded and cut in thin strips	½
1 cup	sliced asparagus or green beans, cut in 1-inch (2.5 cm) pieces	250 mL
2 tbsp	soy sauce	25 mL
2 tbsp	lime juice	25 mL
2½ tsp	chopped fresh red chilies	12 mL
2 tsp	granulated sugar	10 mL
½ tsp	black pepper	2 mL

1. Heat a wok or large skillet over medium-high heat and add 2 tbsp (25 mL) oil. Add tofu and stir-fry for 4 minutes, turning carefully, until golden brown. Remove with a slotted spoon and reserve.
2. Add remaining oil to wok. Add shallots and garlic and stir-fry for 1 minute.
3. Add carrot, red pepper and asparagus and stir-fry for 2 minutes.
4. Add soy sauce, lime juice, chilies, sugar and pepper and cook, stirring, for 1 minute.
5. Return tofu to wok and cook for 1 minute, or until combined and heated through.

Deep-fried Tofu

Cut 12 oz (375 g) firm tofu into 1-inch (2.5 cm) cubes. Pat very dry.

In a wok or deep saucepan, heat 1¾ cups (425 mL) vegetable oil to 350°F (180°C). Add tofu in batches and cook for 2 to 3 minutes. Turn and cook for 3 to 4 minutes longer, or until golden brown. Drain on paper towels. Serve with homemade (page 45) or storebought sweet chili sauce.

Serves 3 or 4 as an appetizer or snack.

Quick Tofu with Peanut Sauce

Makes 3 to 4 servings

Tofu can be deep-fried (page 232) or pan-fried, but do not overcook, or it will be chewy.

In this recipe, the tofu is simply stir-fried and tossed with peanut sauce. It is a good last-minute dish.

Instead of cubes, the tofu can be cut in slices ¼ inch (5 mm) thick.

For a strictly vegetarian dish, use soy sauce instead of fish sauce, or season with salt.

This is a rich-tasting dish. Serve it with steamed rice, fresh cucumber slices and shredded lettuce.

3 tbsp	vegetable oil	45 mL
1 lb	firm tofu, cut in ¾-inch (2 cm) cubes	500 g
1 cup	homemade (page 47) or storebought peanut sauce	250 mL
⅓ cup	water (approx.)	75 mL
2 tsp	fish sauce	10 mL
1 ½ tsp	hot chili sauce	7 mL
2 tbsp	lime juice	25 mL
2 tbsp	coarsely chopped fresh cilantro leaves	25 mL

1. Heat a wok or large skillet over medium-high heat and add oil. Add tofu and gently stir-fry for 4 minutes, until golden brown.
2. Add peanut sauce, water, fish sauce and chili sauce. Stir gently to combine just until hot. Stir in lime juice.
3. Serve sprinkled with cilantro.

Variation

Shrimp with Peanut Sauce: Replace tofu with 1 lb (500 g) peeled and deveined shrimp.

Desserts and Beverages

Sticky Rice with Mangoes

Makes 6 servings

Probably the most popular Thai dessert, this is famous throughout the country and a favorite with both Thais and foreigners. On one visit to Thailand, mango season was just starting, so we ordered it every day. This is an easy dessert to make at home, provided the rice has been soaked ahead of time. Once the rice has been covered with the coconut sauce the dessert can sit for up to three hours (before the rice absorbs all the sauce). Make extra sauce if you wish. It is not usually recommended that you refrigerate this dish, but if there is any left over, I have placed plastic wrap directly on the surface, refrigerated it overnight and cut it into squares (like a brownie) for a snack. You decide!

1 ½ cups	white glutinous (sticky) rice	375 mL
2 cups	coconut milk	500 mL
½ cup	granulated sugar	125 mL
½ tsp	salt	2 mL
3	mangoes, peeled and sliced	3

1. In a large bowl, cover rice with at least 2 inches (5 cm) water. Let stand for 3 hours or overnight. Strain rice and place in a conical basket or cheesecloth-lined bamboo basket or sieve. Place over, not touching, boiling water, cover with a lid and steam for 30 to 35 minutes, or until rice is glistening and tender. Make sure water does not boil dry.
2. Meanwhile, in a saucepan, combine coconut milk, sugar and salt. Heat over medium heat, stirring often, until sugar and salt dissolve, about 2 minutes. Remove from heat.
3. Turn cooked rice into a shallow 8- or 9-inch (2 L) square baking dish. Pour three-quarters of coconut milk mixture over rice and, using a fork, stir rice so sauce is mixed through. Cover and let stand for 30 minutes.
4. Serve rice with mango slices and remaining sauce.

Mangoes

Mangoes are becoming increasingly available in North America. Look for them in supermarkets, specialty food shops, Asian and Caribbean stores. If you can, buy the slim, light yellow-skinned mangoes (often called Alfonso), which are more intensely flavored and less fibrous than some others, but any ripe mango will be delicious.

Black Sticky Rice

Makes 6 to 8 servings

1 cup	black glutinous (sticky) rice	250 mL
5 cups	water	1.25 L
3/4 cup	coconut milk	175 mL
1/3 cup	palm, brown or granulated sugar	75 mL
Garnish		
1/3 cup	thick coconut milk (page 18)	75 mL
1/2 cup	diced fresh mango or pineapple	125 mL

1. Rinse rice with cold water. Place in a saucepan with water. Bring to a boil over medium-high heat, stirring frequently to prevent sticking. Reduce heat to low and simmer, uncovered, for 35 to 40 minutes, stirring occasionally, until rice is tender and most of water has been absorbed.
2. Add coconut milk and sugar and cook for 6 to 8 minutes, or until hot and slightly thickened.
3. Serve warm or cold with thick coconut milk spooned on top and garnished with mango.

Seafood Dinner

Mussels in Coconut Broth (page 184)
Steamed Fish Pudding (page 218)
Stir-fried Mixed Vegetables (page 230)
Jasmine Rice (page 114)
Grilled Fish with Spicy Tomato Sauce (page 179)
Black Sticky Rice (page 237)

Black sticky rice, also known as black glutinous rice, is mostly used in sweet dishes that are served as a snack, dessert or even for breakfast (although some Western chefs are now serving it as part of the main course and even in appetizer dishes). It has a slightly chewy texture similar to red or brown rice and our wild rice. Some cooks soak it and steam it like white glutinous rice. Others simply rinse it, cook it in simmering water until tender and then stir in sugar and coconut milk. (In Thai markets, black sticky rice is topped with sweetened and salted coconut milk and sold in plastic bags.)

Make Ahead

Rice can be cooked, covered and kept at room temperature for up to 6 hours.

Coconut Ice Cream

Makes 6 servings

This ice cream is made with coconut milk instead of eggs and dairy products. In Thailand, ice cream vendors cycle through the markets with their frozen chests of goodies — always a welcome treat in the intense heat and humidity. Top with Coconut Caramel Sauce and toasted coconut (page 245) or chopped peanuts.

Make Ahead

Ice cream can be packed into a freezer container and frozen for 2 weeks.

3 cups	coconut milk	750 mL
3/4 cup	granulated sugar	175 mL
1/2 tsp	salt	2 mL

1. In a saucepan, combine coconut milk, sugar and salt. Place over medium heat and bring to a low boil, stirring until sugar dissolves.
2. Pour into a bowl and refrigerate for 2 to 3 hours, or until very cold. For faster chilling, place over a bowl of ice water and stir frequently.
3. Transfer to an ice cream maker and freeze according to manufacturer's directions or freeze in a metal container until firm, stirring 4 to 5 times during freezing process.

Coconut Caramel Sauce

In a saucepan, combine 1 cup (250 mL) granulated sugar and 1/4 cup (50 mL) water. Bring to a boil over medium-high heat and cook, without stirring, for 5 to 6 minutes, or until mixture starts to caramelize. After mixture starts to color, swirl pan gently for even coloring and cook for 2 to 3 minutes, or until golden, being careful not to burn caramel. Remove pan from heat.

Carefully pour 1 cup (250 mL) coconut milk into saucepan (mixture may seize in a lump). Return to medium heat and cook, stirring, until caramel has dissolved.

Sauce can be covered and refrigerated for up to 2 days. Rewarm slowly in a microwave or saucepan before serving

Makes about 1 cup (250 mL).

Crisp Red Rubies

2	8-oz (227 g) cans whole water chestnuts, drained	2
1 tsp	red food coloring	5 mL
1 1/2 cups	cold water	375 mL
1 cup	coconut milk	250 mL
1/2 cup	granulated sugar	125 mL
1/4 tsp	salt	1 mL
3/4 cup	cornstarch or tapioca starch	175 mL
1 cup	crushed ice (approx.)	250 mL

1. Cut each water chestnut into 4 or 8 pieces. Place in a bowl that will not discolor. Sprinkle with food coloring. Let stand for a few minutes.
2. Add cold water and soak water chestnuts for 2 to 8 hours, or until color has been absorbed. Drain well.
3. Meanwhile, in a saucepan, prepare a sauce by combining coconut milk, sugar and salt and place over medium heat. Heat to below boiling, stirring to dissolve sugar. Remove from heat.
4. Place cornstarch in a plastic bag (or in a shallow baking pan). Add water chestnuts and coat with cornstarch. Place in a sieve and shake to remove any excess.
5. Bring a saucepan of water (enough to cover water chestnuts) to a boil. Add water chestnuts and cook in 2 or 3 batches for 2 minutes, or until they float to the surface. With a strainer or slotted spoon, transfer to a bowl of cold water. Drain just before serving.
6. To serve, place some crushed ice in serving dishes and top with "rubies" and coconut sauce.

Crushed Ice

Place ice cubes in strong plastic bags and roll firmly with a rolling pin. Empty into a bowl and keep frozen until serving time.

Makes 8 servings

This is an unusual dessert. For smaller "rubies," cut the water chestnuts into smaller pieces. Usually red food coloring is used, but I have also seen a few cooks soak the water chestnuts in pomegranate juice overnight.

This recipe can easily be halved.

Make Ahead

Water chestnuts can be soaked and refrigerated overnight. Cooked water chestnuts can be kept in cold water in refrigerator for 2 hours. (Do not refrigerate longer, as rubies may stick together.) Sauce can be made and refrigerated overnight. If it firms, gently reheat over low heat or in a microwave.

Caramel Lime Bananas

Makes 4 to 6 servings

There are at least twenty varieties of bananas in Thailand, and they are used in both savory and sweet dishes. At floating markets, boats laden with bunches of bananas are a common sight. Often used to line the edge of fields, most parts of the banana tree are used. The oval purple flower buds are used in cooking, for animal food and in flower arrangements. Leaves are used for wrappings and as a base for steaming as well as for animal food. The stalks are used for animal food and ropes. Although not truly Thai, this is a simple, quick dessert that can also be served as a snack. Select bananas that are ripe but firm. Serve with ginger or coconut ice cream (page 238).

1/4 cup	butter, melted	50 mL
1/3 cup	lime juice	75 mL
4	regular bananas, or 8 small sugar bananas	4
1/3 cup	palm or brown sugar	75 mL
2 tbsp	shredded coconut, toasted (page 245)	25 mL

1. In a small bowl, combine butter and lime juice. Pour into an 8-inch (2 L) square non-metallic baking dish (or another dish just big enough to hold bananas in a single layer).
2. Add bananas to baking dish and turn to coat all sides (cut regular bananas into 2-inch/5 cm lengths). Sprinkle sugar over bananas.
3. Bake in a preheated 400°F (200°C) oven for 15 to 17 minutes, or until mixture starts to bubble and bananas are just tender.
4. Sprinkle with coconut before serving.

Quick Ginger Ice Cream

Soften 2 cups (500 mL) vanilla ice cream or frozen yogurt. Stir in 1/3 cup (75 mL) chopped candied ginger and 1/4 tsp (1 mL) ground ginger. Return to freezer.

Makes 4 to 6 servings.

Bananas in Coconut Milk

Makes 4 to 6 servings

A popular Thai dessert, this is usually served warm. If available, use the short sugar bananas, otherwise use slightly underripe regular bananas. In Thailand, we also had versions of this dessert that included bananas and pumpkin or just pumpkin.

3 cups	coconut milk	750 mL
1/2 cup	granulated, palm or brown sugar	125 mL
1/4 tsp	salt	1 mL
4	regular bananas, or 8 small sugar bananas	4

1. In a saucepan, combine coconut milk, sugar and salt. Bring to a gentle boil over medium heat, stirring to dissolve sugar.
2. Cut bananas into 2-inch (5 cm) lengths on a slight diagonal. (If you are using chubby regular bananas, cut them in half lengthwise before cutting into pieces.) Add to milk, reduce heat and simmer for 3 minutes. Spoon into serving bowls.

Variation

Sweet Potato in Coconut Milk: Replace bananas with 2 cups (250 mL) sweet potato or butternut squash cut in 1/2-inch (1 cm) pieces. Simmer for 10 to 12 minutes, or until just tender.

Tropical Trifle

Makes 8 to 10 servings

Although not a typical Thai dish, this is a very appealing dessert with a creamy texture and coconut flavor. It is perfect for potlucks and buffets, and I have even enjoyed it for breakfast. Angel cake makes a very light trifle, but pound cake will also work. Tropical fruit can be replaced by blueberries, raspberries and/or sliced strawberries.

Make Ahead

Custard can be made a day ahead, covered and refrigerated. If it is too thick, thin with a little milk before assembling.

1/3 cup	cornstarch	75 mL
1/3 cup	granulated sugar	75 mL
1/4 tsp	salt	1 mL
1 1/2 cups	milk, divided	375 mL
1 1/2 cups	coconut milk	375 mL
2	egg yolks	2
1/3 cup	coconut liqueur or coconut milk	75 mL
1	small angel cake (about 12 oz/375 g)	1
1/2 cup	mango juice	125 mL
2 1/2 cups	chopped pineapple, mango, papaya, or a combination	625 mL
	Fresh mint sprigs	

1. To prepare custard, in a saucepan, combine cornstarch, sugar, salt and 1/2 cup (125 mL) milk. Whisk until cornstarch is mixed in. Add remaining milk and coconut milk.
2. Place over medium heat and bring to a simmer, stirring constantly, until mixture has thickened. Remove from heat.
3. In a bowl, combine egg yolks and 1/2 cup (125 mL) hot mixture. Return to saucepan and return to heat. Cook for 2 minutes. Remove from heat and stir in liqueur.
4. Pour custard into a bowl. Cover surface directly with plastic wrap (to prevent a skin from forming) and cool in refrigerator for 4 hours. If custard is too thick, thin with 3 tbsp (45 mL) milk.
5. To assemble trifle, tear cake into 1-inch (2.5 cm) pieces and spread on a baking sheet or other flat pan. Sprinkle with mango juice.
6. Spoon some custard into bottom of a large 10-cup (2.5 L) glass serving bowl. Alternate layers of cake, fruit and sauce, ending with sauce. Cover and refrigerate for 4 hours before serving.
7. Serve garnished with mint sprigs.

Variation

Coconut Custard: Omit cake. After custard thickens, spoon into individual serving dishes. Cover and refrigerate until cold. Serve with diced fresh fruit.

Makes 6 to 8 servings.

Fresh Fruit Platter

Makes 8 servings

In Thailand, fresh fruit is the typical finale to a Thai meal. Mangoes, pineapples, papayas, mangosteens, custard apples, dragonfruit, lychee fruit, rambutans longans, watermelons, cantaloupes, starfruit and bananas are served on their own (often beautifully carved and presented in a banana leaf-lined basket) or accompanied by a sauce. Select the best fresh tropical fruit available, or supplement with berries such as raspberries, blueberries or strawberries. Canned or bottled mango juice is available in most supermarkets.

Make Ahead

Fruit can be arranged, covered with plastic wrap and refrigerated for up to 4 hours. Sauce can be prepared, covered and refrigerated at the same time.

1/2	pineapple, peeled, halved, cored and sliced lengthwise	1/2
1	dragonfruit, peeled and sliced	1
1	papaya, halved, peeled, seeded and sliced lengthwise	1
1/4	small watermelon, peeled and sliced	1/4
1	mango, peeled, pitted and sliced	1
2	starfruit, sliced	2

Mango Sauce

1/3 cup	mango or pineapple juice	75 mL
2 tbsp	lime juice	25 mL
1 tsp	granulated sugar	5 mL

1. Arrange fruit attractively on a large platter.
2. In a small bowl, whisk together mango juice, lime juice and sugar. Drizzle over fruit just before serving.

Noodles and a Salad

Breakfast Noodles with Seafood (page 112)

Green Papaya Salad (page 70)

Fresh Fruit Salad (page 78) or Fresh Fruit Platter (page 244)

Roasted Pineapple

Makes 5 to 6 servings

Fresh pineapple is available year round in Thailand. Fried pineapple is also a favorite, but roasting it gives the cook a break from stovetop cooking. Serve with coconut or ginger ice cream (pages 238 and 240).

1	pineapple, peeled, cored and cut in 6 to 8 wedges	1
2 tbsp	chopped fresh gingerroot	25 mL
2 tsp	grated lime zest	10 mL
1/4 cup	brown sugar	50 mL
1/4 cup	lime juice	50 mL
2 tbsp	butter	25 mL
3 tbsp	chopped cashews or coconut, toasted	45 mL
2 tbsp	shredded fresh mint leaves	25 mL

1. In a shallow baking dish, arrange pineapple wedges in a single layer. Sprinkle with ginger, lime zest, sugar and lime juice. Dot with butter.
2. Bake in a preheated 425°F (210°C) oven for 20 minutes, or until turning golden.
3. Remove from oven. Let stand for 6 to 8 minutes, spooning juices over fruit.
4. Transfer to serving dishes and sprinkle with chopped nuts and shredded mint.

Toasting Coconut

Place coconut on a baking sheet. Bake in a preheated 300°F (150°C) oven for 8 to 10 minutes, or until coconut is lightly colored. Stir once or twice to ensure even toasting. Cool on pan. Coconut can be toasted, cooled, packaged in a freezer bag and frozen for up to 2 weeks.

Mango Upside-down Cake

Makes 10 to 12 servings

Cakes are not a Thai tradition, yet cookies, squares, cakes, sweet buns and more (including the popular little desserts made from soy bean paste and intricately shaped to resemble tropical fruits) are often sold in supermarkets and bakeries.

Serve this with Coconut Caramel Sauce (page 238) or embellished with mango ice or coconut ice cream (page 238).

Make Ahead

Cake is best served the day it is made but can be baked several hours ahead of time.

1/3 cup	butter, melted	75 mL
3/4 cup	brown sugar	175 mL
2	large mangoes, peeled	2
2 tbsp	chopped fresh gingerroot	25 mL
2 tsp	grated lemon or lime zest	10 mL
1/2 cup	butter, softened	125 mL
2/3 cup	granulated sugar	150 mL
2	eggs	2
1 tsp	vanilla	5 mL
1 1/2 cups	all-purpose flour	375 mL
1 1/2 tsp	baking powder	7 mL
1 tsp	baking soda	5 mL
1/2 tsp	ground ginger	2 mL
1/4 tsp	salt	1 mL
3/4 cup	buttermilk, sour milk or unflavored yogurt	175 mL

1. Pour melted butter into a deep 9-inch (1.5 L) round cake pan. Sprinkle with brown sugar.
2. Cut mango sections from each side of mango and cut into thin slices. Arrange overlapping in pan in a sunburst pattern. Cut any pulp remaining next to seed into small pieces and arrange in center. Sprinkle with fresh ginger and lemon zest.
3. In a large bowl, cream butter and granulated sugar until light. Beat in eggs and vanilla.
4. In a separate bowl, combine flour, baking powder, baking soda, ground ginger and salt.
5. Add dry ingredients to creamed mixture alternately with buttermilk, making three dry and two liquid additions, scraping down sides of bowl as necessary. Spoon batter over mango.
6. Bake in a preheated 350°F (180°C) oven for 40 minutes, or until a cake tester comes out clean. Remove from oven and let stand for 5 minutes. Loosen edges with a knife and invert onto a serving platter. Serve cake warm or at room temperature.

Baked Coconut Custard

Makes 6 servings

Many Thai desserts contain coconut milk, sugar and eggs and are quite sweet and rich. Custards show up in several forms — simply served in a cup, steamed in pumpkin or banana leaves, sliced into squares or factory baked in metal tins. Duck eggs and palm sugar are predominantly used, and some desserts are seasoned with pandanus leaves or jasmine essence. This simple dessert makes a wonderful finale to a lighter meal.

Make Ahead

Custards can be baked, refrigerated until cold, then covered with plastic wrap up to 2 days ahead. Caramelize just before serving.

3	eggs	3
1/3 cup	brown or granulated sugar	75 mL
1/4 cup	sweetened shredded coconut	50 mL
2 cups	coconut milk	500 mL
Topping		
1 tbsp	granulated or brown sugar	15 mL
1/2 cup	diced fresh mango or pineapple (optional)	125 mL

1. In a bowl, whisk together eggs and brown sugar. Stir in coconut and coconut milk.
2. Ladle mixture into 6 lightly greased 1/2-cup (125 mL) ramekins. Set ramekins in a larger baking pan. Pour hot water into pan to a depth of 3/4 inch (2 cm).
3. Bake in a preheated 350°F (180°C) oven for 30 to 35 minutes, or until custard is just set and no longer jiggly (test with tip of sharp knife — knife should come out clean). Remove custards from water and cool on a wire rack.
4. To serve, sprinkle surface with granulated sugar. Place custards under a preheated broiler, 4 inches (10 cm) from heat, for 2 minutes, or until just caramelized. Watch closely to prevent burning. Let stand for 2 minutes before serving.
5. Spoon diced mango, if using, over custards.

Coconut Pancakes

2	eggs	2
3/4 cup	coconut milk	175 mL
1/3 cup	water	75 mL
3/4 cup	rice flour	175 mL
1/4 cup	all-purpose flour	50 mL
1 tbsp	granulated sugar	15 mL
2 tbsp	sweetened shredded coconut	25 mL
1 tbsp	vegetable oil or melted butter (approx.)	15 mL
Filling		
1 cup	diced fresh papaya	250 mL
1 tbsp	lime juice	15 mL
2 tsp	granulated sugar	10 mL

1. In a food processor or by hand, combine eggs, coconut milk, water, both flours and sugar. Pulse to combine thoroughly, scraping down sides of bowl, but do not overmix. Transfer mixture to a bowl and stir in coconut.
2. Heat an 8-inch (20 cm) nonstick skillet over medium-high heat and brush lightly with oil.
3. Pour a scant 1/4 cup (50 mL) batter into pan and swirl around pan. Cook for 40 seconds, or until browned on underside. Turn and cook second side for 20 seconds. Slide pancake onto a plate or tray and keep warm while making remaining pancakes. (To keep pancakes warm, cover with parchment paper and place in a 200°F/100°C oven.)
4. In a bowl, stir together papaya, lime juice and sugar.
5. Place about 1 tbsp (15 mL) filling on one quarter of each pancake. Fold each pancake in half, then in quarters.

Makes 4 servings

Pak Khlong market is a large flower market in Bangkok. Buckets of orchids, lotus flowers, marigolds, roses and greenery line the sidewalks. Since the market is open round the clock, food is constantly being prepared — including coconut pancakes. Some are bite size and topped with sesame seeds, coconut, green onions or cilantro. Some pancakes are made wafer thin, rolled into cones and then packaged in cellophane. This recipe is more crêpe than pancake. Just a squeeze of lime juice and a sprinkling of sugar is good, but any kind of fruit (or even your favorite fruit jam) can be used for the filling.

Toasted Coconut Shortbread

Makes about 6½ to 7 dozen

In Thailand, coconut palms wave in the breeze throughout the countryside. The leaves are used as roofing material, and all parts of the fruit (often harvested by specially trained monkeys) are used. The young fruit has a jelly-like flesh that is used in some dishes. In markets, the tops are removed and the coconuts are sold with a straw, because the juice is a cooling beverage. The meat of more mature coconuts is used to make coconut milk (page 18), as well as being shredded and packaged. Truckloads of coconut husks make their way to factories to be turned into ropes, mats, baskets, serving utensils, jewelry and ornaments. It is also used for fuel.

Make Ahead

Cookies can be cooled, packaged and frozen for up to 3 weeks.

2 cups	salted butter, softened	500 mL
1 cup	granulated sugar	250 mL
2 tsp	vanilla extract	10 mL
3 cups	all-purpose flour	750 mL
½ cup	rice flour	125 mL
½ cup	cornstarch	125 mL
¾ cup	medium unsweetened coconut, toasted (page 245)	175 mL
1½ tbsp	granulated sugar	22 mL

1. In a large bowl, cream butter and granulated sugar until light and fluffy. Beat in vanilla.
2. In a separate bowl, combine flours, cornstarch and coconut. Add to butter mixture and mix until blended. Shape dough into a flattened disc. Wrap in plastic wrap and refrigerate dough for 30 minutes if dough is too soft to roll.
3. On a floured surface, roll out dough until ¼ inch (5 mm) thick, dusting lightly with flour as necessary. Cut dough into rounds with a 2-inch (5 cm) cookie cutter dipped in flour. Reroll dough as necessary, without adding too much flour. Place cookies on parchment-lined baking sheets. Sprinkle lightly with sugar.
4. Bake cookies in a preheated 300°F (150°C) oven for 25 minutes, or until just beginning to turn golden. Cool on wire racks.

Mini Banana Pancakes

Makes 24 to 28 pancakes

Every year, Nay Durant goes to Thailand to visit her family in Uttaradit, and when she comes back she shares her travel tips with me. I made these little pancakes to nibble on while we chatted about all things Thai. Serve them for breakfast with sausages or as a dessert with roasted pineapple (page 245), ice cream or fresh fruit. To satisfy my sweet tooth, I even drizzle them with maple syrup or warmed sweetened condensed milk and chocolate sauce. These are best served right from the pan, but I have also frozen them. The flavor resembles banana bread.

Make Ahead

Pancakes can be refrigerated or frozen. To reheat, arrange in a single layer on a parchment-lined baking sheet and place in a preheated 375°F (190°C) oven for 4 to 10 minutes, or until hot.

2	ripe bananas (about 12 oz/375 g total)	2
1/2 cup	coconut milk	125 mL
2 tbsp	water	25 mL
1	egg	1
2 tbsp	butter, melted	25 mL
1/2 cup	all-purpose flour	125 mL
1/4 cup	rice flour	50 mL
2 tbsp	granulated sugar	25 mL
1/2 tsp	baking powder	2 mL
Pinch	salt	Pinch
1 tbsp	vegetable oil	15 mL

1. In a food processor, puree bananas (you should have about 3/4 cup/175 mL). Add coconut milk, water, egg and melted butter and pulse to combine. To prevent discoloration, do not let mixture stand.
2. In a bowl, stir together both flours, sugar, baking powder and salt. Add to banana mixture and pulse to combine. Scrape down sides of bowl and pulse once more. Pour mixture into a bowl.
3. Heat a large nonstick skillet over medium heat and brush with oil. Add batter, using about 1 1/2 tbsp (22 mL) per pancake (these need to be cooked in batches). Cook pancakes for 2 minutes, or until tops are bubbly and bottoms are golden brown. Gently turn pancakes and cook for 2 minutes, or until golden. Transfer to a parchment-lined baking sheet and keep warm in a preheated 200°F (100°C) oven. Repeat using remaining batter. Serve hot, warm or at room temperature.

White Lotus

2	bananas, cut up	2
1 cup	unflavored yogurt, rice milk or soy milk	250 mL
1/2 cup	coconut milk	125 mL
1/2 cup	apple juice or ginger ale	125 mL
3 tbsp	lime juice	45 mL
2 tbsp	liquid honey	25 mL
1/4 cup	coconut liqueur (optional)	50 mL
	Thin lime slices	

1. In a blender, combine bananas, yogurt, coconut milk, apple juice, lime juice, honey and liqueur, if using. Process until smooth.
2. Pour into tall glasses filled with ice. Garnish with a lime twist on a long skewer and serve with a long spoon.

Makes 2 servings

In Thailand, spas and hotels offer a number of enticing-sounding cocktails and beverages. Most of the time I would order based on the name alone. Some of the non-alcoholic drinks offered at the Royal Princess Larn Luang in Bangkok, for example, included Fresh Complexion, Green Forest, Potassium Power and Beauty Express, to name just a few. This is my version of the White Lotus. It is a combination smoothie and fancy drink. At poolside it is often served in hollowed-out coconuts or pineapples.

Make Ahead

Drink can be made 2 hours ahead, covered and refrigerated. Stir well before serving.

Tropical Smoothie

Makes 6 servings (about 6 cups/1.5 L)

A refreshing drink for breakfast, brunch or a snack. Replace any of the fruit with other favorites such as strawberries or blueberries. Rice milk is available in supermarkets and health food stores.

1 cup	mango pieces	250 mL
1 cup	papaya pieces	250 mL
1 cup	pineapple chunks	250 mL
1 cup	rice, soy or regular milk	250 mL
1 cup	unflavored yogurt	250 mL
1/2 cup	mango or pineapple juice	125 mL
2 tbsp	liquid honey	25 mL
6	lime slices	6

1. In a blender, combine mango, papaya, pineapple, milk, yogurt, juice and honey. Blend until smooth.
2. Pour into glasses. Garnish with lime.

Samui Seabreeze

2 cups	pineapple juice	500 mL
1 cup	mango or orange juice	250 mL
1 cup	apple juice	250 mL
1/2 cup	lime juice	125 mL
1 cup	ginger ale	250 mL
	Pineapple slices	

1. In a large pitcher, combine pineapple juice, mango juice, apple juice and lime juice.
2. Just before serving, stir in ginger ale.
3. Pour into tall glasses filled with ice cubes. Garnish with pineapple slices speared with a long toothpick or skewer.

Variations

Sparkling Samui Seabreeze: Add 1/2 cup (125 mL) — more or less — Prosecco or sparkling white wine to each glass.

Last-minute Seabreeze: In a large pitcher, combine 1 can (12 oz/341 mL) defrosted frozen pineapple juice concentrate and 1 can (12 oz/341 mL) defrosted frozen limeade concentrate. Add 7 cups (1.75 L) cold water. Pour into tall glasses filled with ice.
Makes 8 to 10 servings.

Makes 6 servings (about 6 cups/1.5 L)

Koh Samui is a tiny island in the Gulf of Thailand. The beaches entice tourists from all over the world. It has long been a favorite with backpackers, but now luxury resorts offer stylish seclusion (here as well as elsewhere in Thailand). Many of these facilities include spas, specialty restaurants with impressive wine cellars, bathing pools strewn with frangipani and orchids, and service, service, service. Once they get there, many guests are reluctant to leave and just loll around the resort. Refreshing beverages and specialty drinks like this one are everywhere.

Make Ahead

Make drink without adding ginger ale. Cover and refrigerate for several hours or overnight.

Lemongrass Tea

6	stalks lemongrass, white part only, cut in 2-inch (5 cm) pieces, crushed	6
1 1/2 tbsp	coarsely chopped fresh gingerroot	22 mL
4	strips lime or lemon zest	4
1/4 cup	fresh mint leaves	50 mL
2 tbsp	liquid honey or granulated sugar	25 mL
4 cups	water	1 L
	Fresh mint leaves	

1. In a saucepan, combine lemongrass, ginger, lime zest, mint, honey and water. Bring to a boil. Reduce heat and simmer for 10 minutes. Let stand for 30 minutes.
2. Strain tea into a pitcher. Cover and refrigerate for 2 hours, or until cold.
3. Pour into tall glasses filled with ice. Garnish with fresh mint.

Flavored Water

The Chedi Hotel in Chiang Mai served this simple flavored water in a tall, slender glass pitcher. Just the appearance was refreshing.

Place lime slices and diagonally cut carrots in a clear pitcher. Fill pitcher with ice and water. (Sliced cucumbers and fresh mint or basil sprigs also make a refreshing combination.)

Makes 4 servings (about 3 1/2 cups/ 875 mL)

A thirst-quencher in hot and humid weather. Use a rolling pin, heavy knife or meat mallet to crush the lemongrass and release its flavor. For the strips of lime zest, use a vegetable peeler. For a soothing hot tea, pour into mugs after simmering and straining.

Make Ahead

Tea can be made and refrigerated for up to 2 days before serving.

Iced Coffee

Makes 1 to 2 servings

At street and market stalls, beverages are sold in plastic bags fitted with straws. Shoppers walk along with their beverages, sipping as they go. Even scooter riders can often be seen sipping while waiting for one of the lengthy traffic lights to change.

In restaurants, iced coffee and tea are served in glass mugs or tall glasses. In the early morning the beverage may be served hot, but as the day heats up, iced drinks are preferred.

Dairy products are rarely available, so it is not uncommon to have tea and coffee served with evaporated milk and sugar. Sweetened condensed milk is a good substitute.

Thai coffee and tea can be difficult to find here. Use a strong roasted and brewed coffee or espresso in this shortcut version. Adjust the sweetness using more or less milk. Freeze any extra sweetened condensed milk.

1 cup	hot strong coffee	250 mL
2 tbsp	sweetened condensed milk	25 mL

1. In a measuring cup or heatproof pitcher, combine coffee and milk.
2. Pour into tall glasses filled with ice cubes or crushed ice.

Variation

Iced Tea: In a measuring cup or tea pot, combine 2 tbsp (25 mL) black tea leaves with 1½ cups (375 mL) boiling water. Let steep for 4 minutes. Strain tea and stir in 2 tbsp (25 mL) sweetened condensed milk. Pour into tall glasses filled with ice cubes or crushed ice.

Makes 2 servings.

Snacks and Desserts

Cold Watermelon Soup (page 262)
Ripe Mango Salsa (page 264)
Galloping Horses (page 32)
Coconut Dumplings (page 30)
Spring Rolls with Pork and Shrimp (page 35)
Thai Potstickers (page 36)
Grilled Skewered Shrimp (page 38)
Tropical Trifle (page 243)
Fresh Fruit Platter (page 244)
Toasted Coconut Shortbread (page 250)
Iced Tea or Coffee (page 258)

Beyond Thai

Vegetable Curry Rolls

Makes 30 pastries

An adaptation of traditional Thai curry puffs, with a filling similar to vegetable samosas. Using phyllo pastry makes these easy to assemble, and baking replaces the usual deep-frying. For a vegetarian version, replace the fish sauce with soy sauce.

Make Ahead

Rolls can be baked, cooled, packaged tightly and frozen for up to 3 weeks. To heat, place frozen on a parchment-lined baking sheet and bake in a preheated 300°F (150°C) oven for 15 to 18 minutes, or until hot throughout.

1 tbsp	vegetable oil	15 mL
2	cloves garlic, finely chopped	2
1	onion, chopped	1
1 1/2 cups	diced potato	375 mL
1 cup	diced carrot	250 mL
1/4 cup	water	50 mL
1/2 cup	diced red bell pepper	125 mL
1/2 cup	green peas	125 mL
2 tbsp	chopped fresh cilantro leaves	25 mL
2 tbsp	fish or soy sauce	25 mL
1 tbsp	brown sugar	15 mL
1 tsp	curry powder	5 mL
1/2 tsp	hot chili sauce	2 mL
10	sheets phyllo pastry	10
1/4 cup	vegetable or olive oil	50 mL

1. In a wok or large skillet, heat oil over medium-high heat. Add garlic, onion, potato and carrot. Cook for 2 minutes, stirring.
2. Add water. Cover and cook for 4 to 5 minutes, or until vegetables are almost tender.
3. Add red pepper, peas, cilantro, fish sauce, sugar, curry powder and chili sauce. Cook for 4 to 5 minutes, stirring frequently, until vegetables are tender and moisture has evaporated. Transfer to a bowl to cool.
4. To assemble, cut stack of phyllo crosswise into three equal pieces. Working with one or two pieces of pastry at a time (keep remainder covered to prevent drying), place pastry on a flat work surface. Place a full tablespoon of filling about 1 inch (2.5 cm) from bottom narrow edge and sides of pastry. Fold bottom of pastry over filling and fold in long sides. Roll up pastry to form a cigar shape. Place on a parchment-lined baking sheet. Brush lightly with oil. Continue with remaining pastry and filling.
5. Bake pastries in a preheated 400°F (200°C) oven for 15 to 18 minutes, or until golden and crisp. Serve warm or at room temperature.

Last-minute Guacamole

1/4 cup	chopped fresh cilantro leaves	50 mL
3 tbsp	lime juice	45 mL
1 tsp	fish sauce	5 mL
1/2 tsp	chopped fresh red chilies	2 mL
1/2 tsp	granulated or brown sugar	2 mL
2	ripe avocados	2

1. In a bowl, combine cilantro, lime juice, fish sauce, chilies and sugar.
2. Cut avocados in half, remove pits and peel. Add to bowl and mash to combine ingredients well. Taste and adjust seasonings if necessary.

Thai Flavor Accents

Last-Minute Guacamole (page 261) with Shrimp Crackers (page 28)

Homestyle Thai Meatloaf (page 272)

Breakfast Mashed Potatoes (page 275)

Cabbage and Carrot Slaw (page 265)

Baked Coconut Custard (page 248)

Makes 2 to 4 servings

Guacamole certainly isn't Thai, but while testing recipes for this book, I realized that a few avocados were at their peak – and I was hungry! Since I had all the Thai ingredients out, I made this for my lunch and ate it with a plate of leftover cooked and raw vegetables on one of our hottest days of the year. I almost thought I was back in Thailand!

Make Ahead

Best made just prior to serving, this can also be made ahead. Cover surface directly with plastic wrap and refrigerate for up to 4 hours. Let stand at room temperature for 15 minutes before serving.

Shrimp Cocktail

Makes 5 to 6 servings

Thais grill a lot of shrimp, so it is easy to transform a traditional shrimp cocktail. Make extra sauce for guests who wish to add more.

3 cups	shredded iceberg lettuce	750 mL
1 tbsp	chopped fresh cilantro leaves	15 mL
3⁄4 cup	grated English cucumber (optional)	175 mL
30	grilled large shrimp (page 38)	30
1⁄3 cup	sweet chili sauce (page 45)	75 mL
2 tbsp	lime juice	25 mL
1	lime, cut in wedges	1

1. In a bowl, combine lettuce, cilantro and cucumber, if using. Arrange on individual serving plates or in martini glasses. Arrange shrimp over lettuce.
2. In a small bowl, combine chili sauce and lime juice and drizzle over shrimp.
3. Garnish each serving with a lime wedge.

Cold Watermelon Soup

Makes 5 to 6 servings

Although watermelon is served at the end of many Thai meals, chilled soups are rarely seen. However, this soup makes a refreshing starter, especially in hot, humid weather. Serve it really cold. It also makes a refreshing dessert or tall drink.

Make Ahead

Soup can be covered and refrigerated a day ahead. Stir well before serving.

4 cups	watermelon pieces (preferably seedless)	1 L
1⁄2 cup	lychee, guava or apple juice	125 mL
1 tbsp	lime juice	15 mL
1 tbsp	liquid honey or maple syrup	15 mL
1⁄2 cup	diced watermelon	125 mL
2 tbsp	shredded fresh sweet Thai basil or mint leaves	25 mL

1. In a blender or food processor, combine watermelon pieces, fruit juice, lime juice and honey. Blend until smooth. Chill.
2. To serve, place a spoonful of diced watermelon in serving bowls or glass mugs. Stir soup and pour over fruit.
3. Garnish with basil.

Sweet Potato Soup with Corn

2 tbsp	vegetable oil	25 mL
5	shallots, chopped	5
3	cloves garlic, chopped	3
2	stalks celery, chopped	2
2 tbsp	chopped fresh gingerroot	25 mL
2 tsp	red curry paste (page 196)	10 mL
6 cups	diced sweet potato	1.5 L
2	pears, peeled, cored and chopped	2
5 cups	chicken or vegetable stock	1.25 L
1 cup	coconut milk	250 mL
1 cup	corn kernels	250 mL
1 ½ tbsp	lime juice	22 mL
1 tbsp	fish sauce	15 mL
2 tbsp	chopped fresh cilantro leaves	25 mL
1	green onion, chopped	1

1. In a large saucepan, heat oil over medium heat. Add shallots, garlic, celery and ginger and stir-fry for 4 minutes, or until softened. Add curry paste and cook, stirring, for 45 seconds.
2. Add sweet potato, pears and stock. Bring to a boil, reduce heat, cover and cook for 25 minutes, or until tender.
3. Add coconut milk and cook gently for 5 minutes. Puree with an immersion blender or in a food processor until smooth.
4. Return to heat and add corn. Cook for 4 minutes.
5. Stir in lime juice and fish sauce. Taste and adjust seasonings if necessary.
6. Serve garnished with cilantro and green onion.

Makes 8 to 10 servings

This lovely combination of vegetables with Thai flavors would be a great addition to any winter holiday menu. Asian pears can be used. Corn kernels add texture to an otherwise velvety soup. Unlike most Thai soups, this one can be pureed and frozen.

Make Ahead

Soup can be covered and refrigerated for up to 2 days or frozen for up to 4 weeks.

Chicken Tidbits

Makes 4 to 5 appetizer servings

Chicken morsels wrapped in fresh pandanus leaves and deep-fried is a very popular Thai dish. The leaves act as packaging and add flavor. Since fresh pandanus leaves are difficult to find here, the alternative is to bake the seasoned chicken in the oven.

1 1/2 lbs	chicken breasts, cut in 1-inch (2.5 cm) pieces	750 g
3 tbsp	chopped fresh cilantro leaves	45 mL
2	cloves garlic, minced	2
2 tsp	finely chopped fresh gingerroot	10 mL
1/2 tsp	black pepper	2 mL
3 tbsp	oyster sauce	45 mL
1 tsp	sesame oil	5 mL
1 tbsp	sesame seeds, toasted (page 230)	15 mL

1. Place chicken pieces in a bowl. Add cilantro, garlic, ginger, pepper, oyster sauce and sesame oil. Mix thoroughly to coat chicken.
2. Place chicken in a small baking dish (an 8-inch/2 L square baking dish works well) and cover.
3. Bake in a preheated 350°F (180°C) oven for 30 minutes, or until chicken is cooked.
4. Serve chicken sprinkled with sesame seeds.

Ripe Mango Salsa

Makes 1 1/2 cups (375 mL)

When mangoes are at their peak, make the most of them. Serve this salsa with grilled fish, poultry or meats.

Make Ahead

Salsa is best served fresh, but it can be covered and refrigerated for up to 4 hours.

2	ripe mangoes, peeled and diced	2
1/4 cup	chopped red bell pepper	50 mL
2	green onions, chopped	2
2 tbsp	chopped fresh cilantro	25 mL
2 tsp	chopped fresh gingerroot	10 mL
1/2 tsp	chopped fresh red or green chilies	2 mL
3 tbsp	lime juice	45 mL
1/2 tsp	granulated sugar	2 mL
1/4 tsp	salt or fish sauce	1 mL

1. In a bowl, combine mangoes, red pepper, green onions, cilantro, ginger, chilies, lime juice, sugar and salt.

Cabbage and Carrot Slaw

4 cups	thinly shredded white cabbage	1 L
1 cup	grated carrot	250 mL
1 cup	diced English cucumber	250 mL
1 ½ cups	shredded spinach leaves	375 mL
3	green onions, chopped	3
2 tbsp	shredded fresh mint leaves	25 mL
Dressing		
1 tbsp	chopped fresh gingerroot	15 mL
¼ cup	rice vinegar	50 mL
2 tbsp	vegetable oil	25 mL
1 tbsp	sesame oil	15 mL
1 tbsp	maple syrup or brown sugar	15 mL
1 tbsp	sweet chili sauce (page 45)	15 mL
2 tsp	soy sauce	10 mL
1 cup	chow mein noodles	250 mL
2 tbsp	chopped peanuts (optional)	25 mL

1. In a large bowl, combine cabbage, carrot, cucumber, spinach, green onions and mint.
2. To prepare dressing, in a bowl, whisk together ginger, vinegar, vegetable oil, sesame oil, maple syrup, chili sauce and soy sauce.
3. Pour dressing over salad and toss well. Cover and refrigerate for up to 4 hours.
4. Toss and sprinkle with noodles and peanuts, if using, just before serving.

Makes 6 to 8 servings

A plate of vegetables is often served alongside curry dishes and other spicy dishes to help offset the heat and provide texture, but Western coleslaw is not a common side dish in Thailand, especially with mayonnaise as a base. This recipe combines some popular crunchy Thai vegetables with a tasty non-creamy dressing.

Make Ahead

Salad ingredients can be chopped, combined and refrigerated up to 6 hours ahead. Dressing can be covered and refrigerated up to a day in advance.

Chicken Mango Salad

Makes 6 servings

A popular salad from my Lazy Summer cooking class. In Thailand, grilled chicken is always available at markets and supermarkets, but here at home, deli chicken saves the day. Occasionally I meet people who are allergic to mango. In that case, I substitute nectarines or peaches, adding them just before serving.

Make Ahead

All salad ingredients can be prepared, placed in separate dishes, covered and refrigerated 4 hours ahead. Dressing can be prepared, covered and refrigerated up to a day ahead.

3 cups	cooked chicken, cut in 1-inch (2.5 cm) pieces	750 mL
3	stalks celery, chopped	3
1 cup	snow peas, trimmed and sliced	250 mL
2	mangoes, peeled, pitted and cut in 1/2-inch (1 cm) chunks	2
2	green onions, sliced	2
Dressing		
1/4 cup	rice vinegar	50 mL
2 tbsp	lime juice	25 mL
2 tbsp	chopped mango chutney or peach jam	25 mL
2 tbsp	vegetable oil	25 mL
1 tbsp	sweet soy sauce (page 45) or soy sauce	15 mL
1 tsp	sesame oil	5 mL
1/2 tsp	curry powder	2 mL
1/2 tsp	salt	2 mL
	Lettuce leaves	
	Fresh mint or cilantro leaves	

1. In a large bowl, combine chicken, celery, snow peas, mangoes and green onions.
2. To prepare dressing, in a separate bowl, whisk together vinegar, lime juice, chutney, vegetable oil, soy sauce, sesame oil, curry powder and salt.
3. Pour dressing over salad ingredients. Toss gently to combine.
4. Serve on lettuce leaves and garnish with cilantro.

Homemade Curry Powder

In a small dry skillet, combine 2 tbsp (25 mL) whole coriander seeds, 1 tbsp (15 mL) whole cumin seeds, 1 tbsp (15 mL) hot pepper flakes, 2 tsp (10 mL) black peppercorns, 2 tsp (10 mL) whole cloves, 2 tsp (10 mL) fennel seeds and 2 tsp (10 mL) cardamom seeds. Roast over medium heat for 3 to 4 minutes, or until fragrant but not colored. Transfer to a plate and cool. Grind in a spice or coffee grinder with 1 tbsp (15 mL) ground ginger and 1 tbsp (15 mL) ground turmeric. Store in an airtight container.

Makes 2/3 cup (150 mL).

Red Rice Salad

Makes 6 to 8 servings

Since red rice has a nutty taste and chewy texture, it lends itself easily to this healthful and colorful salad. Cold jasmine rice could also be used, or even a combination of the two. It is a great buffet or picnic dish. Serve with grilled chicken, fish or seafood.

3 cups	cooked red rice (page 115)	750 mL
1 cup	diced English cucumber	250 mL
1 cup	chopped green beans, blanched	250 mL
1	grapefruit, peeled and separated in sections	1
3/4 cup	chopped pineapple	175 mL
1 cup	chopped fresh watercress	250 mL
3	green onions, chopped	3
1/4 cup	chopped fresh mint leaves	50 mL
1/4 cup	chopped fresh cilantro leaves	50 mL
1/3 cup	lime juice	75 mL
1/4 cup	sweet chili sauce (page 45)	50 mL
3 tbsp	fish sauce	45 mL
	Whole lettuce leaves	

1. In a large bowl, combine rice, cucumber, beans, grapefruit, pineapple, watercress, green onions, mint and cilantro.
2. In a small bowl, whisk together lime juice, chili sauce and fish sauce. Add to rice mixture and toss to combine thoroughly. Let stand for 30 minutes and toss again. Taste and adjust seasonings if necessary.
3. Arrange lettuce leaves on a serving platter. Mound rice salad over lettuce.

Rice Pasta with Pesto

Makes 4 to 5 servings

Pasta and pesto are not commonly found on Thai menus, but this Western favorite can be adapted using Thai flavors. Rice pasta works well for those on gluten-free diets, but any kind of wheat pasta can also be used. Serve with grilled shrimp, cold cooked chicken or pork tenderloin. You will probably have pesto left over; use it on pizzas, grilled bread and crackers.

Make Ahead

Pesto can be covered and refrigerated for up to 2 days or frozen for 6 weeks.

2	cloves garlic, peeled	2
2 tsp	chopped fresh gingerroot	10 mL
1 tsp	chopped fresh red chilies	5 mL
3⁄4 cup	packed fresh sweet Thai basil leaves	175 mL
1⁄2 cup	packed fresh cilantro leaves and stems	125 mL
1⁄4 cup	packed fresh mint leaves	50 mL
1⁄4 cup	roasted peanuts	50 mL
2 tbsp	lime juice	25 mL
1 tbsp	fish sauce, or 3⁄4 tsp (4 mL) salt	15 mL
1⁄2 cup	vegetable or olive oil	125 mL
1⁄4 tsp	black pepper	1 mL
1 lb	dried rice pasta (e.g., fusilli, penne, spaghetti)	500 g

1. In a food processor, combine garlic, ginger, chilies, basil, cilantro, mint and peanuts. Process until coarsely chopped.
2. Add lime juice, fish sauce, oil and pepper and process until smooth.
3. Meanwhile, cook pasta in a large amount of boiling salted water for 7 to 10 minutes, or until just tender (do not overcook). Reserve 1⁄2 cup (125 mL) cooking water.
4. Drain pasta and transfer to a large bowl. Add about 1⁄2 cup (125 mL) pesto and toss well to combine, adding enough cooking liquid to moisten as necessary. Serve hot or at room temperature.

Variation

Rice Pasta and Pesto Salad: Cook pasta and drain. Rinse with cold water and drain. Place in a large bowl and toss with 3⁄4 cup (175 mL) pesto, 1 1⁄2 cups (375 mL) halved cherry tomatoes, 1 1⁄2 cups (375 mL) diced cucumber, 2 seeded and chopped red or green bell peppers, 1 cup (250 mL) slivered carrots and 3 tbsp (45 mL) lime juice or rice vinegar. Toss well and transfer to a serving dish. Cover and refrigerate for up to 4 hours. Let stand at room temperature for 30 minutes before serving. Garnish with mint sprigs.

Makes 8 to 10 servings.

Roast Chicken

Makes 4 to 5 servings

Remove the backbone and flatten the chicken for an easy-to-roast and easy-to-carve main course. In Thailand, variations of this chicken are cooked on the barbecue. Serve it hot or cold with a salad and rice.

1	3-lb (1.5 kg) chicken	1
1	½-inch (1 cm) piece fresh gingerroot	1
1	stalk lemongrass, white part only, cut in 1-inch (2.5 cm) pieces	1
4	cloves garlic, peeled	4
2	shallots, peeled	2
1	small jalapeño, seeded	1
1 tsp	red curry paste (page 196)	5 mL
2 tbsp	fish sauce	25 mL
2 tbsp	lime juice	25 mL
1 tbsp	brown sugar	15 mL
1 cup	coconut milk	250 mL

1. With kitchen shears or a sharp knife, cut carefully along both sides of backbone. Remove backbone. Cut off wing tips (freeze to make stock). Spread chicken open and press firmly to flatten. Place in a large shallow dish.
2. In a blender or food processor, combine ginger, lemongrass, garlic, shallots, jalapeño, curry paste, fish sauce, lime juice, sugar and coconut milk. Blend until smooth. Pour over chicken, turning chicken to coat on all sides. Cover and refrigerate for several hours or overnight.
3. Remove chicken from marinade, reserving marinade. Arrange chicken skin side up on a foil- and parchment-lined baking sheet.
4. Roast in a preheated 400°F (200°) oven for 50 minutes, or until juices run clear and a meat thermometer registers 180°F (82°C) when inserted into thigh. Spoon reserved marinade over chicken halfway through cooking time.
5. Transfer to a carving board and cut into serving pieces.

Roasted Pork Tenderloin

2	cloves garlic, peeled	2
1 tbsp	chopped fresh gingerroot	15 mL
2 tbsp	chopped fresh cilantro leaves	25 mL
2 tbsp	hoisin sauce	25 mL
2 tbsp	sweet chili sauce (page 45)	25 mL
2 tbsp	lime juice	25 mL
1 tbsp	fish sauce	15 mL
1 tbsp	palm or brown sugar	15 mL
1 tbsp	sesame oil	15 mL
1/2 tsp	five-spice powder (page 170)	2 mL
2	pork tenderloins (12 oz/375 g each)	2

1. In a food processor, combine garlic, ginger and cilantro. Pulse to puree. Add hoisin sauce, chili sauce, lime juice, fish sauce, sugar, sesame oil and five-spice powder. Puree to make a sauce.
2. Arrange tenderloins in a single layer in a shallow dish just large enough to hold pork. Pour sauce over meat. Turn meat to coat in sauce. Cover and refrigerate for up to 24 hours.
3. Transfer tenderloins to a baking rack set over a foil-lined baking sheet.
4. Roast in a preheated 350°F (180°C) oven for 30 minutes, or until juices run clear and internal temperature reaches 160°F (70°C). Let stand for 5 minutes before slicing.

Makes 6 servings

Roasted red pork is seen in many Chinese meat stores alongside chicken and ducks. If you live close to a Chinatown or Asian supermarket, there is no problem finding it, but since I live in the country, I made up my own substitute. Serve it with pineapple fried rice (page 122) and cabbage (page 75) or cucumber salad (page 72). It is excellent cold or hot.

Make Ahead

Cooked tenderloins can be wrapped and refrigerated for up to 2 days. Slice and serve cold or use in sandwiches or salads.

Homestyle Thai Meatloaf

Makes 6 servings

In Thailand, you would probably never be served meatloaf, but many Thai flavors can be packed into this traditional Western comfort dish. Serve it with Breakfast Mashed Potatoes (page 275).

In one of the markets we visited in Bangkok, a sausage vendor had an amazing selection of sausages, including garlic pork, smoked pepper, fermented fish and pork with hot basil. Some of these flavors are included in this meatloaf.

This can also be served cold with a rice salad (page 268), coleslaw (page 265) and mango salsa (page 264).

1 lb	lean ground pork	500 g
1 lb	ground chicken or turkey	500 g
1/4 cup	chopped fresh cilantro leaves	50 mL
3	green onions, chopped	3
2	cloves garlic, minced	2
3 tbsp	oyster sauce	45 mL
1 tbsp	fish sauce	15 mL
2 tsp	hot chili sauce	10 mL
1/2 tsp	black pepper	2 mL
2	eggs	2
3/4 cup	dry bread crumbs (preferably panko)	175 mL

Topping

1/4 cup	ketchup	50 mL
1 tsp	hot chili sauce	5 mL
1 tsp	soy sauce	5 mL

1. In a large bowl, combine pork, chicken, cilantro, green onions, garlic, oyster sauce, fish sauce, chili sauce, pepper, eggs and bread crumbs. Combine thoroughly.
2. Pack into a 9- by 5-inch (2 L) parchment-lined loaf pan. Bake in a preheated 350°F (180°C) oven for 55 minutes.
3. Meanwhile, in a small bowl, combine ketchup, chili sauce and soy sauce. Spread over top of meatloaf. Return to oven and bake for 20 to 25 minutes, or until a meat thermometer registers 170°F (77°C).
4. Let stand for 5 minutes. Pour off any accumulated juices. Cut into slices.

Thai-flavored Sloppy Joes

Makes 6 servings

One summer, when many of my students wanted quick recipes for the cottage and easy family entertaining, I made a Thai-inspired version of Sloppy Joes. It became a popular addition to their repertoire. I served this with small homemade rolls and coleslaw (page 265), but steamed rice can easily replace the rolls. Any combination of ground meat or poultry works well. Serve with hot chili sauce.

Make Ahead

Sloppy Joe mixture can be made ahead, covered and refrigerated for a day. Reheat gently in a saucepan or skillet over medium heat, stirring often. Mixture can also be frozen for up to 6 weeks.

2 tbsp	vegetable oil	25 mL
2	onions, chopped	2
2	stalks celery, chopped	2
3	cloves garlic, chopped	3
1 tbsp	chopped fresh gingerroot	15 mL
12 oz	ground chicken or turkey	375 g
12 oz	lean ground pork	375 g
1 1/2 cups	chopped canned tomatoes	375 mL
2 tsp	chopped fresh red chilies	10 mL
1/4 cup	hoisin sauce	50 mL
2 tbsp	oyster sauce	25 mL
3 tbsp	lime juice, divided	45 mL
1/2 tsp	black pepper	2 mL
1 tbsp	fish sauce (optional)	15 mL
2 tbsp	coarsely chopped fresh cilantro leaves	25 mL

1. In a wok or large skillet, heat oil over medium-high heat. Add onions, celery, garlic and ginger. Cook for 4 minutes, stirring occasionally, until softened.
2. Add chicken and pork and cook, breaking up meat, for 6 to 8 minutes, or until lightly browned.
3. Add tomatoes, chilies, hoisin sauce, oyster sauce, 2 tbsp (25 mL) lime juice and pepper. Bring to a boil, reduce heat and simmer for 25 to 30 minutes, or until thick.
4. Stir in remaining lime juice and fish sauce, if using.
5. Serve sprinkled with chopped cilantro.

Breakfast Mashed Potatoes

Makes 5 to 6 servings

Potatoes are not considered to be a major ingredient in Thai cooking, though they are added to some curry dishes. But in hotels that cater to an international clientele, potato dishes are often offered at the breakfast buffet. When I saw mashed potatoes for breakfast, I just had to try them. The Thai touches were evident.

2 lbs	Yukon Gold or all-purpose potatoes, peeled and cut in pieces	1 kg
2 tbsp	vegetable oil or butter	25 mL
2	cloves garlic, chopped	2
2	shallots, chopped	2
1 1/2 cups	corn kernels	375 mL
1/2 cup	milk	125 mL
2 tbsp	butter	25 mL
1 1/2 tsp	salt	7 mL
1/4 tsp	black pepper	1 mL
2	green onions, chopped	25 mL
2 tbsp	chopped fresh cilantro leaves	25 mL
3/4 tsp	hot chili sauce	4 mL

1. In a large saucepan, cook potatoes in boiling salted water for 20 to 25 minutes, or until tender.
2. Meanwhile, in a separate saucepan, heat oil over medium heat. Add garlic and shallots and cook for 3 to 4 minutes, until softened and slightly golden.
3. Add corn, milk, butter, salt and pepper and cook for 4 to 5 minutes, or until milk is hot and corn is tender.
4. Drain potatoes and mash. Add corn and milk mixture. If mashed potatoes are too thick, add extra milk.
5. Stir in green onions and cilantro. Drizzle or dot chili sauce over potatoes.

Carrots in Mango Juice

Makes 5 to 6 servings

These Thai-flavored carrots are especially popular with children. Mango juice is available in the juice section of the supermarket.

1 tbsp	olive oil or butter	15 mL
2 tsp	chopped fresh gingerroot	10 mL
1 ½ lbs	carrots, peeled and sliced	750 g
½ cup	mango juice	125 mL
1 tbsp	lime juice	15 mL
2 tbsp	chopped fresh cilantro leaves (optional)	25 mL

1. In a saucepan, heat oil over medium-high heat. Add ginger and cook for 1 minute, or until fragrant.
2. Add carrots and mango juice and bring to a boil. Cover, reduce heat and simmer for 20 minutes, or until carrots are tender.
3. Remove cover and bring to a boil. Cook, shaking pan, until carrots are glazed with juice.
4. Remove from heat. Stir in lime juice and cilantro, if using.

Library and Archives Canada Cataloguing in Publication

Stephen, Linda
Complete book of Thai cooking : over 200 delicious recipes / Linda Stephen.

Includes index.
ISBN 978-0-7788-0180-1

1. Cookery, Thai. I. Title.

TX724.5.T5S84 2008 641.59593 C2007-906806-5

Index

C

D

E

F

G

H

O

P

Q

R

S

T

V

W

Y